MW01711790

Dafina-Lazarus Stewart
Bowling Green State University
Bowling Green, Ohio, USA

ISBN 978-1-137-59076-3 ISBN 978-1-137-59077-0 (eBook)
DOI 10.1057/978-1-137-59077-0

Library of Congress Control Number: 2017934657

© The Editor(s) (if applicable) and The Author(s) 2017
This work is subject to copyright. All rights are solely and exclusively licensed by the Publisher, whether the whole or part of the material is concerned, specifically the rights of translation, reprinting, reuse of illustrations, recitation, broadcasting, reproduction on microfilms or in any other physical way, and transmission or information storage and retrieval, electronic adaptation, computer software, or by similar or dissimilar methodology now known or hereafter developed.
The use of general descriptive names, registered names, trademarks, service marks, etc. in this publication does not imply, even in the absence of a specific statement, that such names are exempt from the relevant protective laws and regulations and therefore free for general use.
The publisher, the authors and the editors are safe to assume that the advice and information in this book are believed to be true and accurate at the date of publication. Neither the publisher nor the authors or the editors give a warranty, express or implied, with respect to the material contained herein or for any errors or omissions that may have been made. The publisher remains neutral with regard to jurisdictional claims in published maps and institutional affiliations.

Printed on acid-free paper

This Palgrave Macmillan imprint is published by Springer Nature
The registered company is Nature America Inc.
The registered company address is: 1 New York Plaza, New York, NY 10004, U.S.A.

For Michael
and all of us who were not raised to be "ordinary children" (GKB)

Foreword

Dr. Dafina-Lazarus (D-L) Stewart is a deeply committed human being. I have known this since meeting D-L years ago at an academic conference. The seriousness, rigor, thoughtfulness, passion, and commitment of D-L are contained wholeheartedly in *Black Collegians' Experiences in US Northern Private Colleges: A Narrative History, 1945–1965.*

Unfortunately, few scholars of higher education pursue historical research. It is not a methodological approach that is encouraged or even taught in most higher education programs. Higher education scholars often don't understand its benefits or its beauty. Perhaps after reading D-L's handsomely crafted book, they will. D-L fastens together historical narratives with skillful representations of educational theory. D-L provides opportunities for voices of Black collegians to shine, roar, sit silently, reflect, and inform throughout the book. The voices of the 68 Black students who attended liberal arts colleges in the North tell the story of Blacks on college campuses—majority White northern college campuses—between 1945 and 1965. However, their stories do more than that as D-L captures their formative years growing up and their experiences after graduating or leaving college. Whereas the focus in higher education research is almost always on students, D-L thinks about these Black students when they are alumni and as vibrant individuals, making their way in various communities across the nation. We get a full picture of their lives.

Black Collegians' Experiences in US Northern Private Colleges tells us about segregation in the North—a topic that is often ignored or overshadowed by the vast manifestation of segregation in the South. D-L shows us the complexities through the lives of these students. Given my interest in Black college students during this time, I found D-L's portrayal of the collegiate lives of these students to be most riveting. I was almost giddy about the ways that I could use this work in my classroom to motivate and empower Black students who often feel left out of history texts—here, they were in full brilliance. And the complexities with which D-L presents them will push back against the flattened and narrowed views of Black students that many White students bring to the classroom.

Knowing so much about these Black students' school experiences, their college choice decisions, their college adventures, and their postcollege contributions changes the presentation of Blacks in the larger history of education narrative. By far one of the most interesting aspects of *Black Collegians' Experiences in US Northern Private Colleges* is D-L's presentation of divergent college experiences based on gender. Far too often gender is not discussed in histories of Blacks, and in history of education overall, gender has referred to women only and typically White women. Because D-L is sensitive to gender issues and challenges in research and practice, gender is a carefully woven narrative throughout the book. D-L doesn't make assumptions and judgments but allows the Black collegians to present their own experiences, fears, and voices.

One aspect of *Black Collegians' Experiences in US Northern Private Colleges* that I found particularly interesting, and D-L's treatment of it unique, was those students who did not finish college for various reasons—joining the military, marriage, and other obligations. Once again, D-L doesn't pass judgment and treat these students as failures like so many scholars do today. Instead, D-L gives them the space to tell their story, avoiding the trap of the single collegiate experience that we often fall into with research. For D-L, graduating from college wasn't the end goal for these Black collegians—it was one step on the way to the rest of their lives and sometimes they took a different pathway—away from college—and that is a respectable choice from D-L's perspective. There is no shame or judgment on D-L's part or in the words chosen to describe the students' choices.

Another area that D-L doesn't ignore, but that is ignored almost systematically by scholars of the history of education and higher education, is the postcollege experiences of students—their lives as alumni. D-L gives us a window into the lives of these Black collegians postcollege by showcasing their careers, families, and roles as alumni of their alma maters. Again, as I read these stories, I thought about how empowering these individual lives are and how they will empower other Black alumni who are often ignored by their institutions and by researchers interested in alumni contributions to higher education.

As D-L, from my perspective, always seems beautifully open to learning, this book is also a learning experience for the author. D-L presents personal experiences and reflections—what was learned in the process of writing this book and from these Black college students. I appreciate D-L's reflections, moments of silence, commitments, and passions throughout the text and think that much is added to the overall book through D-L's inclusion of self.

In the end, *Black Collegians' Experiences in US Northern Private Colleges* is a compelling narrative of beautiful stories, often untold. As readers, we learn students' motivations, goals, desires, struggles, and hopes. From my perspective, D-L lifted the personal narratives and voices of these students off the pages, telling complex stories of social isolation, self-discovery and growth, cross-racial friendships, dating, inter- and intra-cultural learning, and academic learning. D-L has given us individual stories and a larger historical narrative to fill the void that exists in our understanding of Blacks in higher education.

Professor Marybeth Gasman
University of Pennsylvania
July 2016

Preface

The Civil Rights Movement has been well-documented in many respects (Anderson, 1995; Day, 2014; Farber, 1994; Farber & Bailey, 2001; Lewis & D'Orso, 1998; Williams, 2004, 2013), including the educational narratives of those Black students who first sought to integrate southern primary, secondary, and postsecondary institutions (Beals, 1995; Clark, 1992; Doyle, 2003; Halberstam, 1998; Hunter-Gault, 1992, 2014; Meredith & Doyle, 2012; Sayre, 1995). Yet, missing from those narratives are the voices of Black[1] people who were admitted to and decided to attend private, liberal arts colleges in *northern* states after the Civil War and Reconstruction Eras. Some discussion has reviewed northern racial integration in higher education in the early twentieth century (Plaut, 1954; Woodson, 1933/2006), but the literature is largely silent regarding the period between World War II and the passage of the Civil Rights Act and Voting Rights Acts.

Indeed, due to the greater presence of Black people in the South, much of what is known about their experiences in US colleges and universities is geographically focused there. When the education of Blacks in the North prior to the mid-1960s has been discussed, it has been typically in the context of elementary and secondary education (e.g., Franklin, 1979; Harding, 1981). Also, there has been little known and discussed concerning the process of integration as enacted in specific institutional contexts. Public discourses would imply that integration "just happened" uniformly, rather than the more authentic reality of the uneven, partial, and paradoxical juxtaposition of inclusion and exclusion that characterized the era between World War II and the passage of the 1964 Civil

Rights Act. The more gradual integration that occurred on northern college campuses has been mostly ignored in favor of the relatively rapid, and violently contested, racial integration that occurred across the South. The ways in which these northern institutions that were early adopters of limited racially heterogeneous student bodies actually engaged the demands of integration for institutional policy and practice and the nature of Black student experiences with those institutional climates are the focus of this book. Although their numbers were quite small, the backgrounds and college experiences of these Black students who attended these institutions between 1945 and 1965 can reveal much about early racial integration efforts among young adults in residential and social settings. *Black Collegians' Experiences in US Northern Private Colleges: A Narrative History, 1945–1965* also illuminates the ways in which whiteness as an ideology of isolationism and self-involvement implicated and contravened northern engagement in southern discourses of racial terrorism and resistance, respectively.

Rationale for Focus

Studying these institutions in this place and time matters for several reasons. First, as acknowledged by other scholars (Horowitz, 2005; Thelin, 2011), the lack of historical scholarship on private colleges has produced an incomplete portrait of US higher education. Second, during this time period, liberal arts colleges and universities alike grappled with the roles of research, utilitarianism, and religion in the mission of their institutions (Eisenmann, 1999; Horowitz, 2005). For example, at Oberlin College, sectarian dogma advocating racial equality was subsumed by (poorly conceived and executed) research-based arguments that bolstered the segregationist social attitudes that took hold after Reconstruction (Waite, 2001). Considered a bellwether for the nation (Waite, 2001), Oberlin and this set of institutions, collectively, present a unique opportunity to investigate how social attitudes contravened religious equality rhetoric at these campuses, which were similar in size and scope and which had evolved by the mid-twentieth century to commit to educate any student regardless of race. Third, despite general characterizations of this postwar era as one marked by greater access and diversity, rigorous study of these institutions in the North between 1945 and 1965 provides a richer, more complete understanding of the nuances of access and diversity as enacted by colleges and reflected by their students. These reasons support an investigation into the experiences of Black collegians in these geographic (Midwest, Great Lakes region), institutional (private, liberal arts colleges), and chronological (1945–1965) locations.

Black students who attended these colleges between 1945 and 1965 provide the most information-rich sources regarding this topic. People of African descent were the most visible and largest minority group in college and in the Midwest and Great Lakes region during this historical era (Thelin, 2011; Wilkerson, 2010). Rather than seeking a monolithic and essentialist narrative of these students' experiences, I layer multiple stories that overlap, conflict, and interrupt each other to produce an authentic historical reflection on race, institutional climate, integration, and equity at these institutions during this period.

Data Sources

Archival research at each of the member institutions of the Great Lakes Colleges Association (GLCA) was conducted in fall 2012. I reviewed primary documents that addressed questions about the presence of Black students at each institution, and whether and how issues of race and the events taking place around the country, particularly in the South, were discussed on campus. To collect such data, I reviewed yearbooks, student newspapers and other publications, as well as presidential records and minutes of faculty meetings and other correspondence.

During spring and summer 2013, I conducted interviews with 68 Black men and women who attended these institutions between 1945 and 1965 to obtain oral histories of their experiences in college and sense-making of their experiences. I provide an extended discussion of the study's design, including the research paradigms, methodologies, and data collection and analysis methods that informed this study in Appendix 1. I encourage the reader to read that appendix to learn more. A full list of primary sources follows the general reference list.

Organization of the Book

For this study, I drew on multidisciplinary frameworks to produce a layered history that juxtaposes racial animus, disregard, and welcome in the lives of these Black matriculates participating in postsecondary education between 1945 and 1965. I have organized the book into 11 chapters, plus a concluding epilogue and two appendices. These are briefly summarized below.

The introduction explores the social and cultural context of this study, including the historical development of the Great Lakes region and particularly the Northwest Territory and its significance in US racial history; civil rights legislation and Black education in the northern USA; and the development of the institutions that would form the GLCA.

The next nine chapters present the excerpts from the participants' oral histories related to the different themes covered in those chapters as described below. Although the restoried narratives of the participants introduce and comprise the majority of each chapter's content, interpretive essays discussing the central themes across the narratives conclude them.

Chapter 2 focuses on the geographic origins of the 68 Black matriculates. The narratives of those who were born and spent most of their early childhood in the South will be presented first, followed by those who were raised predominately in the North. These narratives, drawn from participants' life history interviews, are meant to illuminate similarities and differences and how their journeys toward entering college were impacted by the geographical context of their childhoods. The relevance of having college-educated parents, middle-class status, and neighborhood context to the encouragement of these collegians to pursue college is also discussed.

Chapter 3 presents the elementary and high school experiences reflected among these participants and the varying roles that Black and White teachers and organizations played in supporting their educational pursuits. Collectively, they attended a variety of high schools: some college prep and others not; segregated public schools and mission schools for Blacks; private White high schools; and integrated public schools. For those participants who were raised in the North, experiences with Northern segregation, often in the context of educational co-curricular activities, are acknowledged. Southerners shared their experiences with or ideas of the North and what it would be like as well as the ways that segregation did not consistently demarcate their lives.

Chapter 4 focuses on the participants' college choice processes and rationale behind those choices. Most of the participants had never heard of the GLCA institution they ultimately chose until a favorite teacher or trusted family friend recommended it. Also, scholarship programs like the National Service and Scholarship Fund for Negro Students (NSSFNS) were critical in making these students aware of their college options and making it possible for them to attend. The negative light in which some viewed historically Black colleges is also apparent, alongside integrationist philosophies that sought preparation for a post-segregationist world.

Chapter 5 describes the participants' experiences traveling to and arriving on campus and their experiences within their first semester of being in college. From this general focus, the chapter sharpens to discuss the participants' adjustment and transition to a new identity as college students. Entering college for many of these students, most of whom were first-generation, was more than just a matter of moving into a residence hall and finding their way around. The participants discussed finances, academic transitions, and the realities of being Black at their traditionally White college.

Chapter 6 focuses on what college life was like for these participants. In their interviews, they spoke extensively about their academic and social lives during their undergraduate years, revealing stark differences related to gender. Both Black men and Black women shared narratives of influential faculty, challenges and successes with classes, deep and lasting friendships, participation in academic and civic service groups, and off-campus excursions. Yet, access to intercollegiate athletics, social clubs, and opportunities for interracial dating significantly differentiated the ways that Black women and Black men experienced their campuses.

Chapter 7 presents the college departure narratives of those who did not graduate from their GLCA institution. Finances, military service, and marriage were among the major contributors to attrition. These factors illustrate the ways in which these small, private colleges were very reliant on a traditional model for college enrollment and the differing effects of gender on these students' opportunities to complete their college degrees.

In Chap. 8 participant narratives and archival data from yearbooks and newspapers will be presented to portray how issues of race, segregation, and the Civil Rights Movement were handled across the 20-year time period and across the 13 colleges. The chapter begins by positioning selected participant narratives in the context of some of the most significant and notable events of the civil rights era. Following these narratives, archival data from the colleges are presented to supplement and speak to the general nature of campus discussions, and lack thereof, about racial justice issues.

Chapter 9 discusses how college impacted the paths these 68 participants took after college. They pursued a variety of fields of study and careers upon leaving their college (whether through attrition or graduation), including education, ministry, civil service, the arts, business and entrepreneurship, and the law. In the narratives that begin this chapter, the participants share what effect they believe their education at their GLCA institution has had on their lives since then.

Chapter 10 features the participants' narratives related to their relationship to their colleges as alumni and former students. Some have been very active with their alma mater, serving as trustees even, while others have not returned to the campus since their graduation. As may be expected, those who were able to make substantive and meaningful connections to faculty, staff, and other students through in-class and out-of-class activities were more likely to be deeply engaged with their colleges presently. Three types of alumni engagement featured among the participants are discussed.

Chapter 11 leaves behind the participants' narratives and presents the lessons learned from what has been shared by the participants and revealed through the archival material. These lessons cover seven topics that speak to the experience of racially minoritized students in predominantly White colleges, institutional responsibility and accountability, and the strength and resilience demonstrated by these participants' narratives.

In the epilogue, I share my own narrative of choosing Kalamazoo College and some of my experiences there as a student and alum. After an interview with one participant, a Black woman who was also a graduate of Kalamazoo, the conversation shifted to my college journey. After hearing about those experiences, the participant commented that our experiences, though separated by 30 years, were not so different. Her insight caused us both to pause in reflective silence. This epilogue then illustrates the pervasiveness of the issues that confronted and challenged institutions and their students half a century ago.

There are also two appendices. Appendix 1 is a compilation of biographies for each of the 68 Black matriculates who participated in this study. These biographies give brief overviews of the lives of this highly accomplished group before and after college. While the narratives of four participants can be traced throughout the text from their origin stories to remembering their alma maters, some portion of each of the 68 participants' narratives is used to tell the story of their experiences at the GLCA colleges. Readers may use the index to trace the individual participants throughout the book, as well as to construct a review of each college's presence in the text.

Appendix 2 provides more thorough details about the methodology used in this study and discusses three issues related to conducting and reporting this type of research. First, college yearbooks and newspapers present interesting challenges and opportunities for historical analysis. Second, the role of racial classifications is discussed and the paradigmatic approach to race used in this book. Third, the cultural and class issues presented by transcription and textual representation of participants' words are highlighted. Finally, the adoption of a more literary approach to writing this book is discussed, and so is its implications for reporting research.

Summary

Black Collegians' Experiences in US Northern Private Colleges: A Narrative History, 1945–1965 tells the largely unknown collective story of what it was like, prior to legislatively mandated educational desegregation, to be a Black collegian in the racially isolated, northern, rural towns of Ohio, Michigan, Indiana, and western Pennsylvania. Through oral history narratives and archival material, I document and reflect on the experiences of Black collegians in the northern USA attending the 13 member institutions of the GLCA between 1945 and 1965. This history illuminates both the empowerment of these collegians and the persistent challenges of enacting institutional values in the face of resistance from both outside and within.

This book is significant because it seeks to understand the nature of progress toward pluralistic diversity in college environments characterized by the paradox of racial homogeneity and interracial engagement. By doing so, I better demonstrate the complex interplay of social movements, institutional context, individual identities, and the experiences of marginalized students in postsecondary education.

Professor Dafina-Lazarus Stewart
Bowling Green, OH
July 31, 2016

Note

1. I use Black as a pan-African descriptor to include various ethnicities and nationalities of people of African descent in the USA, including those born in the Americas, Caribbean, Europe, and Africa.

References

Anderson, T. H. (1995). *The movement and the sixties: Protest in America from Greensboro to Wounded Knee.* New York, NY: Oxford University Press.

Beals, M. P. (1995). *Warriors don't cry: The searing memoir of the battle to integrate Little Rock's Central High.* New York, NY: Washington Square Press.

Clark, E. C. (1992). *The schoolhouse door: Segregation's last stand at the University of Alabama.* Oxford: Oxford University.

Day, J. K. (2014). *The Southern Manifesto: Massive resistance and the fight to preserve segregation.* Jackson: University Press of Mississippi.

Doyle, W. (2003). *An American insurrection: James Meredith and the battle of Oxford, Mississippi.* New York, NY: Anchor Books.

Eisenmann, L. (1999). Reclaiming religion: New historiographic challenges in the relationship of religion and American higher education. *History of Education Quarterly, 39,* 295–306.

Farber, D. (Ed.). (1994). *The sixties: From memory to history.* Raleigh: University of North Carolina.

Farber, D., & Bailey, B. (Eds.). (2001). *The Columbia guide to America in the 1960s.* New York, NY: Columbia University.

Franklin, V. P. (1979). *The education of Black Philadelphia: The social and educational history of a minority community, 1900–1950.* Philadelphia, PA: University of Pennsylvania.

Halberstam, D. (1998). *The children.* New York, NY: Fawcett Books.

Harding, V. (1981). *There is a river: The Black struggle for freedom in America.* San Diego, CA: Harcourt Brace & Company.

Horowitz, H. L. (2005). In the wake of Laurence Vesey: Re-examining the liberal arts college. *History of Education Quarterly, 45,* 420–426.

Hunter-Gault, C. (1992). *In my place.* New York, NY: Vintage Books.

Hunter-Gault, C. (2014). *To the mountaintop: My journey through the Civil Rights Movement.* New York, NY: Square Fish.

Lewis, J., & D'Orso, M. (1998). *Walking with the wind: A memoir of the movement.* New York, NY: Harcourt Brace & Co.

Meredith, J., & Doyle, W. (2012). *A mission from God: A memoir and challenge for America.* New York, NY: Atria Books.

Plaut, R. L. (1954). Racial integration in higher education in the North. *The Journal of Negro Education, 23,* 310–316.

Sayre, N. (1995). *Previous convictions: A journey through the 1950s.* New Brunswick, NJ: Rutgers University.

Thelin, J. R. (2011). *A history of American higher education* (2nd ed.). Baltimore, MD: Johns Hopkins University Press.

Waite, C. L. (2001). The segregation of Black students at Oberlin College after reconstruction. *History of Education Quarterly, 41,* 344–364.

Wilkerson, I. (2010). *The warmth of other suns: The epic story of America's great migration*. New York, NY: Random House.
Williams, J. (2004). *My soul looks back in wonder: Voices of the civil rights experience*. New York, NY: Sterling.
Williams, J. (2013). *Eyes on the prize: America's civil rights years, 1954–1965 (25th anniversary ed.)*. New York, NY: Penguin Books.
Woodson, C. G. (2006). *The mis-education of the Negro*. San Diego, CA: The Book Tree. (Originally published in 1933).

Acknowledgments

I first sketched the idea for this project sometime during 2010 in a red leather-bound journal. I had long wondered what it was like to be a Black student in a traditionally White college when racial segregation was daily life for many Black people. I had read very little that studied Black people in northern colleges prior to 1965 and nothing about their experiences in liberal arts colleges. I was searching to understand what histories had shaped my own experiences at Kalamazoo College in the early 1990s. Finding nothing that satisfactorily answered my queries, I embarked on a project to answer them for myself. This book is a result of those efforts.

There is no way that I could have done this without the support and assistance of my village. At the risk of overlooking someone, I endeavor to name those people here. I am grateful to the Department of Higher Education and Student Affairs (#HESANation), the College of Education and Human Development, the Office of Sponsored Programs and Research at Bowling Green State University, vice president for Research and Economic Development Michael Ogawa, and Provost and Senior Vice President Rodney Rogers. I could not have done this research without the academic-year faculty improvement leave (i.e., sabbatical) I was granted for 2012–2013, the two grants I received through the Building Strength initiative, and the sincere interest, support, and encouragement I received from my HESA colleagues and students, as well as Drs. Ogawa and Rogers. I also acknowledge the invaluable assistance offered by my graduate assistants, Keenan Colquitt Jr. and Tiffany Menard. Their assistance, especially Tiffany's during the 2015–2016 academic year, has helped bring this project to fruition.

I also acknowledge and appreciate the ACPA Foundation for their early support of this research project in July 2012. Next, I am exceedingly grateful to the magnificent alumni office staff and archivists at the colleges in the Great Lakes Colleges Association (GLCA). Alumni staff searched their databases for mailing addresses, labeled dozens of envelopes, and mailed my recruitment letters. The GLCA archivists provided a wealth of knowledge and access to their colleges' materials. You are truly priceless treasures to your institutions and I appreciate your co-labor with me. I am especially grateful to the presidents of DePauw University, Kalamazoo College, and Wabash College in 2014 who saw the value of this project and financially supported it.

During my time in Indiana, visiting the archives at Wabash, DePauw, and Earlham, I was greatly blessed to be hosted in Terre Haute and Richmond by my sorors of Delta Sigma Theta Sorority, Incorporated. To Drs. Mary Howard-Hamilton and Kandace Hinton, thank you for opening your homes to me, for sharing the companionship of Simba and Nala, and for connecting me to our soror in Richmond who opened her home and another who broke bread with me during my sojourn there. Truly, the bonds which connect us are transcendent and everlasting. I am also grateful to my former academic advisor from Kalamazoo, Dr. Marigene Arnold, for engaging me in hours of conversation, thinking through this project, connecting me with resources, and writing several letters of recommendation for ultimately failed grant applications. Your knowledge, experience, and wisdom have been a treasure.

To the 68 Black alumni who agreed to participate in this project and are profiled in Appendix 2, you all have profoundly enriched my life. I feel like I have an extended family of aunts, uncles, and grandparents whose wisdom and life experiences have not only made this book possible but also stretched and challenged my own perspectives and attitudes. I will be forever grateful for your collaboration, for your honesty, for your generosity of time and wisdom. Although at least three of you have passed away since I first began corresponding with you in 2012, it means the world to me to have been able to meet each of you and to learn from you. Your phone calls and e-mails to check on my progress and to encourage me have been sweet succor at times when I feared I would not finish.

As of summer 2015, I had not raised enough funds to complete the interview transcription that was necessary to finish this book. I followed the advice of one of my oldest friends, who encouraged me to use a crowdfunding campaign. I was skeptical, but desperate. Using GoFundMe,

I created a campaign page, and within two weeks, I had raised the necessary funds. This book simply would not exist without the generous financial support of the following individuals: Chris Venable, Heather C. Lou, Daniel Shimmura, Montique Cotton Kelly, Kacee Snyder, Lucas J., Eli Kean, Gavin Henning, Ray Plaza, Kate Graves, Missy Ciavarelli, Stephanie Waterman, Kelly Jo Larsen, Jamie Washington and Sam Offer, Chase Catalano, Niki Messmore, Dan Morrison, Usha Nair-Reichert, Kristen Renn, Keith O'Neill, Rachel Friedensen, Liza Talusan, Steve D. Mobley Jr., Al DeSimone, Dan Tillapaugh, Brenda Armitage, Donna Nicol, Dian Squire, Kathy Sisneros, Sonya Som, Paul Brown, Michaeline Shuman, Joel Pettigrew, Kathryn Palmieri, CJ Levine, Jeremy Franklin, Erin Simpson, Jolene Miller, Donald Mitchell, Nykia Gaines, Keisha E. McKenzie, Erin Peltzman, Conor McLaughlin and Windi Sasaki, Becky Roth, Albert Lunde, and Cynthia Carpenter.

Prior to submitting this manuscript to the publisher, I invited a scholarly powerhouse of colleagues to review the whole book or specific chapters. To Drs. Felecia Commodore, Thomas Edge, Susan Marine, Steve Mobley Jr., and Z Nicolazzo: Many thanks to each of you; your feedback has significantly improved this manuscript. I also am deeply grateful to Dr. Marybeth Gasman for writing the foreword for this book. Your strong support of this project from the beginning has been very much appreciated.

I was so blessed to be in spiritual community from 2009 to 2016 with the congregants of Trinity Episcopal Church in Toledo, Ohio, and the Reverend Elizabeth Hoster and Barbara Clarke, who led the community until 2015. I came to know the prayer for travelers by heart as it was said over me time and time again while I was collecting data. Your steadfast support and prayers were a healing place when I needed one. To my social media networks, you all have been rock-steady cheerleaders. I am connected to the best folks on the planet, because I am in community with you.

I cannot adequately express how much of who I am is because my mother, Dorothy Elizabeth Lazarus, has supported me in every endeavor. Mom, you have always been my biggest fan and most fervent prayer warrior.

To my chosen family in this world, especially my queer and trans* kin: Thank you for building me up, for reminding me that I am worthy of love, for loving me when I did not love myself, for being a safe resting place, for allowing me to love you. You know who you are. Ana Brown,

(Doctors-to-be) Joy L.E. Boggs and Alex Lange, Dr. T.J. Jourian, Rev. Dr. Judy Alston, Rev. Dr. Cynthia Tyson, Rev. Dr. Jamie Washington, and Rev. Sam Offer: You all have been the absolutely best chosen siblings I could have ever hoped for. My love for each of you is boundless. To Dr. Z Nicolazzo, I cannot adequately express how healing, life-giving, and transformative our friendship and academic partnership over these last two years has been.

Finally, to my only child, Michael Ezra Martin: You have been a source of light, love, and grace since the day you were born. As you prepare to head off to college, I hope these stories inspire you to remain resilient in the face of challenges, hopeful in the midst of adversity, and receptive to the support and encouragement of those who will come to walk with you along the way. I am amazed every day that I get to parent you. Thank you for affixing mailing labels to hundreds of envelopes, for helping to cook and clean the house, and for abiding a month's worth of mostly pizza and fast food while I was writing the draft of this book. Nothing I ever achieve in this life will be more important than being your parent, and everything I do is so that your life can be free. I love you beyond life.

August 2016
Bowling Green, OH

Contents

List of Figures

List of Table

CHAPTER 1

Introduction

It is important to frame the present study of the experiences of Black collegians in the 13 colleges of the Great Lakes Colleges Association (GLCA) from 1945 to 1965 in its regional and chronological social and cultural contexts. Rejecting historical objectivity (Novick, 1998), the theoretical perspective of critical race theory (CRT) and the theoretical framework of whiteness as property (Harris, 1993) inform this contextual reading (see Appendix 1 for further discussion). In so doing, I foreground issues of race and White supremacy as inherent characteristics of US society and understand whiteness to be a system of privileges and norms that are not biologically determined, but rather are socially constructed and maintained through a cycle of cultural and institutional socialization in which laws, policies, educational institutions, and religious institutions are complicit (Harro, 2010).

Therefore, this chapter is not intended to serve as a general historical summary of the political development of the Great Lakes region or as a chronological synopsis of national history from 1945 to 1965. Rather, in keeping with the aims of this text, this chapter depicts the ways that racism, colonialism, and White supremacy informed the political and social development of the region in which these institutions were founded. I first discuss the Northwest Territory and the states emerging from it that would host the GLCA colleges and civil rights legislation and activism in these states. Then, the conditions facing Black collegians in higher education

© The Author(s) 2017

D.-L. Stewart, *Black Collegians' Experiences in US Northern Private Colleges*, DOI 10.1057/978-1-137-59077-0_1

between 1945 and 1965 are discussed. Finally, I review the emergence of the GLCA as a consortium and the presence of Black collegians in the GLCA colleges in greater depth than covered in the preface.

The Northwest Territory and Emergent States

The Northwest Territory generally comprised the land west of the Appalachian Mountains and beyond Pennsylvania's western border, north to the border with Canada, east to the Mississippi River, and south to the Ohio River. Of the six states that would emerge by the mid-nineteenth century, only three will be discussed here as they are the states in which the GLCA colleges would develop: Ohio, Michigan, and Indiana (the other states being Illinois, Wisconsin, and Minnesota). Western Pennsylvania[1] is appropriately included in this discussion, because its positioning west of the Appalachian Mountains demarcates it from the eastern half of the state. Western Pennsylvania is more like the Midwest, whereas eastern Pennsylvania is more like the Northeast and Mid-Atlantic regions.

The original inhabitants of the geographic area that is the primary focus of this study were generally members of indigenous tribes belonging to one of three "mother groups": Algonquian, Iroquoian, or Siouan, each with well-developed and established systems of governance, either matrilineal (Iroquoian) or patrilineal (Algonquian and Siouan) kinship systems, and vibrant spiritual belief systems that were highly dependent upon the Great Lakes and its tributaries for fishing, trading, and farming (Treuer, 2010). Specifically, the territory now known as the states of Michigan, Ohio (and western Pennsylvania), and Indiana was inhabited by various Native American nations, including the Potawatomi, Ojibwe (Chippewa), Ottawa, Shawnee, Myaamia (Miami), Stockbridge-Munsee, Wea, and Piankshaw (Horse Capture, 2010; Treuer, 2010). European contact was established first with the French who colonized this area and then later the British and what would become the US colonists. France ceded this area to the fledgling USA in the Treaty of Paris, signed in 1783. However, the territory was occupied and controlled almost completely by either British or indigenous populations until 1796 (Lindley, Schneider, & Quaife, 1937). In fact, Native American resistance to US encroachment on the land west of the Appalachian Mountains would continue through the early nineteenth century, including along the Lake Erie waterway bordering both western Pennsylvania and Ohio.

Northwest Ordinance

The new nation saw the territory adjacent to the Great Lakes as a vital national resource (Lindley et al., 1937; Roosevelt, 1957). The Northwest Ordinance sought to expand US territory and to encourage settlement. The six articles of the ordinance upheld a number of fundamental principles, including freedom of religion, the encouragement of schools and means of education, and "good faith toward the Indians [*sic*]," and the final article declared, "there shall be neither slavery nor involuntary servitude, within the territory, otherwise than in the punishment of crimes, whereof the party shall have been duly convicted" (Chase, 1833, p. 18). This prohibition would also be extended to the states that would emerge from the territory (Chase, 1833). Although later histories of the Northwest Territory would credit the prohibition of slavery in the territory with the later triumph of the Union in the Civil War a century later (Lindley et al., 1937), the issue of slavery loomed large over the discussions (Lindley et al.; Roosevelt, 1957).

The initial draft of the ordinance, written by Thomas Jefferson in 1784, would not have enforced a prohibition on slavery in the territory until after 1800 but this was rejected by Congress (Lindley et al., 1937). Several different committee iterations then produced a number of other drafts that were also rejected until a brand new committee managed to write a completely new draft that passed each of three readings and then was unanimously voted in favor by all states present in 1787 (Lindley et al.). There were 11 states represented in the young Congress at the time the ordinance was passed in 1787; although ratified as states, neither Rhode Island nor New Hampshire yet had congressional representation ("Report of proceedings in Congress," 1787).

In 1787, slavery existed in all but one state (Rhode Island) in the USA, and Lindley et al. (1937) credit Jefferson's insistence for the inclusion of a prohibition on slavery in the ordinance's initial draft and its remaining there through its final passage. Roosevelt's (1957) history of the ordinance would also emphasize the support of the southern states who were part of the drafting committee for the anti-slavery clause, but he noted that the anti-slavery article was actually a compromise measure to appease southern slave-holding states, as well as the White French and US settlers already in the territory who owned slaves. The compromise included not making the prohibition on slavery retroactive; only no *new* slaves could be brought into the territory. In addition, fugitive slaves could be rightfully reclaimed by their owners from any of the existing states, so that the territory would not become a "refuge for runaway negroes [*sic*]" (Roosevelt, 1957, p. 40). As recounted by Lindley et al., Indiana and Illinois tried to get the anti-slavery provision set aside when they pursued statehood, as a means of attracting more settlers and increasing their population and economic development; however, Congress would not allow it.

Native American Removal

Although Native Americans were to be treated with "good faith" by White settlers, treaties were consistently broken and indigenous communities regularly had their land encroached upon (Treuer, 2010; Horse Capture, 2010). Two provisions would effectively remove all Native American inhabitants from the area (Treuer, 2010; Horse Capture, 2010). In 1830, President Andrew Jackson signed into law the Indian Removal Act, which called for all Native Americans living within existing state borders to be removed to unsettled lands west of the Mississippi River (Horse Capture, 2010). The existing states at the time included Pennsylvania, Ohio, Indiana, and Illinois, but not yet Michigan. This would include therefore the Myaamia, Wea, Piankshaw, and Stockbridge-Munsee tribes. The Shawnee in Ohio would face removal through another avenue.

As described by Horse Capture (2010), throughout the early nineteenth century, the Shawnee, who had been driven north into the Ohio Valley from Tennessee by the Cherokee, tried to form an alliance with other Midwestern tribes to resist further Euro-American expansion but were defeated in 1811. Shortly after the Indian Removal Act was passed, the Shawnee still in Ohio signed a treaty in 1831 surrendering their lands to the USA, and by 1832, they were removed to what is now the Eastern Shawnee Reservation in Ottawa County, Oklahoma (Horse Capture, 2010). Consequently, no indigenous communities would remain in the entirety of the states of Pennsylvania, Ohio, Indiana, and Illinois ("Federally recognized Indian Reservations and tribes," pp. 354–355).

There was also ongoing resistance to US colonial expansion and settlement in the Michigan Territory and other territorial lands remaining from the original Northwest Territory (Lindley et al., 1937). In 1833, the Treaty of Chicago, not enforced for several years because it had been fraudulently executed (Treuer, 2010), would mandate that *all* Native Americans living east of the Mississippi River would be scheduled for relocation to either Kansas or Oklahoma (Horse Capture, 2010). By not limiting relocation to only existing states, the tribes in the Michigan Territory were under threat as well. However, the Pokagon and Huron bands of the Potawatomi Indians refused to leave and Chief Leopold Pokagon was able to negotiate for them to remain on two reservations in southwestern Michigan (Horse Capture, 2010). By 1837, free from warfare with indigenous inhabitants, four states would emerge from the Northwest Territory (Ohio—803, Indiana—1816, Illinois—1818, and Michigan—1837, inclusive of the Upper Peninsula; Lindley et al., 1937). One final treaty, signed on July 31, 1855, would remove all the remaining Ojibwe in Michigan to the Upper Peninsula (Horse Capture, 2010), thus reserving nearly the entirety of the Michigan panhandle, save for only a few tribes ("Federally recognized Indian Reservations and tribes," pp. 354–355), for White settlers and the development of their institutions.

Religious denominations were active in missionary activities among the Native American tribes in the Northwest Territory as well. In particular, Treuer (2010) asserted that the Episcopalians and United Methodists "worked tirelessly" Christianizing the Match-e-be-nash-she-wish (Potawatomi) in southeast Michigan (p. 41). Indeed, denominational colleges served the purpose of educating clergy, fortifying lay congregants in the faith, and, particularly in the territories, served as mission outposts (Rudolph, 1990; Thelin, 2011). Therefore, it is notable that of the 13 GLCA colleges, all but one (Wooster) had been founded by the last treaty removing the Ojibwe to the Upper Peninsula in 1855, and of those 12, all but one (Antioch) were founded by religious denominations.[2] The United Methodists had a college in each of first three states to emerge from the Northwest Territory: Albion, DePauw, and Ohio Wesleyan.

Underground Railroad

Although the Northwest Territory and its emergent states were not intended to be a safe haven for African Americans seeking to emancipate themselves from slavery in the South (Roosevelt, 1957), it nonetheless was a thoroughfare for many escaping to Canada. Due to the fugitive slave laws, remaining in even the northern USA was not safe, but free African Americans and White abolitionists, predominantly Quakers, living in these areas enabled safe passage on the Underground Railroad (Gates, 2013). The Underground Railroad was a network of individuals who agreed to hide those escaping slavery in their homes and further aid their journey (Gates, 2013). Prior to and throughout the Civil War, Ohio, Michigan,

Indiana, and Pennsylvania each had stops on the Underground Railroad (National Park Service, n.d.[a]; Switala, 2001/2008). Ohio had the most sites, 13, while Michigan and Indiana had the fewest, 2 and 3, respectively. Although the National Park Service (n.d.[a]) only shows routes in the eastern half of Pennsylvania, Switala (2001/2008) documented the Uniontown–Pittsburgh route which had a branch through Meadville north to Erie. Oberlin College was the only one of the GLCA institutions located in a city that also had a known Underground Railroad station,[3] although other colleges were located relatively proximate to other stations (National Park Service, n.d.[b]).

Civil Rights Laws in GLCA States

The political and constitutional gains for manumission, citizenship, and enfranchisement for Black men as an outgrowth of the Union's victory in the Civil War were quickly undermined by the emergence of White nativist, segregationist organizations (Gates, 2013). Common understandings of the Midwest emphasize it as a hostile place for Black citizens (Finkelman, 2006). However, the states in which the GLCA institutions were located varied greatly in the extent to which laws, social customs, and local activism affected the climate for race relations as the nineteenth century moved into the twentieth century. In this section, the civil rights legislation and activism documented for Michigan, Ohio, Pennsylvania, and Indiana are reviewed.

Michigan

Michigan state law included strong protections against racial discrimination and the State Supreme Court was committed to their enforcement with most of Michigan's early settlers primarily coming from deeply abolitionist areas such as New York and New England (Finkelman, 2006). In fact, Michigan's revised code in 1838—just one year after it became a state—overturned the disenfranchisement of African Americans embedded in the Northwest Ordinance (Finkelman, 2006) that restricted citizenship, property holding, and jury service to White men (Chase, 1833). Michigan legislators and local officials also typically failed to enforce the provisions of Ohio's Black codes[4] that were adopted when it became a state, believing them to be unconstitutional and contrary to public opinion (Finkelman, 2006) and would overturn them by 1850 (Murray,

1951/1997). Consequently, the state's Black population grew rapidly prior to the Civil War. Features of Michigan's laws, including the right of Black citizens to testify against White citizens, caused it to resemble the Northeast more than it did the Midwest (Finkelman, 2006).

Following the Civil War, in 1867, Michigan passed a law prohibiting segregation in its public schools, which faced resistance from Detroit school officials (Finkelman, 2006). As Finkelman (2006) documented, the Michigan Supreme Court definitively rejected the Detroit school board's claims that it should be allowed to segregate its schools. In much of the state, Black students and White students attended school together, and prior to the Civil War, the percentage of Black people in school between 6 and 20 years of age in Michigan exceeded that of the entire North by 9% (Finkelman, 2006). The State Supreme Court would later attempt in 1867 to expand voting rights to its Black citizens though Black residents had already been allowed to vote in school board elections since 1855 (Finkelman, 2006). The state's constitutional convention enthusiastically supported a provision extending suffrage to Black men, but the constitution was defeated because of other provisions related to railroad financing, government salaries, and liquor sales (Finkelman, 2006; Hershock, 2003). By the adoption of an 1883 law repealing the ban on interracial marriage, Michigan had eliminated all forms of legally sanctioned racial discrimination: "Whites, blacks, and Indians [*sic*] were now formally equal in the state" (Finkelman, 2006, p. 5). The Michigan Civil Rights Act of 1885 (Public Act 130; State of Michigan, 1885) defied the US Supreme Court's denunciation of the federal Civil Rights Act of 1875 and guaranteed full and equal civil rights to all those living within the state's jurisdiction (Finkelman, 2006), and these laws remained as of Murray's (1951/1997) review of compiled laws in 1948. Yet, Michigan had no cities with municipal codes banning discrimination listed in Murray's (1951/1997) compilation.

Despite this legal progressivism setting Michigan distinctly apart from the rest of the country, the Jim Crow Era in Michigan did find unequal enforcement of civil rights (Finkelman, 2006). Localities where Republicans were in control generally vigorously enforced civil rights legislation, while those under Democratic control were generally hostile to civil rights for Black people and allowed segregationist policies and practices to develop (Finkelman, 2006). This was particularly the case in Detroit, which had been "successfully ghettoized" by a combination of private business practices such as restrictive covenants, loan refusals to Black residents seeking to purchase in certain neighborhoods, and real estate agents' complicity (Finkelman, 2006, p. 8). In 1925, Finkelman (2006) referred to the case of Dr. Ossian Sweet who had purchased a home in an all-White neighborhood in Detroit and had his home attacked by a mob. In Sweet's ensuing defense of his home, a White man was killed and he, his wife, and several others who had come to assist were put on trial for murder, facing a jury of 12 White men (Finkelman, 2006). Despite the city's virulent racism and the rise of the Ku Klux Klan in the north during this period, the jury upheld Sweet's property rights to self-defense in his own home and acquitted Sweet and his compatriots (Finkelman, 2006). This did not open up Detroit's housing market to Blacks—in fact, it likely further restricted it. Nevertheless, for Finkelman, this case demonstrated both the complexity and conflict within Michigan and how distinct it was from the rest of the Midwest and the rest of the country.

Ohio

Ohio was the first state to emerge from the Northwest Territory, its statehood ratified in 1803 (Chase, 1833). Ohio's Black codes that Michigan would later inherit (Finkelman, 2006) reflected the South's concerns that the Territory and its states not become a refuge for fugitive slaves (Roosevelt, 1957). Any African American entering the state had to register with local officials and provide proof of their freedom, that they would not need public assistance, and references for those who would verify their good behavior (Finkelman, 2006). These requirements made Ohio an unwelcoming place for Black migrants and the laws were not repealed until the mid-nineteenth century. Until this time, Black Ohio residents also could not testify against White residents in court, even for their own self-defense or property interests (Finkelman, 2006). These discriminatory laws coexisted with strong civil rights and abolition activism by both Black and White citizens. As noted earlier, Ohio had the most number of Underground Railroad stations of any of the four states of focus (National Park Service, n.d.[a]). Oberlin and Yellow Springs, near the northeast and southwest corners of the state, were both known for their liberal views (Lester, 2003; Waite, 2001). In 1833, Oberlin College was founded with the mission to educate any student regardless of gender or race (Waite, 2001) and therefore was set apart from state laws.

By the mid-twentieth century, the legal situation in Ohio had evolved. Murray's (1951/1997) review documented that a total of 18 states had "civil rights" laws prohibiting discrimination in "places of public accommodation and amusement" (e.g., restaurants, hotels and inns, movie theaters, bathrooms), including Michigan and Ohio, and provided for both criminal and civil remedies (p. 8). These protections, however, only extended to citizens, not to all persons (Murray, 1951/1997, p. 10). Moreover, Throckmorton's Ohio Code Annotated with Baldwin's 1948 revision included a provision prohibiting discrimination in the awarding of state contracts with penalties amounting to $25.00 per person discriminated against (Murray, 1951/1997, p. 353). In addition, major cities at the time, such as Cincinnati and Cleveland, also had provisions in their municipal codes banning racial discrimination in employment and public housing, respectively (Murray, 1951/1997). Toledo and Youngstown also had municipal codes banning racial discrimination. By 1959, Ohio had passed its own Civil Rights Act covering employment and public accommodations ("Ohio Civil Rights Act of 1959," n.d.).

Regarding education, Murray noted that although Ohio was among nine states that had not passed legislation prohibiting public school segregation, "mixed schools exist in [the state]" (1951/1997, p. 10). The absence of explicit legal prohibitions against school segregation left no means to enforce desegregation uniformly across the state, which would set Ohio up to be a significant test case after 1954 for implementing the *Brown* decision (Clotfelter, 2004). Although Black Ohio residents were afforded legal protection for their public pastimes, they had no codified support for their equal rights to employment or education. Employment and education were prerequisites for having the means and interest for travel and other pastimes.

Indiana

According to Finkelman (2006), the scholarly consensus on Indiana (and Illinois) was that Black people faced discrimination and hostility in the Midwest after the Civil War. Given that political leaders in Indiana and Illinois attempted to have the anti-slavery provisions of the Northwest Ordinance set aside when they pursued statehood (Lindley et al., 1937), this is perhaps unsurprising. In fact, Indiana included the same Black codes that Ohio did when it attained statehood in 1816 and did not repeal them until after the Civil War, during Reconstruction (Finkelman, 2006). Black residents of Indiana were not able to defend their personal safety or economic interests by testifying against White residents in court and were not enfranchised to vote. In 1869, Indiana had mandated that separate schools be provided for Black children and insufficient numbers of children were not a justification for their co-education with White students ("List of Jim Crow law examples by state," 2016).

The twentieth century would see some progress toward desegregation and anti-discrimination legislation, but it was uneven. In 1905, Indiana passed a statute prohibiting miscegenation, and in 1952, the miscegenation statute was strengthened to void any existing Black–White interracial marriages ("List of Jim Crow law examples by state," 2016). By 1949, Indiana laws "abolished and prohibited" racially segregated schools (Murray, 1951/1997, p. 145), including public colleges and universities. This put Indiana ahead of Ohio in this regard. Indiana also prohibited employment discrimination based on "race, color, creed, national origin, or ancestry" (Murray, 1951/1997, p. 148). Murray (1951/1997) noted, however, that Indiana's Fair Employment Practice Acts were "chiefly educational and [had] no strong enforcement powers" (p. 9). Further, in these same statutes, Indiana (as well as Texas, North Carolina, and West Virginia) established racially segregated battalions within its national guard (Murray, 1951/1997). Evansville, in the southwest corner bordering Kentucky on the Ohio River, was the only city in the state that Murray documented as having municipal civil rights legislation as of 1949.

Western Pennsylvania

The Commonwealth of Pennsylvania is one of the original 13 colonies and therefore among the first states in the USA. At one point, the nation's capital was in the eastern city of Philadelphia and its political leaders, such as Ben Franklin, played prominent roles in the founding of the nation. Therefore, one would expect its state statutes to reflect the egalitarianism that was commonly used to describe the Northeast (Finkelman, 2006; Roosevelt, 1957). Indeed, its state laws as of 1949 did prohibit discrimination in public accommodations, though only providing for criminal remedies not civil, and had among the most extensive laws including both a great many types of places covered as well as who could avail themselves of such protections (Murray, 1951/1997). Pennsylvania also prohibited discrimination in the awarding of state contracts and employment of those working such contracts and rail transportation. These state provisions were not necessarily replicated at the local level: Philadelphia was the only city as of 1949 that had municipal laws prohibiting discrimination (Murray, 1951/1997). Pittsburgh, the state's westernmost major city, was not listed in Murray's (1951/1997) comprehensive review as having local provisions prohibiting discrimination.

Like Ohio, Pennsylvania's Black residents were not guaranteed an equal education. In his foreword to the reprinted edition of Murray's text, Davison (1997) noted that "officially sanctioned school segregation persisted in many northern school districts," particularly in Pennsylvania, Ohio, and three other states, "until the late 1940s and early 1950s" (p. xxiii) particularly in their southernmost municipalities. A 2016 listing of examples of Jim Crow laws by state noted an 1869 statute that prohibited Black children from attending Pittsburgh public schools. Even in Philadelphia, however, Black residents faced school segregation and discriminatory funding in the first half of the twentieth century (Franklin, 1979).

Summary

As noted by Finkelman (2006), the history of civil rights protections in the Midwest is complex and uneven. From Michigan's passionately judicially defended civil rights legislation to Indiana's slow repeal of Black codes, the nineteenth century saw a great deal of divergence in how civil rights for Black people were handled across the states. The twentieth century began to see more uniformity in how these states responded to segregation, but there were still laws openly forbidding intermarriage in Indiana and uneven enforcement of employment anti-discrimination state statutes. By the time of this study, only two of the four states in which the GLCA institutions were located had comprehensive civil rights legislation: Michigan and Ohio. Nevertheless, as will be seen in this text, Black matriculates to the GLCA colleges reported uneven experiences with segregation in their off-campus local communities, including in Michigan and Ohio.

Consistent with a CRT analysis, racism and its products, segregation and discrimination, were pervasive and challenging to resist (Delgado & Stefancic, 2012). The existence of legislation was not enough to affect change in discriminatory practices on the local level. Moreover, local adoption and enforcement of state-level anti-discrimination legislation varied, demonstrating the sometimes significant differences in the attitudes of state legislators and governors and those of municipal politicians.

The mob attack on Dr. Sweet's home, discussed by Finkelman (2006), illustrates that people are first guided by internalized beliefs about others not by legislative prohibitions against acting out racial prejudice. Another lesson in Dr. Sweet's story though is that having equal protection under the law (e.g., the right to testify against White people at trial, the right to self-defense and defense of one's property) enables the possibility of justice in individual cases.

The unguaranteed access to equal education—in some cases not offered by the state and in others not enforced or countermanded by localities—reveals a unique enactment of whiteness. Harris (1993) defined whiteness as a form of property that defined social relations and expectations, and functioned to permit White people in the USA to gain tangible property and social mobility. Within this construct, whiteness as property could be used to confer privileges to White people while excluding Black people from attaining those privileges. Although employment and public accommodations were covered by civil rights legislation, being qualified for a job would rely on the extent of one's education and the assessment of the quality of that education by a hiring officer. Segregated elementary and secondary schools often did not have access to high-quality resources and White racial prejudice would deem any Black school and college to be inherently unqualified (Brown & Davis, 2001; Harding, 1981; Minor, 2004). If a Black person is not considered qualified for a middle-class job and thus denied that job, then that Black person cannot afford to avail themselves of the luxuries of traveling, staying in hotels and inns, eating out at restaurants, or going to the theater to see a movie, a play, or other arts performance. Schools therefore become the gatekeepers, protecting and restricting social status, mobility, and wealth for Whites within a locality. A CRT-based examination of civil rights legislation in Michigan, Ohio, Indiana, and Pennsylvania demonstrates the subtle nuances of whiteness to exclude Black residents from sharing most aspects of their public life with White residents and inhibiting their social and economic advancement.

Race and Higher Education, 1945–1965

We now turn to considering the racial terrain in higher education during the time period of this study. Thelin (2011) noted that the period of 1945–1965 had been described as a "golden age" of US higher education, given the significant gains in enrollment institutions experienced.

Federal legislative and judicial actions during these two decades would increase access to higher education for White women, Black students and other racially minoritized people across gender, and students across race and gender from middle-class and working-class families (Thelin, 2011). Although analyses of racial integration in traditionally White northern public universities described progress that was often stunted (Plaut, 1954; Zimbardo, 1966) and featured the social segregation of Black students (Little, 2002), the overall picture is complex.

"Quiet" Activism

As demonstrated in the previous section, the advent of the term "civil rights" predates even the 1940s (see Michigan's Civil Rights Act of 1885; Finkelman, 2006; State of Michigan, 1885). Yet, as Sanders-McMurty (2007) and Hutcheson, Gasman, and Sanders-McMurtry (2011) have pointed out, common perceptions of the Civil Rights Movement (CRM) limit its activity to the late 1950s and 1960s. In actuality, activism to extend civil rights for Black people was prevalent throughout the 1940s and 1950s (Dalfiume, 1970; Hutcheson et al., 2011; Sanders-McMurty, 2007). Black veterans returning from World War II were galvanized to fight at home for the same freedoms they had secured for others abroad (Dalfiume, 1970; Gates, 2013; Hutcheson et al., 2011). Moreover, President Truman's Commission on Higher Education's widely read report included passionate recommendations to end discrimination and expand access throughout public life, including in education (Hutcheson et al.; Thelin, 2011). This activism may have been "quiet" compared to the more televised and reported protest actions of the 1960s, but was nonetheless essential to laying the groundwork for those later successes (Dalfiume, 1970).

Black individuals and civic groups as well as White accomplices sought to expand access to Black people in higher education in the first decade following World War II. These efforts did not always mean fighting segregation directly, but also included expanding support for and improving the quality of Black colleges and universities. Northern White educators and philanthropists had generally come to prefer the education of Blacks in segregated Black schools and colleges (Franklin, 1979; Waite, 2001). Therefore, Black educational philosophers and leaders sought to use White resistance to racial integration to promote the establishment and funding of Black schools and colleges at the turn of the century (Alridge, 2007; Perkins, 1993).

By mid-century, Black civil rights groups like the National Association for the Advancement of Colored People (NAACP) had already been engaged in bringing legal challenges to state supreme courts to overturn separate but equal educational segregation and won some notable victories in *Gaines* in 1938 and *Sweatt* in 1950 that helped lay the groundwork for the *Brown* decision (Miller, 1970; Ogletree, 2004). Other Black civic organizations were also active in the struggle for civil rights for Black Americans. Sanders-McMurtry's case study of Black women's civic organizations, including sororities, illustrated the social activism that motivated these groups (Hutcheson et al., 2011; Sanders-McMurty, 2007). In particular, Black women in these groups raised donations to fund schools and provide loans to their own members to help complete their education and access a middle-class lifestyle (Hutcheson et al., 2011; Sanders-McMurty, 2007). Black women in The Links, Inc., for example, worked directly within communities to support education, intergroup relations, and social uplift as an imperative of living in a democratic country (Hutcheson et al., 2011; Sanders-McMurty, 2007).

White philanthropic organizations also engaged in more vigorous action to bolster educational quality for southern Black residents by getting them enrolled in northern educational institutions (Donohue, Heckman, & Todd, 2002). John D. Rockefeller was among the most active White philanthropists financially supporting Black colleges, as well as providing scholarships to assist Black students to attend private traditionally White colleges in the North (Donohue et al., 2002). Beyond philanthropy, individual White administrators like George F. Zook as head of the American Council on Education (ACE) and other roles (Hutcheson et al., 2011) and Fred G. Wale as director of education for the Julius Rosenwald Fund (Anderson, 1993) sought to broaden access to Black students and Black faculty in northern traditionally White colleges, respectively.

Finally, private citizens in the Black community sought to drive more philanthropic support toward Black colleges. One such effort was led by Harlem postal worker and civil leader, Victor H. Green, the creator and publisher of the *Negro Motorist Green Book* that sought to help Black travelers drive across the country safely finding places where they could buy gas, eat, stay the night, and shop (Burton, 2012; McGee, 2010). In the 1947 edition, Green reprinted a notice from the *New York Times* soliciting donations to support a $1.3 million campaign chaired by Rockefeller on behalf of the United Negro College Fund for 33 private Black colleges (Green, 1947, p. 3). The notice emphasized the need to educate those returning from the war who had proven their capacities fighting alongside White soldiers and to support the colleges dedicated to their education who might otherwise not be able to handle the influx of student demand as these veterans claimed their G.I. Bill benefits (Green, 1947, p. 3). Black college students at Black colleges in the South also found ways to support civil rights activism, despite attempts by presidents at those institutions to dissuade their students from participating in direct action usually for fear of losing funding (T. J. Edge, personal communication, July 2016).

Frustrated Advances

As mentioned earlier, large gains in access and enrollment by African Americans and other groups were realized between 1945 and 1965. Federal legislative and judicial actions spurred much of these gains, particularly the G.I. Bill of 1944, the *Brown* decision by the Supreme Court in 1954, the National Defense Education Act (NDEA) of 1958, the 1964 Civil Rights Act, the 1964 Economic Opportunity Act, and the 1965 Higher Education Act. This massification of higher education (Gumport, Iannozzi, Shaman, & Zemsky, 1997) was not uniformly experienced, however. Geographic segregation patterns and entrenched systemic discrimination distributed expansion unevenly with disparate effects experienced by Black collegians.

The Servicemen's Readjustment Act of 1944, commonly referred to as the G.I. Bill, became law as the country prepared for the eventual end of World War II and the need to reintegrate returning veterans into the nation's economy (Serow, 2004; Thelin, 2011). Although higher education institutions were not intended to be the primary beneficiaries of this legislation, the portable tuition and fee scholarships that the G.I. Bill offered to returning veterans significantly transformed the nation's colleges and universities (Thelin, 2011). According to Serow (2004), 2.2 million veterans used the educational benefits of Title II of the G.I. Bill to pay for undergraduate or graduate education, far exceeding legislators' expectations. However, Black veterans were not uniformly able to take advantage of this entitlement, and its influence on gains in Black collegiate enrollment has been debated (Katznelson & Mettler, 2008; Serow, 2004). Some scholars even argue that the bill actually widened the educational attainment gap for Black Americans (Onkst, 1998; Turner & Bound, 2003).

This debate is due in part to some overestimation of who the bill benefited. As documented by Serow (2004), as a whole, men who served in World War II were better educated and had stronger educational profiles than other men in the general population as well as most other veterans. In addition, surveys of veteran college students during the late 1940s found that only 20% of those veterans would not have enrolled in college without the subsidy provided by the G.I. Bill (Serow, 2004). Particular to Black veterans though, the ability to use their Title II educational benefits was limited by other factors. Elite institutions, contrary to being motivated toward more egalitarian and meritocratic admissions policies, generally admitted veterans who were already similar to nonveteran students (Serow, 2004). Due to racial segregation, most Black collegians remained barred from admission to southern universities, where the vast majority of the US Black population resided and to which most Black veterans returned after the war (Katznelson & Mettler, 2008; Onkst, 1998; Serow, 2004; Turner & Bounds, 2003). The postwar demand for seats at the historically Black colleges and universities (HBCUs) across the South could not be met by these severely underfinanced institutions; an estimated 20,000 veterans were turned away (Serow, 2004) having no other access to higher education due to institutionalized racism in college admissions.

The next decade brought to fruition more than two decades of persistent activism on the part of the NAACP to bring about educational desegregation through legal action (Ogletree, 2004). Led by Charles Houston and his assistant, Thurgood Marshall, limited victories had already been won in undergraduate and graduate education to show the inherent disparities of segregated education. Backed by educational research by psychologists Kenneth and Mamie Clark on the harmful effects of segregation on childhood development, the US Supreme Court would finally overturn the precedent set by the high court's decision in 1896 in *Plessy v. Ferguson* which legitimated Jim Crow laws already being enforced across all areas of public life, including all levels of public education (Ogletree, 2004).

Although the Supreme Court's 1954 ruling in *Brown v. Board of Education, Topeka* began the process of educational desegregation in some municipalities, the Court's later ambiguous mandates thwarted progress (Miller, 1970). Widespread reforms in educational desegregation would take decades to realize (Miller, 1970; Ogletree, 2004). More than 100 southern officeholders signed the "Southern Manifesto" and remained committed to racial segregation, resisting demands to desegregate schools under their purview, including public colleges and universities (Clotfelter,

2004; Day, 2014). Enforcement of the order to desegregate in compliance with the Supreme Court's ruling was uneven and required the support of US marshals and the National Guard (Clotfelter, 2004; Ogletree, 2004).

The students who would integrate these institutions[5] faced significant racial hostility, often as the only Black student on campus or one of just two (Clark, 1992; Doyle, 2003; Hunter-Gault, 1992, 2014; Meredith & Doyle, 2012; Sayre, 1995). The motivation to endure these extremely adverse conditions to receive an education was deeply rooted in a religious conviction that their "mission," as Meredith articulated it, was righteous (Hunter-Gault, 2014; Meredith & Doyle, 2012; Sayre, 1995). They believed that God was on their side and that they had been chosen to carry the race forward on their backs. In these biographies, it is evident, as was the case with primary and secondary school desegregation test cases (Beals, 1995), that these young people were seen as model citizens, good students, and fitting the middle-class respectability perceived as necessary to win support from White advocates.

Black students were also crossing the color lines in northern public and private colleges and universities beyond the GLCA institutions. As documented by historical scholars, social segregation was rife and encounters with racial discrimination on and off campus were common experiences for these students (Little, 2002; Plaut, 1954). Also, typically the only or one of a very few, these Black collegians also experienced friendship and support from White peers, faculty, and administrators (Evans, 2007).

Later in the 1950s, the federal government would again turn to legislative action to broaden economic access to higher education. Although Congress did not fund any of the recommendations that emerged out of the Truman Commission Report in 1947, the passage of the NDEA of 1958 would realize part of the commission's suggestions for national scholarships for college attendance based on financial need (Long, 2013). However, NDEA support was limited to those students pursuing degrees in science, math, and foreign languages related to the country's military interests (Long, 2013). Nevertheless, the National Defense Student Loan Program that was created by the NDEA helped to augment the private philanthropic support that some Black students were receiving via the Ford Foundation's endowment of the National Scholarship Service and the Fund for Negro Students (NSSFNS) begun in the 1950s (Rooks, 2006).

It was not until the US Congress passed the 1964 Civil Rights Act along with other Supreme Court rulings (e.g., *Green v. County School Board*,

Alexander v. Holmes) that local school districts and higher education institutions began to cooperate with federally legislated desegregation mandates (Clotfelter, 2004). The passage of the Civil Rights Act thus enabled the democratic effects of the G.I. Bill and the NDEA to be more fully realized. Passage of the Civil Rights Act would also keep implementation of the Economic Opportunity Act of 1964 (EOA) and the Higher Education Act of 1965 (HEA) from being so hampered by overly discriminatory college admission policies. The EOA and HEA would become the foundation of federal financial aid policies (Long, 2013). Consequently, the greatest gains in college enrollment for Blacks in the USA were realized after 1965.

The Institutions of the Great Lakes Colleges Association

Despite the Supreme Court's unanimous decision in *Brown v. Board of Education* in 1954, most educational institutions, including northern colleges and universities, continued to enact segregationist admission and/or residency policies for Black collegians. Yet, several institutions in the Great Lakes region of the US Midwest had race-neutral admissions policies or sought to admit a racially heterogeneous student body prior to the passage of federal civil rights legislation in 1964. Among these institutions were a set of colleges that first came together formally in 1962 as the GLCA. These institutions included Albion College, Antioch College, Denison University, DePauw University, Earlham College, Hope College, Kalamazoo College, Kenyon College, Oberlin College, Ohio Wesleyan University, Wabash College, and The College of Wooster. Allegheny College, located in western Pennsylvania, joined the association in 1992; it is included in this study because it is similar in historical development, institutional size, student composition, and general character (e.g., reputation for a tradition of academic excellence). Table 1.1 provides more information about these institutions, including their founding date and affiliation, location, gender composition, and estimated size of their Black student enrollment between 1945 and 1965.

Such policies had been in place for a century or longer at several institutions (e.g., Antioch, Earlham, Kalamazoo, Kenyon, and Oberlin) and as private colleges, none of the 13 were required to adhere to state and local laws and could choose to resist local customs, especially when they conflicted with espoused institutional values. Moreover, religious narratives of inclusion and hospitality were often the impetus for these colleges'

Table 1.1 GLCA colleges, institutional characteristics, and Black student enrollment between 1945 and 1965

Institution	*Founded*	*Location*	*Religious affiliation*	*Gender*	*BSE*
Albion College	1835	Albion, MI	United Methodist	Co-ed	66
Allegheny College	1815	Meadville, PA	Congregationalist[a]	Co-ed	32
Antioch College	1852	Yellow Springs, OH	Nonsectarian[b]	Co-ed	133
Denison University	1831	Granville, OH	Baptist	Co-ed	15[c]
DePauw University	1837	Greencastle, IN	United Methodist	Co-ed	49
Earlham College	1847	Richmond, IN	Society of Friends (Quaker)	Co-ed	122
Hope College	1851	Holland, MI	Dutch Reformed	Co-ed	33
Kalamazoo College	1833	Kalamazoo, MI	Baptist	Co-ed	38
Kenyon College	1824	Gambier, OH	Episcopal	Men	21
Oberlin College	1833	Oberlin, OH	Congregationalist	Co-ed	197
Ohio Wesleyan University	1842	Delaware, OH	United Methodist	Co-ed	113
Wabash College[d]	1832	Crawfordsville, IN	Presbyterian	Men	23
The College of Wooster	1866	Wooster, OH	Presbyterian	Co-ed	71
					913

Note: BSE stands for estimated Black student enrollment. Earlham was founded as a seminary in 1847 and the college was added in 1859. Hope College was founded in 1851 but did not receive its charter until 1866. Kenyon College began admitting women in 1969, while Wabash remains a single-sex college

[a]The Congregationalist Church has since become the United Church of Christ

[b]Christian principles still heavily influenced the college's values

[c]Denison's BSE only includes those enrolled as full-time students; there were an additional 14 exchange students from historically Black institutions, who were on campus for either one semester or one academic year from Hampton, Fisk, or Howard

[d]Wabash cut ties with the Presbyterian church during the time period of this study and became nonsectarian

efforts to pursue racial integration on campus. All these colleges, with the exception of Antioch, were sponsored by Protestant Christian denominations. As such, notions of kinship, unity, and community were dominant themes in the institutional archives for promoting the recruitment and retention of Black students. Although Antioch was not a denominational college, it too used Christian rhetoric to support its stance in favor of the full integration of Black students on its campus. Despite this religious fervor, these institutions struggled to realize the hope of Christian kinship, unity, and community in terms of enrollment of Black students and their integration on campus. The conflicts between religious theology and social custom and an unwillingness to directly confront anti-Black social customs often dampened or refuted college efforts to enact their espoused religious values.

The available extant literature regarding these colleges is limited though to mostly personal biographies written by or about renowned Black alumni (Ballard, 1973, 2011; Griffin, Csete, Moerdyk, & Limer, 1983; King, 1993; Lester, 2003) or by institutional historians describing the conditions at a single college (Baumann, 2010; Hamm, 1997; Warren, 1990). These personal and historical accounts all demonstrate similar conflicting and uneven experiences with race relations, discrimination, social isolation, and support as pervasive in the experiences of Black collegians at other northern institutions and in the South.

Although the GLCA was not formed until 1962, all of the 13 colleges were founded in the nineteenth century, and most were founded before the Civil War. As noted above, the Native American removal policies seemingly cleared the land, literally, for the establishment of settler educational institutions, and many of these colleges were established in Ohio, Michigan, and Indiana in the aftermath of such treaties and legislative acts. Moreover, the states of Michigan, Ohio, Indiana, and Pennsylvania had complicated and complex histories with slavery, race relations, and civil rights regarding Black people. Only Oberlin College was located in a city that also had a listed Underground Railroad stop (National Park Service, n.d.[b]). Although both Michigan and Ohio had state-level civil rights legislation, these laws were not rigorously enforced (Finkelman, 2006; Murray, 1951/1997), and racial segregation and discrimination were openly practiced there as well as in Indiana and western Pennsylvania.

A search of four different editions of Green's motorist guides (1947, 1949, 1956, and 1963) did not turn up any listings of safe accommodations for Black travelers in the rural towns in which the GLCA colleges were located, except for the Oberlin Inn in two years, 1947 and 1949. By 1956, the Oberlin Inn was no longer included in the *Green Book* and would not return before its last year of publication in 1963. Although not destination cities in themselves, most of the GLCA colleges were in towns along major thoroughfares prior and which would follow the later developed interstate highway system, especially in Michigan and Indiana. Therefore, they could have served as stops along the way to larger cities, such as Detroit, Chicago, Indianapolis, Columbus, Cleveland, and Pittsburgh. Moreover, some of the colleges were in towns with sizeable Black communities, such as Albion, Kalamazoo, Meadville, Oberlin, and Richmond. Therefore, their absence from Green's travel guides is noteworthy and suggestive of the presence of racial hostility and segregation or the lack of economic means among Black residents to support successful Black businesses and houses large enough to accommodate overnight guests.

Many of the colleges in towns with sizeable numbers of local Black residents saw most of their Black student enrollment come from those towns and surrounding areas, such as Albion and Earlham. Each of these colleges was also close enough to a major metropolitan center (Detroit and Indianapolis) from which they could recruit Black students. Oberlin's already established reputation for educating Black people allowed it to continue to recruit nationally for Black students in a way that was unmatched by other colleges except for Antioch (Waite, 2001). However, some institutions that were not near a sizeable Black population engaged in extensive missionary work to recruit students who had attended denominational schools, such as Hope College's recruitment pipeline from Alabama. The coeducational colleges also had somewhat similarly sized student bodies of approximately 1100–1300 students, though Hope College and Ohio Wesleyan University were the largest with an average of over 2000 students each during this period. Kenyon and Wabash, the only single-sex men's colleges in this set, were the smallest of the 13 colleges with enrollments under 500 students each.

Archival research, institutional chronicles, and alumni biographies confirm that Black students did not constitute a critical mass of the student body at any of these institutions (Ballard, 1973, 2011; Baumann, 2010; Griffin et al., 1983; Hamm, 1997; King, 1993; Lester, 2003; Warren, 1990). Although there were 198 Black students enrolled at Oberlin between 1945 and 1965, they constituted less than 1% of all students during that period, representing a significant decline in Black enrollment prior to the Reconstruction Era (Waite, 2001). Meanwhile, the numbers at other institutions were much fewer: Denison University only had 15 Black students enrolled full-time over the course of these 20 years. The total Black student enrollment at Earlham, Oberlin, Ohio Wesleyan, and Antioch constituted 61.2% (n = 562) of the total Black enrollment of all 13 colleges.

Conclusion

The Northwest Territory, the states that emerged from it and their neighbor to the east, and the GLCA colleges share in common a fraught and complex history with issues of race relations and civil rights. Generally, progressive and liberal policies and aspirations coexisted alongside racial animus and segregationist practices. Whiteness as property inhibited the full enjoyment of Black residents in these areas of the equality promised by state legislation. Moreover, the effectiveness of federal legislation and government programs intended to spur greater access for minoritized students was vulnerable to local and institutional attitudes. Regardless, Black people were consistently pushing for greater rights, especially in the aftermath of World War II. Alliances between Black civic organizations and White philanthropic foundations, as well as individual Whites acting as accomplices in support of increasing access to Black academics in White institutions, led to measured gains and opportunities. Caught between strong public sentiment and inconsistently enacted institutional values, Black students' collegiate experiences were neither wholly negative nor wholly positive. In many ways, the compromises featured in the Northwest Ordinance to appease slaveholders (Roosevelt, 1957) would remain as characterizing features of the states and the private GLCA colleges developing parallel to them throughout this period.

Notes

1. Western Pennsylvania refers to the Pittsburgh metropolitan area and north to Erie, PA. Although the US Census places the entire state of Pennsylvania in the Middle Atlantic region, the industrial economic base and cultural norms of western Pennsylvania have much more in common with the major cities and rural areas of Ohio and Michigan than with cities of Philadelphia and New York, which are also included in the Middle Atlantic region. Personal communications

with several people who have lived and have gone to college in the state, including the participants who attended Allegheny, confirmed this characterization and saw western Pennsylvania as more Midwest than East Coast.

2. See Table 1.1.
3. Likely due to the abolitionist history of both the town and college.
4. Black codes were laws specifically regulating the lives of African Americans.
5. Some of these pioneers included Autherine Lucy (University of Alabama, 1956), Charlayne Hunter and Hamilton Homes (University of Georgia, 1961), James Meredith (Ole Miss, 1963), as well as Vivian Malone and James Hood (University of Alabama at Tuscaloosa, 1963).

References

Alridge, D. P. (2007). Of victorianism, civilizationism, and progressivism: The educational ideals of W. E. B. DuBois and Anna Julia Cooper, 1892–1940. *History of Education Quarterly, 47*(4), 416–446.

Anderson, J. D. (1993). Race, meritocracy, and the American academy during the immediate post-World War II era. *History of Education Quarterly, 33*, 151–175.

Ballard, A. B. (1973). *The education of Black folk: The Afro-American struggle for knowledge in White America*. New York, NY: Harper & Row.

Ballard, A. B. (2011). *Breaching Jericho's walls: A twentieth-century African American life*. Albany: State University of New York Press.

Baumann, R. M. (2010). *Constructing Black education at Oberlin College: A documentary history*. Athens: Ohio University Press.

Beals, M. P. (1995). *Warriors don't cry: The searing memoir of the battle to integrate Little Rock's Central High*. New York, NY: Washington Square Press.

Brown III, M. C., & Davis, J. E. (2001). The historically Black college as social contract, social capital, and social equalizer. *Peabody Journal of Education, 76*, 31–49.

Burton, N. K. (2012, July 9). How did blacks travel during segregation? *The Root*. Retrieved from http://www.theroot.com/print/64178

Chase, S. P. (Ed.). (1833). *The statutes of Ohio and of the Northwestern Territory adopted or enacted from 1788 to 1833 inclusive: Together with the Ordinance of 1787; The constitutions of Ohio and of the United States, and various public instruments and acts of Congress: Illustrated by a preliminary sketch of the history of Ohio; numerous references and notes, and copious indexes* (Vol. 1). Cincinnati, OH: Corey & Fairbank. Center for Archival Collections, Bowling Green State University.

Clark, E. C. (1992). *The schoolhouse door: Segregation's last stand at the University of Alabama*. Oxford: Oxford University.

Clotfelter, C. T. (2004). *After Brown: The rise and retreat of school desegregation*. Princeton, NJ: Princeton University Press.

Dalfiume, R. M. (1970). Stirrings of revolt. In A. Weinstein & F. O. Gatell (Eds.), *The segregation era, 1863–1954: A modern reader* (pp. 235–247). New York, NY: Oxford University Press.

Davison, D. M. (1997). Foreword. In P. Murray (Ed.), *States' laws on race and color* (pp. xiii–xxvii). Athens: University of Georgia Press. Retrieved from https://books.google.com/

Day, J. K. (2014). *The Southern Manifesto: Massive resistance and the fight to preserve segregation*. Jackson: University Press of Mississippi.

Delgado, R., & Stefancic, J. (2012). *Critical race theory: An introduction* (2nd ed.). New York: New York University.

Donohue III, J. J., Heckman, J. J., & Todd, P. E. (2002). The schooling of southern Blacks: The roles of legal activism and private philanthropy, 1910–1960. *The Quarterly Journal of Economics, 117*(1), 225–268.

Doyle, W. (2003). *An American insurrection: James Meredith and the battle of Oxford, Mississippi*. New York, NY: Anchor Books.

Evans, S. Y. (2007). *Black women in the ivory tower, 1850–1954*. Gainesville: University of Florida.

Finkelman, P. (2006, April 27). *The surprising history of race and law in Michigan*. Michigan Supreme Court Historical Society. Retrieved from http://www.micourthistory.org/historical-vignettes/

Franklin, V. P. (1979). *The education of Black Philadelphia: The social and educational history of a minority community, 1900–1950*. Philadelphia, PA: University of Pennsylvania.

Gates Jr., H. L. (2013). *Life upon these shores: Looking at African American history, 1513–2008*. New York, NY: Alfred A. Knopf.

Green, V. H. (1947). *The Negro motorist Green book*. The New York Public Library Digital Collections. Retrieved from digitalcollections.nypl.org

Green, V. H. (1949). *The Negro motorist Green book*. The New York Public Library Digital Collections. Retrieved from digitalcollections.nypl.org

Green, V. H. (1956). *The Negro motorist Green book*. The New York Public Library Digital Collections. Retrieved from digitalcollections.nypl.org

Green, V. H. (1963). *The Negro motorist Green book*. The New York Public Library Digital Collections. Retrieved from digitalcollections.nypl.org

Griffin, G., Csete, J., Moerdyk, R. A., & Limer, C. (1983). *Emancipated spirits: Portraits of Kalamazoo College women*. Kalamazoo, MI: Kalamazoo College Press.

Gumport, P. J., Iannozzi, M., Shaman, S., & Zemsky, R. (1997). *Trends in United States higher education from massification to post massification*. National Center for Postsecondary Improvement. Stanford, CA: Stanford University. Retrieved from http://web.stanford.edu/group/ncpi/documents/pdfs/1-04_massification.pdf

Hamm, T. D. (1997). *Earlham college: A history, 1847–1997.* Bloomington: Indiana University Press.

Harding, V. (1981). *There is a river: The Black struggle for freedom in America.* San Diego, CA: Harcourt Brace & Company.

Harris, C. I. (1993). Whiteness as property. *Harvard Law Review, 106*, 1707–1791.

Harro, B. (2010). The cycle of socialization. In M. Adams, W. J. Blumenfeld, C. R. Castañeda, H. W. Hackman, M. L. Peters, & X. Zúñiga (Eds.), *Readings for diversity and social justice* (2nd ed., pp. 45–51). New York, NY: Routledge.

Hershock, M. J. (2003). *The paradox of progress: Economic change, individual enterprise, and political culture in Michigan, 1837–1878.* Athens: Ohio University Press.

Horse Capture Sr., G. P. (2010). Chapter four: The plains. In A. Truer, K. Wood, W. W. Fitzhugh, G. P. Horse Capture, T. L. Frazier, M. R. Miller, M. Belarde-Lewis, & J. Norwood (Eds.), *Indian nations of North America* (pp. 142–193). Washington, DC: National Geographic Society.

Hunter-Gault, C. (1992). *In my place.* New York, NY: Vintage Books.

Hunter-Gault, C. (2014). *To the mountaintop: My journey through the Civil Rights Movement.* New York, NY: Square Fish.

Hutcheson, P., Gasman, M., & Sanders-McMurtry, K. (2011). Race and equality in the academy: Rethinking higher education actors and the struggle for equality in the post-World War II period. *Journal of Higher Education, 82*(2), 121–153.

Katznelson, I., & Mettler, S. (2008). On race and policy history: A dialogue about the G. I. Bill. *Perspectives on politics, 6*(3), 519–537.

King, C. S. (1993). *My life with Martin Luther King, Jr* (Rev. ed.). New York, NY: Henry Holt & Co.

Lester, J. S. (2003). *Fire in my soul: Eleanor Holmes Norton.* New York, NY: Atria Books.

Lindley, H., Schneider, N. F., &Quaife, M. M. (1937). *History of the ordinance of 1787 and the Old Northwest Territory (A supplemental text for school use).* Marietta, OH: Northwest Territory Celebration Commission. Folder pOG 1113. Center for Archival Collections, Bowling Green State University.

List of Jim Crow law examples by state. (2016, May 18). *Wikipedia: The free encyclopedia.* Retrieved from https://en.wikipedia.org/wiki/List_of_Jim_Crow_law_examples_by_state

Little, M. H. (2002). The extra-curricular activities of Black college students, 1868–1940. *Journal of African American History, 87*, 43–56.

Long, B. T. (2013). Supporting access to higher education. In M. J. Bailey & S. Danziger (Eds.), *Legacies of the war on poverty, The national poverty center series on poverty and public policy* (pp. 93–120). New York, NY: Russell Sage Foundation.

McGee, C. (2010, August 22). The open road wasn't quite open to all. *The New York Times* [digital reprint]. Retrieved from http://www.nytimes.com

Meredith, J., & Doyle, W. (2012). *A mission from God: A memoir and challenge for America.* New York, NY: Atria Books.

Michigan, State of. (1885). *Public acts and joint and concurrent resolutions of the legislature of the state of Michigan, passed at the regular session of 1885, with an appendix.* Lansing, MI: W. S. George & Co.

Miller, L. (1970). Very deliberate speed. In A. Weinstein & F. O. Gatell (Eds.), *The segregation era, 1863–1954: A modern reader* (pp. 280–293). New York, NY: Oxford University Press.

Minor, J. T. (2004). Decision making in historically Black colleges and universities: Defining the governance context. *Journal of Negro Education, 73*(1), 40–52.

Murray, P. (1997). *States' laws on race and color.* Athens: University of Georgia Press. Retrieved from https://books.google.com. (Originally published in 1951).

Novick, P. (1998). *That noble dream: The "objectivity question" and the American historical profession.* New York, NY: Cambridge University Press.

Ogletree, C. (2004). *All deliberate speed: Reflections on the first half century of Brown v. Board of Education.* New York, NY: W. W. Norton & Co.

Ohio Civil Rights Act of 1959. (n.d.). Ohio history central. Ohio History Connection. Retrieved from http://www.ohiohistorycentral.org/w/Ohio_Civil_Rights_Act_of_1959

Onkst, D. H. (1998). "First a Negro…incidentally a veteran": Black World War Two veterans and the G. I. Bill of Rights in the deep south, 1944–1948. *Journal of Social History, 31*(3), 517–543.

Perkins, L. M. (1993). The role of education in the development of Black feminist thought, 1860–1920. *History of Education, 22*, 265–275.

Plaut, R. L. (1954). Racial integration in higher education in the North. *The Journal of Negro Education, 23*, 310–316.

Report of proceedings in Congress, Wednesday, Feb. 21, 1787. (1787, February 21). *Avalon project.* Yale University College of Law. Retrieved May 20, 2016 from avalon.law.yale.edu/18th_century/const04.asp

Rooks, N. M. (2006). *White money/Black power: The surprising history of African American studies and the crisis of race in higher education.* Boston, MA: Beacon Press.

Roosevelt, T. (1957). *The Northwest territory, 1787–1790.* Fort Wayne, IN: Public Library of Fort Wayne and Allen County. (Originally published in 1896).

Folder pOG 3088. Center for Archival Collections, Bowling Green State University.

Rudolph, F. (1990). *The American college and university: A history* (2nd ed.). Athens: University of Georgia.

Sanders-McMurty, K. (2007). *"Linked together in service": A history of education and philanthropy among the Black elite: The Links, Incorporated, 1946–1996.* Unpublished doctoral dissertation. Atlanta: Georgia State University.

Sayre, N. (1995). *Previous convictions: A journey through the 1950s.* New Brunswick, NJ: Rutgers University.

Serow, R. C. (2004). Policy as symbol: Title II of the 1994 G. I. Bill. *The Review of Higher Education, 27*(4), 481–499.

Switala, W. J. (2001/2008). *Underground railroad in Pennsylvania.* Mechanicsburg, PA: Stackpole Books.

Thelin, J. R. (2011). *A history of American higher education* (2nd ed.). Baltimore, MD: Johns Hopkins University Press.

Treuer, A. (2010). Chapter one: The northeast. In A. Truer, K. Wood, W. W. Fitzhugh, G. P. Horse Capture, T. L. Frazier, M. R. Miller, M. Belarde-Lewis, & J. Norwood (Eds.), *Indian nations of North America* (pp. 16–63). Washington, DC: National Geographic Society.

Turner, S., & Bound, J. (2003). Closing the gap or widening the divide: The effects of the G.I. Bill and World War II on the educational outcomes of Black Americans. *Journal of Economic History, 63*(1), 145–177.

Waite, C. L. (2001). The segregation of Black students at Oberlin College after reconstruction. *History of Education Quarterly, 41*, 344–364.

Warren, S. (1990, October). *The Black behind the black and gold.* Retrieved August 27, 2010, from http://www.depauw.edu/library/archives/find/articles/warren.html

Zimbardo, P. G. (1966). *Physical integration and social segregation of northern Negro college students.* Paper presented at the Eastern Psychological Association conference. ERIC Document Retrieval Service no. ED 025568.

CHAPTER 2

Origins

The South

Frances Walker-Slocum (b. 1924)

Washington, District of Columbia

Oberlin College, 1941–1945

Everything—I didn't even know there was a White world—everything I grew up with was Black. The policemen were Black. The minister, the doctor, every doctor, everybody who did any work on the house, the carpenters, everything. It was a wonderful way to realize that Blacks had skills.[1]

John Herbert Niles (b. circa 1937)

Washington, District of Columbia

Allegheny College, 1955–1959

I grew up in Washington, DC, in an all-Black neighborhood; no interactions with White people except the mailman, the milkman, the insurance man, etc. No contact at all with White children my age except when I appeared on a TV program with other White students my senior year in high school. I had a lot of experience with segregation. I attended

© The Author(s) 2017

D.-L. Stewart, *Black Collegians' Experiences in US Northern Private Colleges*, DOI 10.1057/978-1-137-59077-0_2

segregated public schools all my life, visits in the summer to visit my paternal grandmother in South Carolina from the time I was nine until the summer before attending Allegheny. DC was a hybrid of the rigid segregation of the Deep South. Some examples in the 1950s: In DC, the buses weren't segregated and one didn't have to sit in the back of the bus unless you took the bus to Virginia then you would have to move from the front of the bus to the back of the bus. The public libraries weren't segregated; you could go to the Library of Congress. Some movie theaters were open to all, but only those theaters that showed foreign films. All the rest of the movie houses were segregated; one couldn't even use the second balcony as in Southern states. All restaurants were segregated and you could only get take-out orders at the local drug store soda fountains.

Robert Wedgeworth (b. 1937)

Ennis, Texas and Kansas City, Missouri

Wabash College, 1955–1959

I was born in a small town in Texas. Ennis, Texas—*[Spelling it out.]*—E N N I S, which is in Ellis County. It's southeast of Dallas. It's the end of the railroad line, and at the time that I was born, my dad was a laborer in the roundhouse for the railroad company. My parents left Texas when I was about three years old and moved to Kansas City, persuaded by my maternal grandfather to move there. That's where I grew up. I grew up in Kansas City, Missouri. It would've been just before the beginning of World War II. The first thing that I would remember was that my dad was unable to get a job similar to what he did in Texas because those jobs were restricted racially in Kansas City. He worked at a number of odd jobs in service stations, just to support the family, but then when the war started, he was able to get a steady job at Lake City Arsenal, which was a federal arsenal. He held that job throughout the war.... Kansas City was a racially segregated city. We lived in a totally Black neighborhood. After my grandfather died, we moved into his house, which was on the fringes of that Black neighborhood, but my elementary and secondary schools were all racially segregated. They were all Black. I think racial segregation in Kansas City was more by custom than by law. For example, Blacks were not accepted in the theaters downtown—movie theaters. They were not accepted in the restaurants and lunch counters downtown. I didn't have regular contact with any White people. It was occasional. There were school things. There were school exchanges—not exchanges, but there were school activities that brought us into contact with White kids, but that was only occasional. Then I took private lessons as a musician. I was a drummer. I took private lessons from two professional White drummers, downtown Kansas City. I would go down for my private lessons, so that was a regular contact that I would have about once a month, as my parents could afford it. Those were one of the few regular contacts that I had with any Whites, but that was not a problem. Jack and Johnny treated me like any of their other students, and that was just it. The subject of race just never came up. They were jazz musicians, so they knew a lot of—Black musicians, and so it just wasn't an issue.

Elizabeth Kitterman (b. 1944)

Charlotte, North Carolina

Earlham College, 1962–1966

I'm an only child. I said that, and only grandchild. I was really close to my grandmother who tended to—they have property in the area, so I was kind of spoiled, you might say in that I pretty much—I was never on an allowance, but I was able to pretty much buy what I wanted to buy. Not extravagantly rich or anything like that. It's just that I always had what I wanted. Well, education was very important because in our neighborhood my mother was a teacher, and my dad was a principal. Other people in our area were mainly like lawyers or doctors. They were considered high in professional society. It's Black. I lived in an all-Black neighborhood. After having talked to some of my other friends, I never encountered really any segregation or biases or anything as a child. I joined the Congress of Negro Protestants, Catholics, and Jews. I enjoyed mixing with other people and not being rigid as far as Blacks would be concerned or anything like that. There was a bussing issue, but I was never exposed to it. Because the bus came out of our neighborhood and went to the square where they would change busses. I never had to change a bus where I was confronted with people of another race.... Oh, now that was one reason that I was attracted to the Catholic Church because the priests always tended to have somewhat of a foreign accent. Therefore, I realized they were exposed to another world other than just the world that we were living in. When we would go shopping sometimes the White sales ladies would come up and say, "Girls, can I help you," when my mom was with me and my cousin that I was brought up with. I finally told the ladies, "Please, don't call my mother girl." *[Laughter]* My mother very quickly put them in their place. Or they call her "Aunt," and she would say,

"Oh, I'm sorry. Which of my relatives is your mother? Which one was your father?" I don't know. I was never really exposed to that. I think it might be Charlotte. We were brought up in Charlotte, North Carolina which is, I guess, one of the more progressive cities in North Carolina. We don't really associate North Carolina to South Carolina or anything South. I think I probably had a different type of upbringing.

Faye Hines (b. 1945)

Louisville, KY

Hope College, 1963–1967

Blacks, in particular, when I grew up in Louisville—we lived all in one area. It was actually called "Little Africa." There's still a little sign memorializing that. It was on and in the swamp of Louisville right next to the river. I lived in a house on a double lot where my grandmother lived in front and we lived in a two-room house in the back. That's where I was born. I don't think I saw White people until I was probably—I wasn't aware that I had—until I started school, and then I only saw them when we got on the bus, or trolley at that time, to go to the downtown area. At that time, of course, we weren't allowed to buy anything, but we could go down there to do some shopping, especially groceries and things. Blacks couldn't get really top jobs, so the teachers and lawyers and people like that, funeral home directors, were like the society of the place. The teachers were all very, very well educated people, because I can remember my kindergarten teacher. Miss Brown had been a missionary in Africa, and she came back and told us all about Africa. They were all very educated.

The Northeast

Leonard Yorke (b. 1935)

The Bronx, New York City, New York

DePauw University, 1952–1956

I loved growing up in The Bronx. Right after the war, there were a lot of street gangs, but we weren't involved in that. Like I said, my parents didn't have none of that business. My father's family, his mother, sisters, brother, and grand uncle lived close to us in The Bronx, and they were like my second—they were my second family. My mother had uncles who lived in The Bronx not far from us, and they were a secondary sort of a family. I enjoyed The Bronx. We were active in street sports. The church was a serious social outlet for me and my brother. My parents being fairly strict as far as partying, going to parties and carrying on like that. The word normal is cliché, but I don't know what else to say about it. Well a lot of things were accepted, but New York—New York was fairly liberal by the prevailing social standards at the time. One of the things that I remember hearing, I don't know if this was specific—it wasn't specific to my family but, "You have got to be better. You've got to be twice as good as."[2] *[Interviewer: What was the racial composition of your block?]* Just about all Black. We rented from a White family. The block had been—well, we moved into White neighborhoods in the forties. Yeah, we moved into White neighborhoods in The Bronx. I always went to school with White kids. In junior high school, elementary school, and in high school, all of my schools were integrated. We could go anywhere we wanted except a couple of places in Harlem we couldn't go because no Blacks could go. Isn't that ironic?[3] On 125th Street, yeah. A couple of places, a couple of restaurants down there that you couldn't go in at one time or another because they were White-only. Segregation, discrimination was a fact of life, we knew about it. It was everywhere. Places, neighborhoods you didn't feel comfortable going into. By and large, New York was fairly open.

Mamie Cavell Adderly (b. 1939)

Columbia, South Carolina, and Philadelphia, Pennsylvania

Earlham College, 1957

I'm a southern girl. *[Chuckle]* Yes. My roots are in the south. I spent my summers in Richmond, Virginia, with my father's parents. My father got a job in Philadelphia with the federal government. My elementary school days started in Philadelphia, and I was in Philadelphia through high school. While I was in elementary school, or just beginning, my father became a Quaker. I was raised as a pacifist along with conscientious objectors and civil disobedience people, I guess, kind of thing. When I got into high school, I met up with another group of high school students who were going to a place we call fellowship house, they were called fellowship houses then. It was founded by a Quaker in Philadelphia also. Anyway, we ended up doing little plays about civil rights in Philadelphia because every place was not open either. We ended up doing boycotts and sit-ins at the Woolworth's and going to other little roller skating rinks and bowling rinks that weren't open to us. This morning, I was laughing because Dick Clark had his bandstand in Philadelphia. Some of us, well, two of my friends at least, could pass.[4] We would go in. We would try to get in; they wouldn't let us in. Then Elaine and them would come right behind us and go in. We would go home laughing and couldn't wait for them to get back to tell us what happened. The first neighborhood I grew up in, it was—let's see. How can I say it? Blacks on one side of the street, and very much a mixture on the other side. A lot of Europeans coming in from World War II, mixing into the neighborhood. When I got to, I guess sixth grade, we moved out of that neighborhood to a bigger house. That neighborhood was integrated. I guess we integrated it. *[Laughter]* I remember my parents looking at houses and a lot of brick walls coming up. "No, you can't go here; you have to go here." This kind of thing. "We can't show you that house." That kind of thing. When we finally got onto a block, it was almost half and half. Growing up, in elementary school, I was the only colored girl in my elementary school and there were two boys. The other kids all went to an all-Black school but my mother said, "No, we're not doing that." At first, they had enrolled me for that school and she says, "No, we're not doing that. This is Philadelphia, and we're going to change things." That school was okay with me.[5] I had friends there. That was good. Philadelphia wasn't open. They didn't tell you that you had to sit at the back of the bus. You could sit anywhere you wanted to on the bus. You could go anywhere you wanted to. In the theaters. You could shop. Most of the time, everything was neighborhood oriented. You mostly shopped in your neighborhood, you went to church in your neighborhood, you went to school in your neighborhood and that was that. Once you got outside, say if you wanted to go to a certain roller skating rink—which we didn't have in our neighborhood—that was a different story. You had to fight your way in. *[Laughter]* They stopped you at the door.

Sarah Lawrence (b. 1943)

Hempstead, Long Island, New York

Oberlin College, 1961–1963

At the time I was born it was like the hub of Long Island or a major place and I think my parents were some of the original African American business people in the community. I lived in a place called Hempstead

Heights. There were three areas where mostly Black people lived and that was the Heights, most of those were blue collar workers, and then there was the Hill, which were projects.[6] That was on the other side of town. And then as I grew older, another more middle-class, upper-middle-class neighborhood arose. I guess a much richer community and at that time, unfortunately, there was a lot of color discrimination.[7] Most of the light skin African Americans lived over in an area called Circle Drive and in that area. The racial composition of the neighborhood I grew up in was—I would say my neighborhood itself was 90% maybe African Americans. We were Negroes and Colored people back then. I was brought up in a very integrated atmosphere. My mother was the first African American president of the Jackson Street School PTA. That's where I went for kindergarten to eighth grade. That was very historic. My parents were very active in the community in terms of the civic association and my father was an auxiliary policeman. My mother was president of just about every African American club. I was brought up very equally or knowing that White people were just like Black people. They were in and out of our home so much. We were very integrated into what was going on even though my parents worked for all White people. Those people were also friends.... Oh yes, segregation was everywhere. Especially when we went South as a child, it was hard for my parents to try to explain to us. We would travel down the New Jersey Turnpike and I remember as a child when we would go back and forth, we had to use a potty because we couldn't use the restrooms. There were places that we weren't allowed to eat, so my mother always packed lunches. One year they took us to Tennessee and I remember driving around for two or three hours because they were looking for a place for us to spend the night. It was just hours before we found a place.

Tanya Summers (b. 1947)

Brooklyn, New York, New York

Kalamazoo College, 1963–1967

Well, let me see. Brooklyn is the—I think it's probably the largest borough. I mean Brooklyn could be the size of Chicago. It's three million people,[8] so it's a huge city actually. I think the difference is it's not as dense as Manhattan. You have more family homes, double family homes. It's not as dense as Manhattan. On my block, for example, I lived on a small two-block street. There was maybe one, two, three—three, four apartment buildings on the whole street. Everyone else had either a single-family home, or a double family, something like that. Then you have a lot of ethnic diversity. Again I grew up on a block where you had people from—let's see. If I go down the block, Puerto Rico, Haiti, Jamaica, Barbados, Eastern Europe, Germany. You could just go down the block and then people from the South, so you had such a mix of people. That was just part of the scenery. It was no big deal. We weren't aware of overall patterns, but yes, it was very segregated. We lived across the street from a White family that owned the corner fish market. Over the years that situation changed—I guess especially after maybe the riots in the early 1960s when Whites moved out. We lived there long enough to see Whites and a racially mixed, ethnically mixed street and now it's reverting back. The schools were segregated and there were lots of—I think in the early 1960s—there were a lot of demonstrations against segregated schools, so there were a lot of those issues in Brooklyn as there were in other places. I went to a school—the schools that I went to, the classes that I was in were racially integrated throughout my schooling. Then I went to a high school that was in Williamsburg. Williamsburg was a heavily Eastern European immigrant community at that time. Let's see. When I went there, I always described it as like one-third Puerto Rican, one-third African American, and one-third White. The Whites were from—many of the White students were first-generation Americans. Their parents were from Poland, Hungary, Czechoslovakia, the Soviet Union, like that. The Puerto Rican students that I knew were often not first,[9] but they themselves may have been immigrants because Spanish was their first language. Then the Blacks were from a variety of places, Caribbean, and the New York/Brooklyn area, and the south. Many of the Blacks I knew were first-generation New Yorkers like I was. No, I was actually second generation. Many of the Black students in my class, their parents may have come in from Georgia or Alabama. They were first-generation New Yorkers. The same thing with the students from the Caribbean. Their parents were from Barbados, or Jamaica, or Trinidad. I had a lot of friends whose parents came from Trinidad.

The Midwest

Richard Hammond (b. 1934)

Chillicothe, Ohio

Ohio Wesleyan University, 1952–1954

Growing up in Chillicothe, in my neighborhood, I was happy. I was happy and I was friends with everyone. I lived in what was called the south end. It was three streets. I lived on the corner of Seventh and Mechanic. The boundaries were Walnut Street up to Sixth Street and from Seventh Street down to Paint Street. Those were the boundaries. In the West End, they were segregated by a couple of streets. Anyway people lived primarily on a couple of streets. North End was just a couple of families who lived in the North End of Chillicothe. The East End which is—that's where the really poor Whites lived and some of the Black. The East End, you were at the bottom of the totem pole. Then the South End, you were in the middle, and the West End—you were better off if you lived in the West End. The town to me was very prejudiced, very prejudiced. I was always envious of the White children that I went to school with when I was able to go to school. I was in a segregated school for the first six grades. Even at the time we went to it, it was condemned. The building was condemned. I guess architects or engineers say it's condemned, but it was still in use. *[Int: You talked about being envious of the White children when you were growing up.]* Right. *[Int: What were you envious of?]* Oh, their homes and it was just the fact that you knew there was a difference and didn't understand why. Why did they have televisions way before we did? In sports and in the middle school, they were given preference to everything. Then, when I look back on it, it doesn't bother me at all. The fact is their homes—the middle class—wasn't that much different than our homes. They had bathrooms. *[Laughter]* Very few of us had a specified bathroom with the showers and everything. I remember going when I went to middle school and got involved in sports, I was able to shower and that was great. Some of them had it in their homes and I thought they were really fortunate. We had indoor plumbing but not—we didn't have a shower, we didn't have a tub. Most of us didn't even have—we had the tin tub. *[Laughter]* Some of them, some families didn't even dump the water. The oldest got to bathe first and then the younger one. The water wasn't *[laughter]* that clean when you got down to the youngest one. We had a tin tub—but we did get to empty the water. *[Laughter]* At first we had the hydrant outside. We had to go out and bring the water in. It was just a few steps. Finally my father got his cousin, no, his nephew to bring the water inside, to put the plumbing inside. That was a big event; we didn't have to go out there in the winter. You'd build a fire and hold newspapers on it so it would thaw it out. We always had an indoor toilet and the water was piped in for that purpose. That was great *[laughter]* because some people didn't have it and—you can imagine. My grandparents lived in Jackson, Ohio. They had the old path down the back of the property to use the bathroom. I thought I was pretty fortunate to have a bathroom in our house.

Bill Lowry (b. 1935)

South Side, Chicago, Illinois

Kenyon College, 1952–1956

My family used one entrance and the White family used another at St. Lou's Hospital when I was born. In terms of when I was born and where we lived, I would say that [our neighborhood was] basically all Black. Down in what we used to refer to as the "Dirty Thirties." Also, around 50th and Indiana, and then we were like the Jefferson's, "moving on up."[10] Moving up to 61st Street, but when we started going up 61st Street, and I'm going to say—and it was at 62nd and what used to be South Park Way, which is now King Drive. We were moving into areas as they were changing. As I recall, and I was at that time, six years old or something like that. We were moving into changing areas. They were still predominantly Black, but there were some few White stragglers. We moved further east, and it was the same thing. Whites move in, they moved on. Then after I moved over to 64th and Fairlawn, which was a little bit further east, that was Black and remained Black. Solely Black. We might have one or two Whites that were part of a blended family. It might have been a stepson or something like that. By and large it was Black. It was a Black community. Most of the exposure I had with Whites up until the time I was 13 was with a few vendors and storeowners in the block. Because although the blocks had turned Black, there was a plumbing office down the street from us near the corner, and he was White. The plumber there was White. The produce store was White. The person who had the drugstore was

White. We had that kind of relationship that a lot of Blacks have. In terms of people my age and stuff, we were mostly athletically involved. I played organized football when I was 12 years old for the park team. We were the only Black team in the league. Outside of that, very little. We didn't—there weren't that many in the neighborhood, as I say. They weren't there long, and they moved out. We didn't have a great deal of interaction.

Harvey Hawks (b. 1937)

Marshall and Battle Creek, Michigan

Albion College, 1955–1959

Where I grew up at, there in Battle Creek, of course, there were a fair number of colored families. In Marshall, there were three colored families, and we were one of them. My father is, oh, I guess you might say relatively light-skinned. I think that probably helped his acceptability by other farmers in the area, although some never did accept it. Because we weren't able—like, for example, we could not sell milk. We had a farm and so we had milk cows, but we could not sell our milk to the dairy because we were colored. We had the CCCF, the Calhoun County Colored Farmers. It was a way of—for the colored farmers to kind of help each other out, and it was through that organization that we set up a retail—kind of retail business selling our dairy products: our milk and cream and butter. Then we would also sell chickens and turkeys and eggs and meat. We would sell it to the people that lived in town that, particularly toward the end of the Second World War, they weren't able to get a lot of these products because of the rationing.... We would run into various forms of segregation, and of course, in Michigan, it wasn't overt. It was very subtle. There weren't labels on the drinking fountains or anything like that, but if there was something, we weren't supposed to do, they would let us know. My father always told us, he said, "Just don't worry about what other people do. Just worry about what you do." He said that—he always told us, "For every action there's a reaction." He said sometimes you can't control the action, but you can always control your reaction. So that—in other words, that's a way of telling us to think twice before we act. When our—we had some neighbors across the street that were very—they were quite prejudiced, but us kids, we didn't pay any attention. The White parents wouldn't let their kids play with us at first, but then we went to school together and it was hard to keep us apart. We got so that—and we went to a one-room schoolhouse. It was about a mile away. We would walk to and from school together, but their parents didn't like that. So what we would do is we'd walk together until we got about a quarter mile from home and then we'd start calling each other names and kicking and scratching and so that would make the White parents happy.

Willis "Bing" Davis (b. 1937)

Dayton, Ohio

DePauw University, 1955–1959

I was two weeks old when we came to Dayton. With the migration—yeah, they were sharecroppers in South Carolina and working on somebody else's land. You know that history. Every year ended up in debt to the man. My father had a brother in Cincinnati, so he came up and decided to relocate. Got a job here in East Dayton driving a coal truck. He came back to get my two sisters and a brother and my mother and me. Yeah, came up, got a job, and then came back. I was able to travel, and so we moved to East Dayton. East Dayton had a pocket of only four streets of African Americans. Blacks coming to Dayton came to East Dayton first, even though it's perceived as West Dayton as being the Black community. Because it was a small enclave, I've come to learn that the extended family concept was in action, because there's just a few of us—about less than 60–100 families in that enclave, surrounded by our Appalachian brothers and sisters. That Southern way of being in that extended family way where the children belong to the community and you could get chastised by anybody in the community—okay. That helped to structure and formulate, too, a sense of purpose and direction. Well, [East Dayton] was different from the standpoint there's still people in Dayton that don't realize that there were Black people on the East Side, even to this day. Even when we played athletics, White students at the high schools were surprised to see us come out. *[Drawing a map while talking.]* Here's East Dayton here, and here's the two main streets, but there's a river that runs here—the Miami River that separates West Dayton from downtown. Most people see where we're physically at today as being West Dayton, as the Black community, but it was really like many other places. It used to be Hungarian, it used to be Polish, used to be German, used to be Jewish, and then African American. What happened here in East Dayton *[pointing back to the map he's drawn]* was that you had Blacks who would come down and live a little closer to downtown for work, and then there was one last street called Robert Drive here, before you cross the river. Then they would come in and live around here on the east side. *Then* they began to cross the bridge and move over to the larger area of West Dayton that people now today just assume it's always been African American, and it has not.

Ronald Spann (b. 1943)
Ann Arbor, Michigan
Kalamazoo College, 1961–1965

I'm a fifth-generation Ann Arborite. Of course, Ann Arbor is very university dominated. A very class-stratified town. I mean I don't think I appreciated that as much as a child. I was just a naïve kid growing up. I can look back and look at Ann Arbor now and appreciate the realities of class. Through Second Baptist Church, we were part of a community that included many veteran people—veteran families in that area. I mean we served as a point of entry for some families. Our home was like a boarding home over the years. There were always other adults living with us, like an extended family. When my mother was growing up in the house, her adopted father used it as a boarding house. We had that in our DNA I guess. All of us kids—all our godmothers came from somebody we knew living with us. There were two Black community concentrations. One on the north side where I grew up and one on the southeast side of the town closer to the university campus. I know less about that end of town because you just didn't get around that much although I knew people through church and stuff.... Pretty early on, my mother arranged for me to be Ann Arbor's first experiment in bussing I guess. Jones School. What a great name. In our neighborhood, that was the concentration of where Black kids in our part of town went to school. I mean it actually was never by any means exclusively Black. I mean if there was a concentration of Black kids that was one of the couple of schools in town where that would be the case at the elementary level. I don't know how she worked it for me to go to some schools outside the neighborhood for my first three years. Then from third grade on I was going over to the east side in a neighborhood very much on campus in Ann Arbor. It had a wonderful and symbolic name. Instead of Jones School, I went to Angell School.[11] There were never more than three or four of us who were Black kids in that school—in the entire school. I mean I was the only one in my classroom for most of my time there.... By the time I was in high school, my brother would have been just getting ready for junior high, the family moved to another part of the north side. That was a big thing; finding a place where a Black family could move to another neighborhood which was also integrated. Residential segregation was very rigid. I mean you just had housing covenants that prescribed where people could live or not live. The real estate industry was totally involved in that. My father says the tradesmen—he and my uncle, his brother, who eventually relocated to Ann Arbor—had a hell of a time just getting union status. Because the unions were very resistant to letting the Black workers be involved with any labor. That's class stuff as well as race stuff going on there. You knew the eating places in town. You knew what restaurants were likely to refuse Black patrons and so on. I mean there was the up-north version of Jim Crow stuff.

***

The Pervasive Yet Contradictory Effects of Segregation

The 14 narratives shared above reflect the diversity of backgrounds and childhood experiences with race, segregation, and race relations with White children and adults among the 68 participants in this study. Three areas of the country were represented among the participants' birthplaces and upbringings: the South (n = 33), the Northeast (n = 9), and the Midwest (n = 26). The narratives shared here are more evenly distributed with 5 narratives from southerners, 4 from those raised in the Northeast, and another 5 from those raised in the Midwest.

As reflected in these narratives and across all the participants, racial segregation was known to each of them, though there were a couple, such as Elizabeth Kitterman born and raised in Charlotte and Ruth Ann Hatcher born and raised in Chicago, whose reflections indicated that they had been spared its indignities. Moreover, this familiarity with segregation was pervasive across all three of these geographic areas. In both the North and Midwest, as well as the South, there were variances in whether segregation was enforced by custom or by law. In the Northeast and Midwest, segregation did seem to be mainly enforced through custom. Chicago stood as a glaring exception, where there were municipal Jim Crow codes prohibiting racial integration in housing, schools, and even hospitals (Moore, 2016).

Despite the prevalence of racial segregation in these geographic communities, most participants did not recount a strong conscious awareness of its effects on their daily lives. The neighborhood was the center of activity, as Mamie Cavell Adderly's narrative reflects, and the neighborhood could fulfill all one's needs and many of one's wants. Moreover, as Frances Walker-Slocum asserted, segregation provided opportunities to "realize that Blacks [*sic*] had skills" in a variety of skilled trades and professional occupations. When correlated with parents' educational attainment and social class, the more rigid segregation of the South does not illustrate an economically depressing effect on these families' means.

Economically, the participants' described childhoods experienced across the expanse of social class, from just one family headed by a pair of great-grand aunts living on government assistance to 33 two-parent families occupied as stoutly middle-class professionals. The greatest plurality (49%) of participants described middle-class upbringings, including trips to visit relatives in other parts of the country and in the case of one, Adine Ray Usher, a childhood largely spent in Europe during her father's military deployment. Lower-middle-class families comprised the next largest group (32%) and then families who labored among the working poor (18%). When social class status is overlaid with geographic region (see Fig. 2.1), the South is shown to have the greatest number

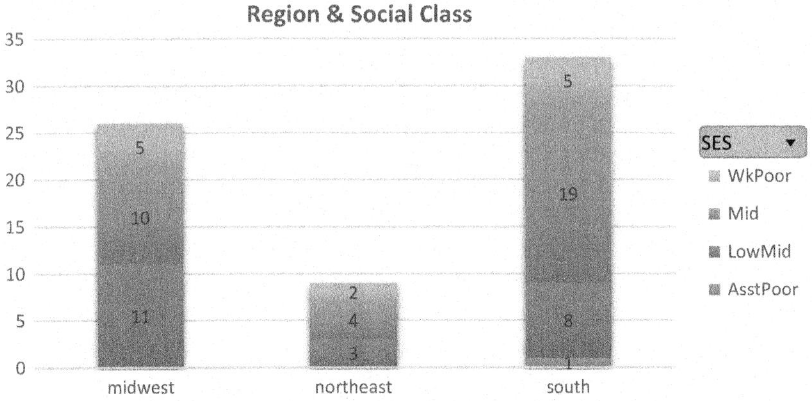

Fig. 2.1 Region and social class status of participants. Key: *WkPoor* working poor, *Mid* middle class, *LowMid* lower-middle class, *AsstPoor* state-assisted poor

of participants whose families were middle class (57.5% of Southerners). Although several participants whose parents or earlier generations had migrated north to take advantage of perceived better job opportunities, those who were raised in the Northeast or Midwest were as likely to be lower-middle class as middle class in both regions. Moreover, a higher percentage of the parents of those raised in the Northeast (22%) and Midwest (19%) were among the working poor than of those raised in the South (15%).

Parents' educational attainment also was not reliably related to social class status among these participants. I tracked parental educational attainment across five categories: no college attendance by either parent or guardian (n = 31), mostly in the Midwest and South (n = 14 and 13, respectively); one parent or guardian with some college attendance but not completed (n = 5); two parents or guardians with some college attendance but not completed (n = 2); one parent or guardian with at least a bachelor's degree (n = 11); and two parents or guardians with at least a bachelor's degree (n = 19), nearly twice as many from the South (n = 11) than the Midwest (n = 6). Combining these into three categories (no college, some college, at least bachelor's degree) reveals that the participants are nearly evenly split between those whose parents or guardians had no college experience (n = 31) and those for whom one or both parents or guardians had attained at least a bachelor's degree (n = 30).[12] Seven participants had at least one parent who had begun college but not been able to complete it, typically due to finances. Of those whose parents were college graduates, they were usually accompanied by siblings and/or other extended relatives who were also college graduates, mostly but not exclusively from southern historically Black institutions. These participants who would themselves go on to attend and, for the overwhelming majority, graduate from the elite private colleges of the GLCA were just as likely to be first-generation college students as those who were the second generation or more to attend.

What is most interesting about these data is revealed when parent education is overlaid with social class (see Fig. 2.2). One would expect to find the vast majority of those in households with two college graduates to be middle class, as is the case here where 18 of the 19 families with 2 college graduates described their families as middle class. Even 1 college graduate in the home produced 9 middle-class households out of 11 total in that group. However, middle-class families can be found across all educational levels among these participants. Moreover, those in families where

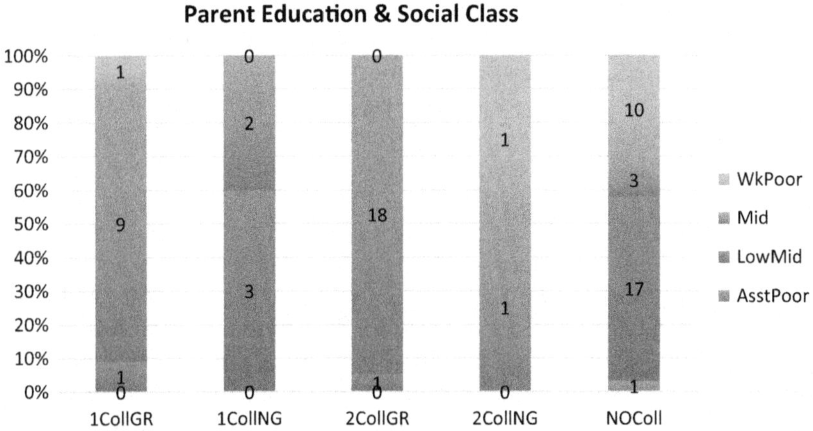

Fig. 2.2 Parent education and social class. Key: *WkPoor* working poor, *Mid* middle class, *LowMid* lower-middle class, *AsstPoor* state-assisted poor, *1CollGR* one college graduate, *1CollNG* one college non-graduate, *2CollGR* two college graduates, *2CollNG* two college non-graduates, *NOColl* no college attendance

neither parent nor guardian had the opportunity to attend college, still more than half were stably employed and lower-middle class (54.8%). As Nidiffer (2010) also found, parent occupations were not reliable indicators of financial wellbeing. Although mostly employed in civil service or industrial occupations, the number of lower-middle-class households was still twice as high as those who were the working poor among families with some college experience or none at all.

Variance among parents' educational attainment and social class status was also not reflective of variance in their attitudes about education for their children. Among the 68 participants, only two would report having one of their parents or guardians try to dissuade them from pursuing a college degree. Donald Peppers, who would graduate from Kenyon College as a first-generation student from a lower-middle-class family in the Midwest, noted in his interview that his stepfather wanted him to enter the military after high school and noted that he "didn't get much help going to college, financially or encouragement." Jeane Bounds Williams, who was raised by her great-aunts who had not gone to college and were on state assistance, shared that she was told she needed to get a job. Although Robert Wedgeworth's parents, who were lower-middle class and had no college experience, "expected that [he] would do well in school," they did not have a "vision of college," though as he commented, "I was the one who had the expectation and they supported that."

Otherwise, each of the other 65 participants shared stories similar to Geraldine Copeland who grew up outside Chicago in Harvey, Illinois in a lower-middle-class home. Geraldine's mother, a single parent who did not attend college, "started early," telling Geraldine, "You're going to go to college, Gerry. Gerry, you're going to go to college." It was repeated so often at home that Geraldine said she started saying it to herself as well. In like manner, these participants came from families that almost universally saw a college education as necessary for economic and social mobility. Although Denise Baisden's father began college before she was born, he did not complete his degree until Denise was about seven years old. Nevertheless, Denise, who graduated from Ohio Wesleyan, was taught by her parents that "In order to get ahead in life, you needed a college degree." Denise would go on to say that these messages came not only from their parents, but also from other family members and adults in their communities.

Both Alridge (2007) and Perkins (1993) have discussed the high value placed on education as a means of social uplift among Black people during the early twentieth century. A college degree was understood as providing social capital and entrée into economic stability and social respectability. This was in fact one of the intended outcomes of the nation's historically Black colleges and universities (HBCUs) at the turn of the century to fully realize the promise of the previous century's emancipation (Brown & Davis, 2001). These participants, born between 1924 and 1946, were students of this tutelage and it set the tone for their entire educational careers. We turn to these narratives in Chap. 3.

Notes

1. Referencing the system of racial segregation.
2. This was a reference to Blacks having to be twice as good as White people.
3. Harlem is a collection of neighborhoods in the Borough of Manhattan, north of Central Park, and its residents have been predominantly Black since the early twentieth century. In light of this, Leonard considered it ironic that there were businesses that would not serve Black patrons.

4. They could be perceived racially as White because of their lighter skin and more European phenotypical features.
5. Referencing the White school that her mother had her integrate.
6. Projects, or the projects, is a colloquial term for a subsidized housing apartment complex. Residents were typically on state assistance or otherwise qualified due to low incomes.
7. Color discrimination, or colorism, is a system of discrimination and bias in which those with lighter complexions are privileged over those who have darker complexions and are more identifiably of African ancestry.
8. As of the 2010 Census, the Borough of Brooklyn had a population of over 2.5 million people and was in fact the largest of New York City's five boroughs (NYC Department of City Planning, 2016).
9. As in not the first generation to be born stateside.
10. The theme song for the sitcom television show *The Jefferson's* was about "moving on up to the east side" as a sign of improved social class status, being able to afford a higher-rent neighborhood.
11. So named for a prominent figure in the development of the University of Michigan.
12. Only 9.3% of all those in the USA had attained a four-year college degree in 1940 (Statista, 2016), so it is striking that so many of the students in this sample (44%) had parents who had obtained a bachelor's degree. This is a historical illustration of the contemporary conclusion that earning a college degree significantly raises the likelihood of one's children going to college as well (Pascarella & Terenzini, 2005).

References

Alridge, D. P. (2007). Of victorianism, civilizationism, and progressivism: The educational ideals of W. E. B. DuBois and Anna Julia Cooper, 1892–1940. *History of Education Quarterly, 47*(4), 416–446.

Brown III, M. C., & Davis, J. E. (2001). The historically Black college as social contract, social capital, and social equalizer. *Peabody Journal of Education, 76*, 31–49.

Moore, N. Y. (2016). *The south side: A portrait of Chicago and American segregation.* New York, NY: St. Martin's Press.

New York City Department of City Planning. (2016). *NYC Population: Current and projected populations.* Retrieved May 28, 2016 from http://www1.nyc.gov/site/planning/data-maps/nyc-population/current-future-populations.page

Nidiffer, J. (2010). "Poor" research: The historiographical challenges when socio-economic status is the unit of analysis. In M. Gasman (Ed.), *The history of U.S. higher education: Methods for understanding the past* (pp. 137–149). New York, NY: Routledge.

Pascarella, E., & Terenzini, P. (2005). *How college affects students: A third decade of research* (Vol. 2). San Francisco, CA: Jossey-Bass.

Perkins, L. M. (1993). The role of education in the development of Black feminist thought, 1860–1920. *History of Education, 22*, 265–275.

Statista. (2016). *Percentage of the U.S. population who have completed four years of college or more from 1940 to 2014, by gender* [chart]. Retrieved July 23, 2016 from http://www.statista.com/statistics/184272/educational-attainment-of-college-diploma-or-higher-by-gender/

CHAPTER 3

Black Disciples and White Missionaries

Samuel Lewis (b. 1928)

Brewton, Alabama

Hope College, 1947–1951

Of course, there was segregation as we were coming up. There were no really bad incidents of any kind, but there were in neighboring towns around us. I went to the county grade school through the ninth grade. In the tenth grade, I didn't go to the city school. I went to the private school, which was a Dutch Reform school. The church had a school there. That was where I went from the 10th through the 12th. We knew nothing about the Dutch Reformed Church before then. [*Laughter*] We only knew that it was there for us, and it was free. It was something unusual to have White people come from up North and provide a school for us. Of course, we were really proud of that. Now, what happened was maybe 10 or 20 years earlier, that was a Black man named Dooley who founded that private school. He got money from the surrounding people in the county. Then he took a group of Black singers up North. It was a choir, and they sang at different churches in the North: Michigan, Ohio, and others. Somehow, the Dutch Reformed folks decided to support that school. It was all Black teachers.

As a child, I wasn't very smart. I was in the lower half of my class up to the eighth grade. In eighth grade, I moved to the top of the class.

© The Author(s) 2017
D.-L. Stewart, *Black Collegians' Experiences in US Northern Private Colleges*, DOI 10.1057/978-1-137-59077-0_3

I don't really know what happened, but I had a teacher in the eighth grade who was a new teacher. He was good. He really taught me. He took time to sit down and to help me with the problems that I had. From there, I began to understand, and I began to become interested. I began to learn. When I got to this school in the tenth grade, the classes were really crowded. That was when I became the top student in the class. I led the class from the 10th through the 12th. My math teacher—very good. [*With emphasis*] In the grade school, the teachers were good, and in high school, they were even better. I really didn't realize I could do as well as I did. I never thought I'd be at the top of the class. It seemed that something just inspired me with the teaching that I got. They encouraged me. They gave me books to read and all of this just inspired me.

Cynthia Carpenter (b. 1930)

Portland (Jamaica) to Newtown (Pennsylvania)[1]

Earlham College, 1947–1951

I didn't look forward to this, but it's customary in Jamaica—which was not independent at that time. It was part of the Commonwealth of Great Britain. It was customary that you send your children away for higher education. My sister got sent to a school in South—oh, I'm trying to remember the name of that—ah, Middlesex Hospital South—Middlesex Hospital in England, to become a nurse. I was then sent to George School to be, as I said, the first Black Quaker student. Later on, my brother and the youngest sister went to the University of Massachusetts. What I heard about George School also was that the year that they made the decision to send two Black students, it would be a boy from New York, whose family was a lawyer, and me, from Jamaica, whose father was a doctor and a headmaster. I ended up getting there, but this lawyer's son never did show up. One of the things we learned afterward was that there were people who protested, hearing that these two Black students were going to be enrolled in the campus at George School. That was surprising to me. Well, I'd rather say shocking and appalling that people—I mean here they were, the Quakers—were making a good effort. Those were the Germantown Friends, because they held the annual meeting that supported George School.

Jeane Bounds Williams (b. 1931)
Philadelphia, Pennsylvania
Allegheny College, 1951–1952

By being in the top percentile of my classes from elementary school on up, and finally when I got to high school which was predominantly Jewish, and therefore the top level of achievement was predominantly Jewish, I could compete with them. The schools were segregated too, I forgot to tell you that, but my aunt refused to send us to the Black school, which you had to walk a long distance across town to get to it. A couple of other parents joined in with her, so there were like six of us who went to the White schools, which were right around the block from us with these Italians. We got along with them fine, we really did because they—well, it just didn't matter to them. I remember the fight that my aunt put up not to send us to the Black school, and they couldn't point to the law that we had to go, and all they could say was "customary."[2] Again, when I got to junior high, that was the first time I went to school where there was kind of a good mix of both. There were fights every day, and I remember one day the assistant principal called me to her office and she asked me why I was never involved in the fights. Well, even then I was young, but I thought, "She doesn't know my aunt. If I go home with my clothes torn, she will kill me." I said to her, "Well, one thing, I'm used to them and they're used to me. They know me." The kids from North Camden, which were mostly Black, they weren't used to getting along with White kids. The White kids weren't used to them, so they were fighting all the time. Now by the end of the year, they would be friends, but in that first two or three months of school, there were fights all the time until they settled down. But they could not compete academically. There were a few Blacks in the academic track, but most of them took the business or the general track. Too much work to be in the academic track. Well, I took the academic track because I thought it was a challenge. I decided I wanted to be a metallurgist. Now, don't ask me why I decided I wanted to be an engineer, and then after that I decided on being a metallurgist. I guess it was because I knew what all the other engineers did but I didn't know what a metallurgist did; it was a challenge.

Ruth Holland Scott (b. 1934)
Albion, Michigan
Albion College, 1952–1956

In high school, I ran into a lot of challenges. Kids were divided into college-bound and non-college-bound classes. My grades were so good that they could do whatever they wanted to, but they couldn't claim that I was not capable. I was in the college-bound classes. I had a teacher in home economics, though, and we had group work. We did group assignments. Everybody in this group got an A because they were all White, except me. I got a C. I went to the teacher and I asked her why I had received a C. She said, "Because I can't give a grade above C to a Negro child." Yes, that's exactly what she said. But it was interesting to me, because I had a number of experiences where somebody tried to discriminate against me, and my classmates raised Cain. In some cases it was changed, and in other cases it was not. For instance, I was voted by my class to go to Girls State, but in those days the DAR[3] was not willing to take Negro students as part of their summer leadership program. The high school principal just said that they weren't going to send me and they chose another girl. My classmates said, "Well, if you don't send Ruth to Girls State, then no one is going." The girl they chose instead of me refused to go. Somehow the suggestion was made that they should send me to the Junior Red Cross Leadership Training Institute. Red Cross had a leadership training thing that was very much like Girls State, and a wonderful experience it was, I have got to tell you. I learned more about leadership there than I ever learned in my life. My high school sent me to that one. I still have the leadership creed from that year, 1951, and have often used the words in my speeches and writing. Then, when we got to the end of the senior year, I was supposed to be salutatorian. It was widely believed that somehow the grades were jimmied[4] so the White girl who took all secretarial courses became the salutatorian. The kids said, "We don't care whether she is salutatorian, but she is our best speaker in our class, and you have to let her speak." So, they created another category, which was class orator. I got to speak for graduation. On the other hand, I had a debate teacher, who identified me at seventh grade as a potential star. I was in her homeroom. As I said, I did talk a lot. She had this strict rule about kids being quiet during homeroom period, and so she'd send me on errands so I didn't have to sit still in the class and not talk. She just kind of adopted me. She wanted me to be a debater, and so when I got to eighth grade, she had me be in the storytelling contest. Then, when

I got in ninth grade, I became a debater. She taught me very well. I won a lot of debates across the state of Michigan, and my colleague and I won the state championship debate. As a result of that, being one of the top debating schools in the state, I was chosen by my debate teacher to represent our team and went into a scholarship contest. I don't know if every school had an opportunity to send somebody or not, there were over 100 kids there though. We vied for a scholarship from the *Detroit Free Press*. I won second.

Russell Davis (b. 1935)

Washington, District of Columbia

Ohio Wesleyan University, 1952–1956

My schools were excellent. Elementary, junior high, and high—excellent schools. Of course, Dunbar was the epitome of excellence. It was really—it was run like a prep school in the sense that everybody had to take a foreign language or two, and everybody had to take science, and so on. Most of my teachers from elementary school through Dunbar had at least a master's. Most of them had 30 points higher than a master's or something. It was via a curriculum that they pursued at New York University (NYU) and Columbia that gave them another level of certification that enabled them to qualify for higher salaries, although it was not the EdD or the PhD. You had your master's plus 30, that's how they termed it.[5] At Dunbar, of course, I had a significant number of the teachers there who had doctorates, and a whole lot of them were finishing their dissertations, and they had all but the dissertation. I can't say enough about the excellence of the schools there in DC, and, in particular, the ones that I attended.

Willis "Bing" Davis (b. 1937)

Dayton, Ohio

DePauw University, 1955–1959

You know what? Being in a small—I've shared that many times—neighborhood, we talked about a practicing-up system. It went like this: being small, we didn't have a lot of kids in different age groups, and so we would as peewees, which is 11 and under, in order to have a practice, you'd have to have some of the 12- and 13-year-olds with you. Those boys were better, bigger, more developed, and so it caused you to develop more. It was consciously done in our community, where the older guys would work with the younger guys, very much an extended family kind of structure. As you move from peewee to the junior level, which is 15 and 16, then you would be practicing with 18- and 19- and 20-year-old men, and that was to toughen you up. I did have a natural interest in athletics. As an elementary school kid, even though I was drawing and doing artistic things, to everybody in the community, I was one of the up-and-coming artists. Athletics was just a matter of course. It was not perceived to be contradictory. Number one, there were many people who were involved—boys and girls in my neighborhood involved themselves in the arts—dancing, drawing, painting, and so it was okay. Then also I had definite peers and role models on the street or in the community. What was different for me is that I had that nurturing in the church and the community center, at home, and on the playground, which was all within the block. I had that nurturing that it was okay to be expressive. The athletics were just a natural outlet. I had that dexterity. I was perceived as, "Oh he's going to be an outstanding athlete." I just insisted that, "Hey, I'm also going to be an artist." My high school coach[6] left his comfortable community and would come into the Black community and was comfortable there. There were some other athletes he had before me, but he had a positive relationship with me, in particular, because of his sincerity. His sincerity about my interest in the arts was appealing to me to the point that I would say, "Hey, I'm going to go to Wilbur Wright. I'm not going to the other school." In junior high, there used to be a system. We were a feeder school to a high school. The high school would have some athletic events, like particularly track, and they could invite their feeder schools to participate. They'd have the high school running a relay, then they'd have the elementary schools running relays. They'd have the high school high jump, then they'd have high jump for the feeder schools coming in. He was able to develop a rapport with me and other athletes even before we got to the high school level.

Robert Wedgeworth (b. 1937)

Kansas City, Missouri

Wabash College, 1955–1959

All my schools were segregated, but had well-qualified staff. All of my teachers had degrees from reputable universities. Many of my high school teachers had advanced degrees, so they were well qualified. For example, my English teacher had a master's degree from Yale. My psychology teacher had a PhD from Michigan State. My math teacher had a master's degree from the University of Kansas. They were among the leaders of the high school teaching staff where I was. All of the teachers had bachelor's degrees from reputable universities, including traditionally Black universities like Lincoln University—not Lincoln University in Pennsylvania, but Lincoln University in Jefferson City, Missouri. Oh, I started playing sports in elementary school. [*Chuckles*] I played everything. I played baseball. I played football. On the elementary level when I was young, I did it all: football, basketball, baseball, yeah. I didn't start concentrating on basketball until I got to high school.

~May 1954: U.S. Supreme Court Decision in *Brown v. Board of Education* reverses "separate but equal" precedent set by the Court in *Plessy* in 1896 ruling unanimously that racial segregation is unconstitutional~

Rose Jackson Enco (b. circa 1940)

Atlanta (Georgia) and Cleveland (Ohio)

Ohio Wesleyan University, 1958–1962

Honey, listen, I will tell you something. When I was in Atlanta, I was, of course, on the college track. We did a lot of partying, honey. We had such a good time in Atlanta. We danced. My father said, "You go to too many—you're going to too many parties." I said, "No." Then I came to Cleveland, and when you come to Cleveland from the South in my day then, they automatically tested you to see if you could really be in—see, I was supposed to be a senior. You had to take a test to see if you would be placed there or placed back. They usually put you back a grade, but because I was a senior, they gave me the test, and said I could stay with my grade, but, honey, I had to work. Do you hear me? I felt a definite difference in the workload. I would come home, and I would sit at this desk, eat dinner, and then get back on those books. I really had to work. I was thrown in the college prep track then. You know what they did at lunchtime? They were looking at the Scholastic Aptitude Test (SAT) books and quizzing each other on the words. They weren't doing that in Atlanta, honey. We were looking at clothes and who did what, planning the next party. I said, "Oh, dear God." Don't let anybody tell you there wasn't any difference between the North and the South because it was Black down there and Black up here. That transition in the fall—I had to work pretty hard. Oh, from that college prep track, they all went to college. They went to places like Wellesley and Vassar. This one girl was really bright. She went to Vassar. They went to these really elite colleges. Oh, yeah, they went to college. I had friends in that group. Ohio State, too. Two or three of them went to Ohio State.

Mabel "Midge" Winston (b. 1941)

Kansas City, Missouri

Oberlin College, 1959–1963

I went to high school, freshman year, in 1954. The first year of integration. My experiences were different than either one of my siblings. I kind of embraced challenge. Well, I can remember, you know, as I said, being part of the first wave of integration. In my high school, they had about 350 people in my class, maybe 55 Black people. I tried out for everything. [*Laughter*] I tried out for cheerleader. I didn't really get it, but it was the principle of the thing. Whatever was going on in high school, I was not shy about it and I never said I couldn't do something just because I was Black. It was more like, "Oh I'm going to try." [*Laughter*] I'm going to try, kind of thing. I was in the honor society and a whole lot of other things; but that was what I said, is that you have to have an air of confidence.

Sybil Jordan Hampton (b. 1944)[7]

Little Rock, Arkansas

Earlham College, 1962–1966

I was in eighth grade. Four of the Little Rock Nine went to my church. Their parents were friends of my parents. I think that it's very fascinating that although we went to church with them, we did not ever engage them in conversation about what was happening to them. People said this is not entertainment, this is not for your curiosity. What needs to be done is to keep their lives outside of that as normal as possible. One of the things I'm always struck by is that I knew what was going on. My parents were avid newspaper readers and we watched TV. Central High School is at 12th and Park.[8] I lived at Seventh and Park. I literally lived in the neighborhood. What happened is that we used to walk past Central on our way to junior high school. What we had to do is we had to change the way we went to school because we could no longer walk through that neighborhood. That was one big change. My parents and others who were involved in the NAACP were constantly going to meetings, and we went with them where people were talking strategy. What was going to happen, what were people going to do, and who was going to be the young people who were going to be in the queue. Because, of course, the whole way in which students got selected to go was they had to be in a queue, and then they had to be screened and undergo psychological testing, and then the school board.[9] I was in the queue in that year to go. Central was 10, 11, 12. I was in the eighth grade, so Central was a three-year school, not a four-year school. I was in the eighth grade and my parents were already saying to me, "If you want to," because I said that I would really like to be in the queue of people who were going to be perhaps able to go to Central High School. My parents really encouraged us to do it no matter what was going on at Central because they said not a lot of people have the kind of flexibility and freedom that we have with my father working for the post office as a federal job. He wasn't going to get fired. Many people were in service where they worked as cooks and maids and chauffeurs, and so a lot of people were threatened, and they were fearful. My parents were not fearful, and they felt that because they were in a position of some privilege that their children could be good candidates to go to Central High School. My parents were always talking about what it meant, that it wasn't something for an individual, but this was something for the race. I was raised as a child to think of what I did, of what I accomplished as being something for the race. It wasn't that you were going to go and you were going to get rich. You weren't going to get an education to be a doctor, a lawyer and live this wonderful life. It was that you formed part of the body of proof that our people are people who are strivers, and you formed the body of proof that our people are capable of taking their rightful place in this society, and leadership roles when the society opens up. That was the kind of conversation that was going on in my home. There was a constant focus on what this meant and its value. So people, both in my family and in the community, were not sitting around talking about how terrible things were. They were not sitting around being fearful. Certainly they were being very cautious, but really my parents were very strategic, and they were very much a part of the adult cadre who were planning and preparing for what was going to come next. I went in the second class that entered, and initially only two others were admitted because they really didn't want to expand.

They wanted to say, "We'll stay with the original nine people, blah-blah-blah." My parents were very persistent in the court struggle, and, in fact, had some real tussle with the NAACP Legal Defense Fund people because they were quite willing to strike out on their own along with the other two parents if my parents thought the Defense Fund was dragging its feet. We were admitted later, so those first two entered when school opened. Several weeks later, three more of us entered, so there were five of us in all.[10] There were two people who entered as juniors and then another two as seniors—and I was placed in the tenth grade by myself. [*With emphasis*] I was placed in the tenth grade by myself. A White man who was a member of the school board called my parents when I went away to college. He said, "I need to meet with you," and he was crying, and he said, "I participated in an act of cruelty." He said, "Your child was placed in the tenth grade by herself because the school board members were so stunned at how poised she was throughout that everybody reported that she was the most poised and self-possessed little person during everything that happened, including the big interview." After, when they were making the selections, he said the comment was, "Well, let's see just how poised she is." They literally placed me in tenth grade alone as a test. That's really important that my parents probably didn't know that at the time because I'm sure it would have been very upsetting. I went in as the only tenth grader. I was the youngest, and there was never another student placed in my class. When I graduated in 1962, my class at that time numbered 544 students who graduated, and I was the only Black student. We were shunned. Nobody ever spoke to me except my French teacher, because he was from France, and his niece who came. I also had one social studies teacher who had been very grievously wounded in the war, and he was disabled, and he was a very kind person. He'd talk with me, and he also had me participate in activities in the classroom in which I had to be with other students. The only time any of those people in my homeroom heard me speak was when I had to read the Bible, because you read the Bible and everybody had to pick a turn. [*Pause*] All those things that my parents actually had been doing all those years before really became extraordinarily important, because I had been in Junior National Honor Society. I was editor of the student newspaper. All of a sudden I go into this situation where not only am I banned by law from participating in anything extracurricular, no Beta Club.[11] There was a state law passed and Governor Faubus was absolutely clear: Okay, niggers can go to school, but you're certainly not going to do anything more than go to school. My parents had said to me, "No matter what happens to you, you will never cry because if you cry and they see you crying, they will say, 'We've got her, and we'll just keep getting her.'" That was a wonderful lesson that you can maintain your composure. They said cry when you come home, but do not cry there because then you will make yourself vulnerable. When they see that you're strong, they'll leave you alone. I didn't do a lot of crying at home, because this is how my parents were: "Okay, you're feeling upset about this. Cry. Let's get over your crying because we have to think about what's the strategy." Always. That was true about Central. My parents always said, "Remember this is a rehearsal. You are going to go places as the world opens up, and people are going to not speak to you, and people are not going to be kind to you. You're not going to lose your way, and you're not going to lose your focus because this is your rehearsal." They were absolutely right.

Tanya Summers (b. 1947)

Brooklyn, New York City, New York

Kalamazoo College, 1963–1967

We lived in New York City that had a settlement house movement.[12] We had opportunities that settlement houses provided, so I took piano lessons for years. This is Hennessy Settlement, so at the settlement house when you took music lessons, you were required to take music theory. I had music theory classes every week. I had piano lessons every week. I had dancing lessons every week. I think we also had to do drama. I remember having to do drama lessons. Those were a lot of my activities. Yeah, I was in what they call honor school, so I was in the intellectually gifted program from elementary school. That's what they called it. I don't know if we were intellectually gifted or not, but that's what they called it. I always read. My explanation for that was that I was always years ahead in terms of reading. Let's say when I was in 7th grade, I tested for reading, I think, at the 12th-grade level, something like that. Anyway I loved to read. I was always in those gifted classes. I was in the honor school at Eastern District High School. That's where I went to high school. Again that was it. Oh. At that time, New York City had the track, the different kinds of diplomas. You were tracked. I was in the academic track, so the academic track had all of the college prep requirements. Three or four years of math, three or four years of science, foreign language, social studies. We did all that.

***

Preparation for Progress

The 11 narratives featured in this chapter are organized chronologically by participants' dates of birth and separated into two groups: those whose high school experiences preceded the Supreme Court's 1954 decision in *Brown v. Board of Education* and those whose high school years followed that decision. Prior to *Brown*, as noted in Chaps. 1 and 2, northern school districts engaged in racial segregation to varying degrees, often enforcing "custom" as policy as was the case for Jeane Bounds Williams in Philadelphia. Housing segregation practices, through racial exclusion clauses and other covenants, in cities like Cincinnati and Dayton in Ohio, allowed White schools to operate as nearly exclusively White spaces. The absence of specific legal prohibitions, although not masking the effects of racial segregation, did provide rational explanations for why the schools were not racially diverse. The validity of using residential housing patterns as the sole reason for the racial exclusivity of the schools was tested, however, when Black residents began moving into previously all-White enclaves. As noted by Ralph Jones, who grew up in Indianapolis,

> Washington Township School District was exclusively White until the Blacks started moving into the Golden Ghetto. My mother wanted us out there because of the school system. Other families followed because of the school system. The junior high, I think there were like no more than ten Blacks in the junior high. When I got to high school, there was a dozen maybe. We all caught the bus at the same point. We had no problems. The Washington Township Schools accepted the fact that Blacks were moving into their area. The White folks did not leave. We just were part of the school.

However, other locales did not simply accept the integration of their schools as inevitable and sought to leave. Washington, DC, would enact the desegregation mandate of *Brown* immediately the following school year, 1954–1955. Another participant recounted how the demographics of McKinley Technical High School changed post-*Brown*:

> The population of the school in 1957 when I entered was about 2,300, and when I entered in that fall, about 10% of the 2,300 were Black. By the end of the next year, there were about 10% Whites there. White flight had kicked into overdrive, and it was one of the most rapid, from my observation point, demographic changes that I've ever experienced. The changes were happening both in terms of faculty, as well as in students.

In these ways, schools sometimes were emblems of whiteness as a property interest enacted through the educational institutions of a community.

Fostering Black Excellence

As noted by Clotfelter (2004), the *Brown* decision did not immediately end racial segregation in public schooling, especially across the South. The speed with which desegregation was enacted by local school districts varied considerably, with some districts desegregating their high schools, but not the elementary or junior high buildings. Moreover, some Black families had the choice to move their children to the traditionally White school, like Jacqueline Tolliver and Margaret Ralston Payne in Louisville, as well as Vivian Hopkins Jackson in Norfolk. Black parents did not always choose to move their children, however. Vivian shared that when desegregation came, it was her senior year of high school and her parents decided not to move her: "They just thought that would not make sense. It was a very hostile environment, so those children who did go encountered quite a lot of abuse." Margaret's parents were so motivated to keep their daughter in a predominantly Black school that they moved to another school district, because they were "not sure that the White teachers would be as supportive of smart, Black kids." Other participants simply stated that there was no reason to move to another school, there was no disadvantage to being in a segregated school, because their teachers were so exceptional. As Jacqueline shared, "But when we got to high school, we had the option if you wanted to, to attend any White school. I went to the Black high school because it was an excellent school." They were "well qualified" as Robert Wedgeworth's narrative above asserts. These participants were not uniformly convinced that Black primary and secondary schools were inherently inferior institutions. On the contrary, segregation produced the unintended consequence of incubating Black excellence and role modeling it for the youth in their classrooms and communities.

Black excellence served as a mantra of sorts for many of these youngsters. Students with academic talent were cultivated through high academic expectations and participation in a wide variety of extracurricular activities to be prepared to participate in the racially integrated society that they knew was coming or which had dawned. Again from Margaret:

> All that was conscious training on the part of our teachers. For going into an integrated society.... We were really the first group that were going to

> go to schools that were not historically Black or even predominantly Black. Even the folks that were going to work, you were going to go work in an environment where they were predominantly White people.

Betty Johnson described the faculty and students at Dunbar High School in Washington, DC, as "all pretty much strivers" for their dogged determination to prepare every Dunbar graduate to be admissible to any elite college in the country.

Dunbar High School, Washington, DC, despite being racially segregated, was an academically excellent school with teachers who had advanced degrees in their fields and a record of not only high school graduation but also college matriculation (Hundley, 1965; Sowell, 1974; Stewart, 2013). Graduates from Dunbar attended academically elite historically Black colleges, as well as Ivy League and other elite predominantly White institutions. This enviable educational pedigree was also reflected among the teaching staff at the school, who had been educated at the nation's best academies (Sowell, 1974; Stewart, 2013).

Dunbar was founded as the nation's first public high school for Black youth in 1870 as the Preparatory High School for Colored Youth and then renamed as the "M" Street School, before finally being renamed in the early twentieth century for the poet Paul Laurence Dunbar (Stewart, 2013). Anna Julia Cooper is commonly regarded as its most influential principal, governing the school by 1902 and later pushed out by 1930. Cooper's educational philosophy refused to accept that Black people were not capable of a classic liberal arts education. She held an unfaltering commitment to promoting education as "an instrument to social, economic, and political empowerment" (Johnson, 2009, p. 45).

As acknowledged by the seven participants in this study who attended Dunbar High School, its teachers were undeniably highly qualified, having earned advanced degrees in their fields of study (Stewart, 2013). However, employment segregation in DC would prevent them from pursuing other careers. What other industries lost, generations of Black students gained through the benefit of being taught by Black men and women who were experts in their fields of study.

However, as indicated by a few of the participants with whom I spoke, Dunbar was not idyllic. Legacies of classism and colorism soured some students' experiences, while going completely unnoticed by others. Patricia Daly and Russell Davis, whose high school tenures perfectly overlapped, graduated from Dunbar in 1952 and then both matriculated to Ohio

Wesleyan University. Although acknowledging "there's no question that Dunbar has a reputation of being class conscious," Russell felt he had been treated "very ecumenically" and referenced his older sister's very positive experience as a brown-skinned woman with a noticeable physical disability. In contrast, Patricia definitively attributed the lack of explicit college guidance she received to "class differences" because she "wasn't from one of the old line DC families" and therefore she did not receive what she called the "special grooming, to [be] put on the success track." Moreover, she referenced issues of colorism by stating, "I think I fit in some ways being light-skinned…but not in the old line class structure." Russell's impression was that all of that was "more historical than factual" but admitted that light-skinned students were the majority at the school.

Following the *Brown* decision, segregated schooling in DC would be discontinued. The reputation of Dunbar changed considerably from a school that had functioned more like an elite private school to a neighborhood public school without its cadre of teachers with enviable pedigrees subjected to disadvantaged school funding formulas (Stewart, 2013). The building was even at risk of demolition in the 1970s (Wiley, 2013). The paradox of integration is that segregationist policies allowed Dunbar and its students to thrive only to be undercut and undermined by supposed racial progress.

In northern schools, whether Black students had experience attending racially integrated schools or not, Black excellence still mattered. Rose Jackson Enco's narrative in this chapter describes the academic intensity of her predominantly Black Cleveland high school, an intensity she sharply contrasts with her first high school in Atlanta. Jeane's delight in being able to compete with the predominantly Jewish students at her high school is also clear in her narrative. The desire to provide their children with the best opportunity for a high-quality education led many parents, including those without college experience themselves as noted in Chap. 2, to manipulate policies and systems of school placements to position their children to attend the most advantageous schools they could access. Parents used multiple strategies: having children live with other relatives; using a grandmother's address and taking their child to her house in the mornings, so they would be seen getting on the bus to school from that address; literally moving to another area in the city; and demanding their children be allowed to attend segregated traditionally White schools. In these ways, parents across social class strata showed significant interest and made substantial investments in their child's education. The risks these parents were taking to manipulate the system in these ways are evident in the modern-day example of Kelley Williams-Bolar, who was arrested, tried, and jailed for using similar methods to get her child into a better school in Akron, Ohio, from 2006 to 2008 (Ali-Coleman, 2014). This case was brought to mind every time I heard one of my participants talk about the lengths their parents took to ensure they got the best education available.

White Accomplices

This striving for excellence was definitely supported by most of the Black teachers that these participants encountered with very few exceptions. However, there were also influential White teachers who more than just practiced fairness in applying academic standards, but also went above that to provide opportunities to the promising Black students in their classes. In the opening narratives, Ruth spoke of the teachers who supported her, especially the debate teacher who helped to develop her oratorical skills, and she also talked about an English teacher who broadened her exposure to literature. Marylyn spoke passionately about a Jewish teacher at her junior high school, who used her time after school to tutor Marylyn and other students so that they could score well on the standardized tests required for admission to New York City's academically elite public high schools, easing their pipeline to a good college.

Beyond individual teachers, religious denominational groups also supported high-quality education for Black students. This sometimes happened through the establishment or support of mission schools, like the one Sam Lewis attended in Brewton, Alabama. The Dutch Reformed Church then also recruited the best students from these schools to go on to their sectarian colleges, like Hope College. In other cases, denominational groups sought out Black students to integrate their boarding schools. The Quakers used this approach in both Cynthia Carpenter's and Edward Carroll's schooling at The George School and Friends' Seminary, respectively. Though these efforts were substantive and life-changing in many respects for these students, individual White teachers and White religious denominations were not the primary instruments of excellent schooling among these participants. Rather, for most of these participants, Black excellence was fostered, sustained, and nurtured by Black teachers and communities for Black students.

Interracial Engagement

With a few notable exceptions, such as Laura Simms Wiltz and Bill Lowry in Hempstead and Chicago, respectively, the participants had limited interracial engagement even if they did attend integrated schools. Either neighborhoods were so self-contained by residential segregation that they never saw White people at all in social interactions or, as Leonard Yorke explained,

> My relationship with my White school mates seemed to become less intimate the further along I went in the public school system. By the time I got to high school, I knew nothing at all about what my White classmates did after the doors closed for the day.

When I asked Leonard why he thought this was happening, his response was uncertain but suspected White miscegenation fears lay at the root. For those with heavy church involvement in racially segregated denominations, summer camps provided annual periods lasting a couple of weeks to associate with White peers. For others, restricted to the men in the study but not all of them, athletics—both organized and on the playground—sometimes provided a chance to compete against White children and build friendships. Richard Dean remembered an amusing story of his childhood in DC in which he made note that it was White adults, not their children, who typically fostered racial separation:

> Where I lived in Washington, near the Navy Yard, we were maybe the third Black family in an all-White neighborhood. At the time, the playground… was segregated. They'd let people in, lock the gate, and I would go up there and look through the fence, and I'd climb over the fence. The kids would play….It's the parents that keep this stuff going. I'd go over the fence, they'd play with me no problem, but the playground worker would come and say, "You can't stay on," so they'd open up the gate, put me out. He'd walk off, I'd climb back over the fence and keep playing. So I had a lot of interaction with White kids.

The role of athletics in helping to foment relationships among men across race would become apparent again in the participants' college experiences, discussed in Chap. 6.

Throughout their primary and secondary educations, Black students and their families were disciples of the message that being academically excellent would lead to increased opportunities to participate and lead in a world heretofore dominated exclusively by White people. To be able to compete on equal terms was a point of pride. White teachers and organizations helped to support this belief and in some cases committed themselves to helping Black students achieve. The role this would play in these participants' college choice decisions is explored in Chap. 4.

Notes

1. Cynthia Carpenter was born in the USA, in Boston, Massachusetts, to Jamaican immigrant parents who had been educated in the USA. Her father, a Harvard graduate, got a faculty position at Hampton University and the family moved there during Cynthia's elementary school years. When her parents were called by the Quakers to run an American Friends School in Jamaica, Happy Grove School, Cynthia and her siblings returned to Jamaica with them until it was time for high school. From there, Cynthia was recruited to go to a Quaker boarding school in Pennsylvania. Cynthia's narrative here picks up from that point.
2. The fight was to not send them to the segregated Black school. As pointed out in Chap. 1, Murray's (1951/1997) review found that the educational desegregation laws on the books in Pennsylvania were not generally enforced. Jeane's narrative shows that school segregation happened in the eastern part of the state as well as the western.
3. Daughters of the American Revolution (DAR).
4. "Jimmied" is a colloquialism meaning "rigged" or "manipulated."
5. Education Specialist (EdS) programs are post-master's programs requiring a minimum of 30 credits.
6. This coach would become Bing's homeroom teacher, as well as his coach for both track and basketball at Wilbur Wright High School.
7. Sybil Jordan Hampton's narrative about her experiences at Central High School in Little Rock, AR, is presented here at length because of the power of her narrative and the little attention that has been placed on the experiences of those who continued to "queue" up to integrate the school after the first nine students did so in 1957. Although Melba Patillo Beals' (1995) book reflects many similar experiences, Sybil's own narrative highlights the great fortitude shown by the students, as well as the highly politicized nature of

the process to integrate this school. Several times while listening to Sybil recount her experiences at Central, I found myself overcome by emotions and weeping silently during our phone interview.

8. Central High School is currently located two blocks further south on Park, between 14th and 16th Streets. It was still in Sybil's childhood neighborhood.
9. Black students who were going to integrate Central High School had to have an interview with the school board, in addition to the academic and psychological testing that Sybil describes here.
10. This is the second group of Black students who entered Central High School. The first nine entered in 1957.
11. Beta Club is over 80 years old and currently boasts that it is "the nation's largest, independent, non-profit educational youth organization" and is focused on leadership development (National Beta Club, n.d.).
12. A settlement house, also known as a neighborhood or community center, is an organization that provides a wide range of programs and activities intended to "identify and reinforce the strengths of individuals, families, and communities" (United Neighborhood Houses, n.d.). Settlement house history goes back to the late nineteenth century, and the first settlement house was founded by Stanton Coit on New York City's Lower East Side. Jane Addams would later found another settlement house, Hull House, in Chicago. From their beginnings through the mid-1900s, staff who worked in settlement houses also lived in the communities they served and participated in programs and activities with their "neighbors." The United Neighborhood Houses of New York (UNH) was founded in 1919 to unify the settlement houses in the city under one umbrella organization (United Neighborhood Houses, n.d.).

References

Ali-Coleman, K. Z. (2014, March 20). Mom jailed for enrolling kids in school tells her story in new book, film. *Ebony*. Retrieved from http://www.ebony.com/news-views/mom-jailed-for-enrolling-kids-in-school-tells-her-story-in-new-book-film-405#axzz4AMUoTnb7

Beals, M. P. (1995). *Warriors don't cry: The searing memoir of the battle to integrate Little Rock's Central High*. New York, NY: Washington Square Press.

Clotfelter, C. T. (2004). *After Brown: The rise and retreat of school desegregation.* Princeton, NJ: Princeton University Press.

Hundley, M. G. (1965). *The Dunbar story, 1870–1955.* New York, NY: Vantage Press.

Johnson, K. A. (2009). "In service for the common good": Anna Julia Cooper and adult education. *African American Review, 43*(1), 45–56.

Murray, P. (1997). *States' laws on race and color.* Athens: University of Georgia Press. Retrieved from https://books.google.com. (Originally published in 1951).

National Beta Club. (n.d.). *About.* Retrieved June 1, 2016 from https://www.betaclub.org/about

Sowell, T. (1974). Black excellence: The case of Dunbar High School. *Public Interest, 35*, 3–21.

Stewart, A. (2013). *First class: The legacy of Dunbar, America's first Black public high school.* Chicago, IL: Chicago Review Press.

United Neighborhood Houses. (n.d.). *About UNH. Settlement house history. What is a settlement house?* Retrieved June 1, 2016, from http://www.unhny.org/about/index.html

Wiley, A. N. (2013). The Dunbar high school dilemma: Architecture, power, and African American cultural heritage. *Buildings & Landscapes, 20*(1), 95–128.

CHAPTER 4

College Choices

Ritten "Edd" Lee

Brighton, Alabama

Earlham College, 1946–1950

After high school, I went into the service in 1943 and remained there until 1946, serving two years four months and ten days. I had enough of that regimented life! I wanted to get back in school. I had already seen Earlham in 1942. I had sung in one of our choirs in school and we had a two-week trip through the Midwest singing in mostly churches and schools. Our first concert was at Antioch, I believe. It was an interesting experience to meet young White people about my own age, some a little bit older, and with such a spirit of openness and a sense

In this chapter, these 11 narratives represent the varying ways that participants ultimately came to choose what college they would attend and are organized by the participants' years in college, with the earliest matriculate first. These individuals were chosen for the particular issues they raised, allowing for the breadth of diversity in the group to come to light. I did not include birth years as I did for the previous chapters because I believe that when they entered college is more important to situating these narratives in the social and cultural contexts of the period. The participant biographies in Appendix 2 include birth years and can be referenced if desired.

© The Author(s) 2017
D.-L. Stewart, *Black Collegians' Experiences in US Northern Private Colleges*, DOI 10.1057/978-1-137-59077-0_4

of camaraderie. I loved it, because I had never seen that kind of interaction between White and Black youths. Then it was on to Earlham. Being on the Earlham campus was a richer experience than it was at Antioch. In fact, we were on the Earlham campus much longer than we were at Antioch. I got a chance to talk to a lot of students. There was an outpouring, a welcoming to us there. Some immediately wanted to know if we were going to come to Earlham. Of course, nobody knew what was going to happen, but I knew that after I got there and saw and felt the sense of a community, which they emphasized at the college and still do, I had the feeling that was really where I wanted to be, because I loved the people. The teachers were kind and outgoing and giving of lots of time and so forth. They talked about the sense of community, of course. They talked about Quaker meetings and that sort of thing, which nobody was forced to go to, but it appealed to me. All of that appealed to me very much. I knew that I had struck up a love relationship. Of course, I went back home and I was drafted, and I didn't come back until 1946, when I was a freshman at the college. I did consider going to a Black college, very much so. I considered Alabama A&M. I considered Alabama State. I considered Tuskegee. I considered Hampton. I had college catalogues from practically every school in the South by the time I graduated from the 12th grade. I wanted to explore them and see what they were like and how much it cost to go there, because I would've had to pay my own expenses pretty much, as most children did who left coal-mining communities or farm communities and went off to school. Their parents didn't have money. You had to work if you went off to these colleges. I considered, yes, very much going to college down South. With the G.I. Bill of Rights,[1] a government program that provided for your tuition and books and part of your lodging if you were a veteran, you got time in school commensurate to the time you had been in the service. I got that. As a result of having the G.I. Bill, I still had to work at Earlham, but not much, not like some kids did. With the G.I. Bill of Rights, I decided that I would opt for an integrated school. One that was already integrated. One where Black and White people could sit down and treat each other like brothers and sisters. I would prefer that experience rather than continuing in the South, where there was a great deal of segregation and discrimination. Of course, going to Indiana, in time, proved it was not the best of what could be offered in the North. Some people called it—what did they call it?—"Indiana up South" or something like that they used to say. A very conservative state, which I didn't know when I opted to go to Earlham. I didn't know all of these facts, but I learned them very quickly.

Ed Rhodes

Cumberland, Maryland

Kenyon College, 1951–1955

One of the reasons why I wanted to go to a White college was that I knew I wanted to be able to succeed economically. If you're going to have a good job, you're going to have to work with Whites. If you live in a segregated town like I did, we had contact with them. I had friends. But it was different. You never had an opportunity to deal with them in the labor market in the same jobs. As far as a government job or an office job for a company, that was something that was just out of the realm of possibility if you didn't go to college. Oh yes, an integrated college would give you the opportunity to interact with Whites as equals, as peers. That was the reason why I wanted to go. Kenyon, although it was a very small school at the time, there were only about 500 men there. It was very prestigious, very well known. I found out about this scholarship fund[2]—I can't remember the name, but they didn't give money back then. I don't remember exactly how I found out about it. I wrote to them and indicated my interest in going to an integrated college. At that time, they had brochures on every college in the country that was integrated. I indicated I was interested in going in the Midwest, so they sent me brochures. They were just little squibs, really. Wasn't any multi-page thing, but literally about a page or so on each college, but maybe even a little less. They covered schools in Pennsylvania, Ohio, and Indiana, or something like that. At that time, I think I started off at Kenyon it was a little under $1000.00 a year, and that was for everything. That was a princely sum to my parents. I got 60% of my tuition from the state of Maryland. Well, interestingly enough, Maryland and all states south of the Cotton Curtain, if you will—did not want Blacks to go to their state universities. In order to preclude a person applying and perhaps the Civil Liberties Union[3] or whoever their equivalent was, instituting a suit that would be expensive and perhaps if they would lose, they offered scholarships to Blacks to go anywhere they wanted to go. The only stipulation from Maryland was that the course of study you took had to be one that was not offered in a traditional Black college that was in Maryland. That was really funny because when I went [*laughter*] there, I recognized that [*laughter*], well, this is going to be kind of hard to pull this rabbit out of a hat. I told them I wanted to major in *research* chemistry. Now, as everyone knows, there's no such undergraduate course. It's just chemistry. You take chemistry. When I said "research," the response was, "Okay, fine, that's fine." Now, I went to Baltimore for an interview before the board. The way that I got there was because my father, through working at the station,[4] knew one of the state senators. He made certain that my name got down there and that I was one of the candidates for the scholarship. I think you could have gotten there probably easier, but anyway, this guy really greased the slides. When I went there, the one Black representative knew my aunt, who had gone to, I think, Morgan at the same time that he did. She was the only person in the family that had gone to college. Anyway, he said, "Oh, you're Rhodes' nephew," and I said, "Yes." Anyway, when I told him I wanted research chemistry, everybody clucked and clucked and I answered a few more questions, and finally they said, "Fine, you got your money."

Willis "Bing" Davis

Dayton, Ohio

DePauw University, 1955–1959

In this small enclave that we were in, it was almost tradition or expectation that once you turned 16 and you could drop out—school hasn't been so cool anyway, now you can work and help out at home.[5] Most of the boys did that. There were two little small industries out there: a meat packing company, where you could just get a job, learn how to butcher and how to slaughter; and then there was a bleach bottling company where you could get a job. That was the assumption. Athletics was just something fun to do. I was in football, basketball, and track, so I was always in season. I never viewed art as being a real possibility, but I just knew I enjoyed it. When I was considering dropping out of school like everybody else, it was because I was the only one of the six kids without some kind of hustle helping out at home. I was looking forward to dropping out of school, and this coach, he just encouraged me to not drop out, try to see if I could use my potential. I would have dropped out had he not talked to me. That was just my intention. I think it was probably guilt and shame over having to ask my mother for lunch money when all my siblings were working to help her out and support me too. Sure, I played athletics. I'm already all-city now. I'm one of the top athletes in town, but, hey, we were struggling. Well, Coach[6] [*laughs*] took away that excuse. His father was a surgeon here at Miami Valley Hospital, our biggest hospital at the time, and he called his dad, "Bing needs a job." His dad got me on with housekeeping at Miami Valley Hospital. He took away that excuse that I had. Then, in the summer—this is how the DePauw thing came in—his dad said, "Look, I could use some help." I would go out there into the suburbs and just be at the house in the summer for a couple of days just doing odd jobs and stuff. It would come time for lunch or come time for dinner and I'd go in with the family, Coach's mom and dad, to eat. Every time, the maid would have a place set for me at the table and over here is a DePauw alumni magazine, usually folded to the sports section. They never said, "You ought to consider DePauw." They would just talk among themselves. They would just be talking about how great college was, and the fun, and the camaraderie, and the friendship. Another time—we didn't have a car, so the coach—he was my homeroom teacher and my Civics and Social Studies teacher, so I was around him a lot—he took me out and taught me how to drive. Yeah, he was a father figure. Yeah, yeah. On the way back from the Fort Wayne Northside Relays—it was in April or May, almost ready to graduate—Coach says, "What are you doing Sunday?" I said, "Nothing I know of, Coach. What's up?" He says, "I'll pick you up at 9:00 a.m." He came by Sunday. He told my parents, "I'm taking him to see DePauw. I'm taking five students from Wilbur Wright High School." It was me and four of the Appalachian, poor White kids on the team. Drove us over. The admissions director had played ball at DePauw in the forties with my coach, so they had a friendship. We didn't get to know him on a campus tour or fraternity parties. No, we went to his house, and Coach says to him, "I got five young kids out in the car, and I'd like you to talk with them and see if they possibly could get a scholarship to see if they could do college work." He said, "One is a tall Black kid named Bing Davis. Now, he hasn't taken any college prep classes, but he's got a lot of potential." All five of us, on his recommendation, got scholarships to DePauw. Two of us were in basketball, one in football, and two academic. I made the assumption that if you went to

DePauw, you were going to be a good person, and you were going to help others, because the first three people I met from DePauw did that.

Robert Wedgeworth

Kansas City, Missouri

Wabash College, 1955–1959

My counselor in high school took a special interest in me in my sophomore year, and she arranged for me to take the SAT exams in the spring of my sophomore year. As a result of that, a man who represented a scholarship program that was funded by the Ford Foundation but based in New York called the NSSFNS—National Scholarship and Service Fund for Negro Students. He came through, and he had seen my SAT scores. He started talking to me about going to college. They had this special program at that time. After several interviews and some other exchanges, he offered me a scholarship to go to Fisk at the end of my sophomore year in high school. Their idea was that they were losing too many talented African American students between the sophomore and the senior year in high school. They felt that if they could take them out at the end of the sophomore year and send them to college right away, they wouldn't lose as many. I was enrolled at Fisk as a freshman for the fall of 1953, but as the summer rolled on and I would've been a junior, I knew I was going to be a starter on the basketball team, and thinking about the relationships that I had developed among my high school friends, I had some misgivings, but I didn't share them with my parents. Then they began to raise some questions and talk to people. I think what it finally boiled down to was they said they thought that I was too young to go away at that time, which was kind of a relief for me because I was having misgivings myself. Okay, but what that did was set up a relationship between me and NSSFNS. I can't remember the man's name, but every spring he would come through Kansas City and talk to me. The next year, my junior year, he came through and talked to me. By then, I had gone to some college fairs, and I met the Wabash recruiter who had the area of Kansas City. I met the Wabash representative at the college fair in the spring of my sophomore year, when this business with Fisk was going on. The next year, he came back again and I talked with him, but this time more seriously. I was very interested in Wabash for two reasons. One was I was an all-state basketball player, but I knew that I didn't want to go to a big athletic school like the University of Kansas. I liked the combination that Wabash offered of high-level athletic competition and high-quality academics. I knew from another friend who was playing basketball at the University of Kansas that the coaches controlled your academic program, and they wouldn't really allow you to take any challenging courses. I didn't want that kind of control. Wabash appealed to me for this balance. Then when I was a senior, my mother fell ill, and she died in January. Then my father lasted until Easter Sunday, and he died. Just before he died, he was in the hospital, and I went off to Honor Scholarship Weekend at Wabash with his blessing. I came back and I told him this was great; I'd love to go to school there and all. But he died Easter Sunday. My counselor was concerned about my being able to go to college, so she arranged for me to have a part-time job. Instead of going to that last period, I got out of school early, went downtown, and I'd work from 4:00 until 10:00 in the evening throughout the spring and summer. Just so that I could have a little extra money to support myself and I could save a little money for whatever reason. Then this is when everything happened. She arranged for me to be an applicant for a full scholarship to what was then the University of Kansas City.[7] She arranged for me to have a full scholarship at the University of Kansas City, which included being able to live on campus in one of the dorms so that I would be completely out of my environment where I grew up. Then the visitor from NSSFNS came through and asked me what I was planning to do. I told him that I had had some unfortunate circumstances, that my parents had died, and that I had this opportunity to go to the University of Kansas City. He said, "What do you want to do?" I said, "I'd really like to go to Wabash." I said, "But they only offered me a tuition scholarship, and I can't afford to do it for that." He said, "Don't make any decisions for a couple of weeks, and I'll get back to you." He got back to me in about ten days. They offered me a supplementary scholarship that would pay all of the rest of my expenses to go to Wabash because their objective was that they were trying to get students out of their immediate environment and going to predominantly White schools, as distinct from the earlier objective of just getting you to college early, where they were sending them to all-Black schools, like Fisk, Morehouse, Howard University. I was determined that I was going to go to Wabash. I accepted the supplementary scholarship, and that's how I got to Wabash.

Adine Ray Usher
Chicago, Illinois
Oberlin College, 1957–1961

I was two years at the Lab School, then the last two years at Morgan Park. During my junior year, I started looking at colleges. I knew that I wanted small liberal arts colleges. That was the time when there were a lot of first Blacks at a lot of these schools. I looked at Sarah Lawrence, but I wanted co-ed. I looked at Beloit. Beloit desperately wanted me because I would've been the first Black. Then, Lawrence College in Appleton, Wisconsin offered me the sun, the moon, and the stars because they wanted the first Black. A very very very good friend of mine, African American, had gone to Oberlin. Her parents had graduated from the University of Chicago with my parents and were very close friends. I had spent a weekend on the Oberlin campus with her during my junior year. My mind was just swimming. What should I do? What should I do? None of my family or none of my friends would make the decision for me. I said, "Okay, Oberlin is where I need to go. I don't need to be the first Black in such a wonderful place." Even though I'm going to be in the college, they had this wonderful aura of music. While I was there, I studied at the college, but was allowed to study piano free of charge, for four years. It just felt cozier. I looked for more of a relationship with professors. I also loved Oberlin's history. I knew the Black thing wouldn't be an issue. When I went to Oberlin, you'd ask the college president how many Black students were on campus, and he'd say, "I don't know. I don't care." Because it was—now I have to say at Oberlin, at that time in the fifties, most of the kids at Oberlin, Black kids, were the sons and daughters of professionals, many of whom had gone to Oberlin themselves. Why not a historically Black college? Because my parents looked down on them. I married a man from Hampton and my mother didn't want that included in the wedding announcement. You want an honest interview? Well, you have to know that's part of our experience, too. Please, no, not even Spelman. I mean when my father drove around town in the late fifties with an MIT sticker on one side of the back of the car and an Oberlin one on the other, this man was happy. He had arrived. He graduated from the University of Chicago with an A average in chemistry but wasn't allowed to eat in the lunchroom. Think about that pain.

Rose Jackson Enco

Cleveland, Ohio

Ohio Wesleyan University, 1958–1962

I'll tell you what really did it. My mother was one of those people that loved to help people. Many young women came, and they sat on her couch, talking. Sometimes I'd hear them talking. They would cry because when they came from the South, they couldn't get a job. If they wanted to be a teacher, they had to take extra courses. Their employers assumed their education had been inferior. They'd sit there crying on the couch, talking to my mother. I'd hear this stuff. I said, "Mother, I"—I wanted to be a teacher. I said, "I don't want that. I want my credentials to be accepted no matter where I go in the United States. That's my goal." It was because I heard those women moaning. That knocked out all the colleges in the South because I'd seen them coming up, sitting on the couch, crying. Now, probably that wasn't wise in some ways because a lot of people said that's the time to get your MRS. "If you want to find a man, you need to be going and looking at one of these historically Black colleges. You should be looking at Howard." But I said, "I can't—no. I want to be able to go and get a job anywhere." That made an impression on me. You talk about things that hit you. I heard one too many people sitting on that couch. I think I decided I wanted to go in my state, so I applied to Ohio Wesleyan and to Antioch. Ohio Wesleyan—somebody told me that they were very good in education. Yes, yes. That meant when I came out, my degree would be accepted. Two, I think I wanted to stay fairly close to Cleveland. I didn't want to go too far. One of my ideals of college was walking across the lawn with a professor—talking in small groups. That was somehow in my head. [*Laughter*] I liked the campus. I think I went and looked at the campus, and it looked like what I had vaguely imagined—you know?—and the size would facilitate the speaking, I felt. Because I was in Ohio, a lot of people said that was a good school. My parents supported it. I didn't have to fight to go or anything like that. Some people would say, "Are you sure you don't want to go down South? You were down there in Atlanta. You could go to Spelman." I said, "Oh, no! No. Dear God." Even when I was little, I was aware of some of the ranking, plus I heard that Howard was a party school, and I said, "That's a no."

Jeannette Phillips

Toledo, Ohio

Ohio Wesleyan University, 1958–1962

In high school, I had fantastic teachers. They encouraged me to go to a college that was up to the standards they felt were important. I knew I wanted to stay in Ohio, because I thought that would lessen the expenses. With one exception, because I did apply to Howard, I kept my choices within Ohio. That was easy to do, because there are a lot. I wanted to go to a small school. I did not think I would fare well at a very large university. I applied to Oberlin, Ohio Wesleyan. What was the third one in Ohio? Hmm…it was Heidelberg. One of the reasons I applied to Howard is because a friend of the family, who went there, was encouraging my going to Howard and even had arranged that I would be guaranteed a scholarship. I don't remember how much the scholarship was at this point were I to get accepted. My college advisor happened to be one of the science teachers. When I went to see her, and by that point I had the three universities I was going to apply to, she said to me, "You might want to think about this," talking about Howard. She said, "Because after all you want to find a husband while you're there." I was livid. I was very upset. I said, "That's not what I'm going to college for," and so forth. The more I thought about it, the more upset I got, so I ended up going to the principal. Now, the principal at Scott High School, where I went, was a fine man. He probably didn't weigh more than 120 pounds soaking wet. He had a high voice. He was the most fantastic person. He meant a lot to me and to the student body as a whole. This is the time when the Little Rock episodes and everything was going on. I went to see him, and I said, "I really would prefer to have somebody else as my college advisor." I began to tell him what had happened. He started getting red in the face. I knew he was a professional, so he did not lambast the teacher in front of me. He said, "Well, congratulations, you just got me as your college advisor." [*Chuckles*] He worked with me. I went to visit Ohio Wesleyan one weekend, because a friend of mine—a White friend who was a year ahead of me in school—invited me to come down. She was at Ohio Wesleyan. I spent a weekend with her. I sensed from some of the girls in the dormitory a coldness, a coolness. My friend was such a warm person. She offset that a great deal. I liked what Ohio Wesleyan stood for academically. When it all came down to it, I probably would have gone to Oberlin, but it was going to be tougher for me financially because my parents were always a little on the stingy side when it came to what they were willing to put out for my education. I knew I was going to have to work while I was in school for extra money. All of the factors together, plus the fact that my friend was at Ohio Wesleyan, I ultimately chose that one. I did get a scholarship, but it was not enough to prevent me from having to work through school.

Jacqueline Huggins Burt Tolliver

Louisville, Kentucky

Albion College, 1962–1966

The guidance counselor looked for scholarships for students all over the United States. He would actually travel to those universities. He would not send us where he hadn't visited. He spent his money in the summer to visit colleges and learned about those colleges, made sure they were the right institutions for us and then narrowed it down and gave us choices. He was unbelievable. That's the kind of teachers and counselors we had. They wanted the best for us. They always told us that we could be in the White House if we wanted to be. At that time, they told us that. He was responsible for my knowing about Albion College. He gave me a selection of three colleges, I think. It was Albion, Wittenberg, and another school. I applied to Albion, and they gave me a scholarship, a full scholarship.

Sybil Jordan Hampton

Little Rock, Arkansas

Earlham College, 1962–1966

I was so absolutely clear about why I was at Central and what the payoff was going to be for the race and for me. My parents said, "You want to go to a really wonderful college. We don't think that after your experience here that we want you to go to Howard or Fisk or Hampton because we don't want you to feel the pressure of sororities and all that kind of stuff. You won't do well in those places where they're so class—they may be all Black, but they're very much bound by class. You don't have money. We don't have money. We have education. We're good people, but we don't want you thrown into that whole status bourgeoisie stuff. You're going to do well, and some other types of schools will be interested in having you come." Remember there was a time when there were not a lot of Black students in the White colleges in this country. Well, what you have to know is that one of the most magnificent things that the Quakers have done is that when there are cities that have crises, particularly racial crises, Quakers always send what they call "a mission." Little Rock had a Quaker mission. Two people, one who came out of the southwest regional office in Austin, Texas came here. They were the catalysts for the conversations during '57–'59 for people, across the races, who wanted to come and talk, and needed to do that safely. My brother and I knew Quakers here, and we were then also selected to do Quaker work camping. I knew Quakers, but my desire—I applied to Wheaton College in Massachusetts. I applied to Bryn Mawr because that was where my heart was set on going. I wanted to go to a women's college. I really wanted to go to one of the Seven Sisters.[8] I really felt that that would be the kind of learning environment that would be very nurturing. My parents were looking at me like, "We don't think so. We don't want you at an all-girl school. We don't want you at Howard, but we certainly don't want you in an all-girls school." Just because they just felt that I had to live in a world with men, so they wanted me to go to college with men, okay? The big intervention in my life was Earlham was not on my list. The National Scholarship Service and Fund for Negro Students, do you know it? It had money either from the Ford Foundation or the Rockefeller Foundation, and it may have been involved with National Merit, as an offshoot of National Merit because they took students based on their SAT scores, Black students, and identified cadres of Black students, and then they had a profile that they sent out to us. Based on this profile, we were matched with colleges. They were a matching service to help White colleges find Negro students who would be academically capable and who would fit into that particular learning environment. NSSFNS matched me with Earlham. I went to Earlham after never having gone to the campus.

Tanya Summers

Brooklyn, New York City, New York

Kalamazoo College, 1963–1967

So, the teen magazine *Seventeen*, I guess they profiled different colleges. I was a regular reader of *Seventeen* and they had an article about this college that had this very interesting program where you did study abroad and career internships.[9] It sounded very interesting. It was different from anything I've heard about. I thought, "Oh that sounds interesting." I wrote a letter to Kalamazoo College and asked them to send me some information. They wrote back. They would interview on the East Coast. I guess they always had a group of people from Connecticut, New Jersey, and New York. The admissions office had come and interviewed me at a hotel in Manhattan. I was admitted. I got a scholarship and there I was. Nobody I knew had ever heard of Kalamazoo. I remember my mother saying, "What is this college?" No one had ever heard of it. I had applied to Brandeis. I didn't get in. That was my mother's idea. I didn't know anything about Brandeis. Oh, I remember. There was the Negro Student something or other.[10] There was some kind of like the United Negro College Fund. The equivalent of that. Of course, it was called Negro Student something or other back then. I remember applying to that. I think they recommended the kind of schools you should apply for. Okay. I think I remember Northeastern was one of them. Earlham College. I think that was one of them. There may have been a couple of others in that Midwest group. I don't know if I applied or not. I don't remember. I do remember not being interested in whatever they were recommending. Let me see. Then my mother had friends who went to Bennett College.[11] They said, "Oh, you should go to Bennett." My sister was there. I said, "Oh, I don't want to be my big sister's little sister, so I'm not applying there," so I didn't apply to Bennett. What other schools were people telling us about? Howard? Maybe. I don't remember. [*Pause*] I got it. I know where I applied. I applied to Brooklyn College, because I got a regents' scholarship. That's right. I think when you take those regents exams. I don't know if you apply for the scholarship or you're considered automatically. I guess all this shows how little I knew. I don't know if my mother did all this stuff, or did people do it for us, or did we do it. I don't remember any of this stuff. Okay, so Brooklyn College. I think I applied to Brooklyn College, Hunter College, and CCNY.[12] I'm pretty sure I did not get in to Hunter. I don't know. I know I got a scholarship to go to Brooklyn College, but I didn't want to stay home and go to college. That was my issue with the city colleges. See, I had to get away. My main objective in life was getting away. To wherever I went I didn't care, just as long as it was not Brooklyn, New York. I got a good financial aid package and off to Kalamazoo I went.

***

The Right College: A Utilitarian Mission

In many ways, the college search and decision-making processes of these 68 participants, reflected in the 11 narratives above, foreshadow the key factors and issues that would come to characterize current college choice models (Cabrera & LaNasa, 2000; Callendar & Jackson, 2008; Hossler, 2000; Hossler, Braxton, & Coopersmith, 1989; Hossler & Gallagher, 1987; Hossler & Stage, 1992). In particular, Hossler and Gallagher's (1987) three-phase college choice model (predisposition, search, and choice) is evident in the participants' stories. The predisposition to college was demonstrated in Chaps. 2 and 3; each of these participants was already motivated to attend college by a combination of family, school, and personal attributes. Moreover, as reflected in Chap. 3 and these narratives above, participants had varying degrees of assistance and support in the search phase. High school teachers and guidance counselors were often critical to informing the college search phase for students whose parents had not attended college. For those who were not first-generation college students, awareness of possible colleges was developed through knowledge of parents' alma maters, siblings and other relatives, and/or older peers. Finally, the actual choice of one institution over another was influenced by academic reputation, familiarity with the institution, distance from home, institutional size and related characteristics (e.g., relationships with faculty), and particularly for the many students from modest means, cost of attendance.

Yet, there are many ways in which these participants' narratives of their college choice processes contradict today's extant literature. First, although acknowledging the significance of parents to students' college choices, particularly in shaping predisposition (Cabrera & LaNasa, 2000; Hossler & Gallagher, 1987), the nature of those influences according to other literature differs. Hossler and Stage (1992) found that students whose parents had not attended college were less likely to reach for elite, high-quality institutions. However, among these participants, the institutions in the GLCA were high-quality institutions, some well known for their academic rigor generally and in specific areas (e.g., Oberlin in music, DePauw in science, Kenyon in pre-med, Ohio Wesleyan for education) and others understood to be fine institutions through their connections with private philanthropic organizations, such as the NSSFNS (e.g., Kalamazoo and Wabash). This variance may be related to the specific circumstances that confronted these individuals as Black students on the front edge of institutional desegregation in the mid-twentieth century in the USA.

Other research has found that family socioeconomic status (SES) suppressed students' aspirations to attend academically elite colleges (Hossler et al., 1989). Again, these participants defy that expectation. On the whole, they sought to attend high-quality, elite colleges on the urging of parents, teachers, and/or school counselors regardless of cost. This is illustrated in Tanya Summers' and R. Edd Lee's narratives in this chapter. Each of them, both first-generation students from lower-income families, had a wide range of institutions in their choice set, from low-cost historically Black and/or local city colleges to elite, academically rigorous, and more expensive institutions. Also, the NSSFNS played a critical role in broadening the awareness of ten of these participants to the existence of the schools in the Midwest. Other than Oberlin, for participants who were not raised in Ohio, Michigan, or Indiana, those institutions were mostly unknown, overshadowed by the greater name recognition wrought by the northeast Ivy League and Seven Sisters colleges. The matching service run by the NSSFNS, well described in the narratives from Sybil Jordan Hampton and Robert Wedgeworth, enabled academically talented Black students to discover college options they would not otherwise have considered.

Instead of family SES, cost of attendance and availability of financial aid were more relevant considerations for participants when actually selecting a specific college to attend. At that point, as found by current researchers (Callendar & Jackson, 2008; Hossler, 2000), closing the gap between cost of attendance and out-of-pocket expenses was the deciding factor for many of these individuals. Robert Wedgeworth's narrative most clearly illustrates how receiving additional financial aid, in the form of a supplementary scholarship provided through the NSSFNS, allowed him to attend his first-choice institution, Wabash College, after the untimely death of both his parents. Although his other option, the University of Kansas City, also provided him a full-ride scholarship, including campus housing, that was not his first choice. Once the additional scholarship made it a choice between equals—zero cost of attendance at both institutions—Robert was able to follow his passions over his purse strings.

For others in less dramatic circumstances, they chose the institution from which they received the most financial aid. As Henry Deering recalled, the advice was to "Get a ship. Get a ship out of here," where "ship" was shorthand for scholarship. Coretta Scott,[13] whose older sister was attending Antioch College, was "offered an interracial scholarship by the Race Relations Committee" at the college (Scott, 1948, p. 1) that was necessary for her poor Alabama family. Institutional status then functioned somewhat unexpectedly in their decisions. Both academically elite and highly reputable private Black institutions such as Morehouse, Spelman, and Hampton, as well as segregated state colleges, were equally out of bounds for some students from poorer families. On the other hand, the academically elite GLCA colleges were able to offer more generous financial aid, reducing the cost of attendance to levels even lower than what would have had to be paid at a segregated state college or an elite Black private college. As Sam Lewis would share, although he had a scholarship to attend Alabama State, the Hope College scholarship was enough that all he had to cover were his book, and incidentals.

In these ways, the search for the right college was ultimately a utilitarian mission, driven by practical considerations. In addition to finances, institutional size mattered to some of them. In Adine Ray Usher's and Rose Jackson Enco's decisions to attend Oberlin, its small size was attractive and reflected what Rose considered to be an "ideal" college environment. For others, distance from home drew them to their ultimate choice, either because it was near home or because it was further away from home. Jeannette chose Ohio Wesleyan because it was in the state and she didn't want to be far away from home in Toledo. Meanwhile, for one participant in DC, the desire to "keep warm parents at least 500 miles away from me wherever I went to school" made their ultimate choice appealing. Academic reputation also mattered to these participants. Laura Simms Wiltz wanted to be able to study the harp and Oberlin was the only school she was considering where she could do that. For those interested in science, DePauw's reputation was a draw. As mentioned in Rose's narrative, Ohio Wesleyan's positive reputation in teacher preparation reassured her that it would be the best choice for her.

At this point, I would be remiss to close this chapter without addressing these participants' decisions not to attend a Black college. For some, as indicated above, it was a matter of feasibility: costs and lack of financial aid made Black colleges inaccessible. However, for others, perceptions of Black colleges and their own integrationist philosophies made attending a Black college both undesirable and impractical. As Coretta wrote, going to college in the North was important to learning about and working with White people committed to working for racial equality, but moreso "a good education…should be as free as possible—and that means free from Jim Crow as well as free in classroom teaching" (1948, pp. 1–2). Although the more vibrant social life presumably available at Black colleges was appealing to several participants, uniformly that appeal was also seen as counterproductive for fulfilling their goals. They were worried about being distracted and not being encouraged to commit seriously to their academics. As Rose mentioned, hearing that Howard was a "party school" eliminated it from consideration.

Yet, for others, Black colleges were simply devalued. As Adine openly admitted, her parents perceived these colleges to be "inferior." This is not explained by simply presuming these individuals had internalized racism. To denote these participants as believing that anything White was automatically better than what Black people did ignores these participants' clear understanding that White people were only able to have better schools because they had access to the resources necessary to produce them: highly trained teachers, financial resources to provide books and materials, and capital infrastructure budgets. These were people who knew that Black excellence existed independent of whiteness within their segregated communities. They knew that White racist presumptions of Black educational inferiority had material effects. Ed Rhodes understood that getting a job in the professional sector of the labor market beyond the veil of segregation required a degree from a White college. The young women that Rose overheard complaining to her mother provided further evidence of the consequences of not complying with the standards and criteria set by White people for success in White society where greater wealth, social status, and freedom were reserved.

Moreover, the mission to prove one's equality through intentionally associating with Whites was worth being the only one or only one of a few other Black students on campus. To be the "first Black" as Adine put it came with pressures for a certain level of comportment and academic success, not dissimilar to the "test" that Sybil was put through at Central High School. Although Adine opted to attend Oberlin, where she would not have to be the "first Black," others like Sybil, Robert, and Janet Williams enthusiastically embraced the opportunity to disrupt myths of Black inferiority, to excel and prove that they could "compete" as Jeane shared about her high school experience.

Ultimately, using a CRT lens, the choice by these participants not to attend a Black college was highly utilitarian and demonstrated critical race idealism (Delgado & Stefancic, 2012) in four ways. First, they directly challenged dominant ideologies of whiteness by breaking out of the silos of racially segregated educational spaces. This is significantly important to their families as well, as demonstrated in Chap. 2. Second, they sought to gain access to the places that would best help them to affect the structures from which they could redistribute resources. By gaining access to coveted professional and managerial jobs with higher salaries in White-owned companies, they could redistribute wealth toward their families and communities. Third, they would develop a transdisciplinary proficiency, being conversationally fluent in the language of whiteness that informs how society operates. Fourth, the participants harnessed interest convergence to make issues of access central to institutional conversations. These traditionally White colleges had a vested interest in admitting and supporting the persistence of Black students to enact their espoused religious and ethical values. The participants' integrationist philosophy that underlay their college choices was motivated by allegiance, not to whiteness, but rather to a vision of liberation through resistance from within. In Chap. 5, we go to college with the participants and see how their integrationist visions were either strengthened or began to fracture as they arrived and made the transition to becoming college students.

Notes

1. The official name was The Serviceman's Readjustment Act of 1944.
2. This was likely the NSSFNS mentioned by a total of 10 of the 68 participants.
3. The American Civil Liberties Union.
4. Ed's father was a Pullman Porter.
5. Although this was the common course in Bing's neighborhood, his family was highly supportive and encouraging of him graduating from high school and going to college.

6. This was the same coach introduced in Bing's narrative in Chap. 3, who inspired his decision to go to Wilbur Wright High School.
7. The University of Kansas City, which had been a private institution, became part of the University of Missouri system in July 1963 (Curators of the University of Missouri, 2016).
8. The "Seven Sisters" are a group of elite, private women's colleges in the northeast founded in the mid- to late nineteenth century as a parallel to the all-men's Ivy League colleges. The Seven Sisters are Mount Holyoke College, Vassar College, Wellesley College, Smith College, Radcliffe College, Bryn Mawr College, and Barnard College.
9. The "K-Plan" had just been approved by the faculty earlier in 1963 and incorporated career internships, study abroad, and a senior individualized project into a four-year degree plan, which included taking classes over the summers following the second and third years (Pope, 2012; Zipp, 2013). Although these elements are standard practice now across many colleges and universities in the USA, when Kalamazoo debuted this curriculum in the early 1960s, it was considered so unusual that it drew national attention and nearly doubled its enrollment from 750 students to over 1200 within the first decade of its implementation (Zipp, 2013).
10. This is a reference to the NSSFNS.
11. Bennett College is a historically Black women's college in Greensboro, North Carolina.
12. The City College of New York is now the City University of New York, a multi-campus system of undergraduate colleges across the five boroughs and a graduate college in Manhattan.
13. Coretta Scott would later marry Martin Luther King Jr. It is unclear what prompted Scott to write this article.

References

Cabrera, A., & LaNasa, S. (2000). Understanding the college-choice process. *New Directions for Institutional Research, no., 107*, 5–22.

Callendar, D., & Jackson, J. (2008). Does the fear of debt constrain choice of university or subject of study? *Studies in Higher Education, 33*(4), 405–429.

Curators of the University of Missouri. (2016). *History*. University of Missouri-Kansas City. Retrieved from http://www.umkc.edu/history/

Delgado, R., & Stefancic, J. (2012). *Critical race theory: An introduction* (2nd ed.). New York: New York University.

Hossler, D. (2000). The role of financial aid in enrollment management. *New Directions for Student Services, 89*, 77–90.

Hossler, D., Braxton, J., & Coopersmith, G. (1989). Understanding student college choice. In J. C. Smart (Ed.), *Higher education: Handbook of theory and research* (Vol. 5). New York, NY: Agathon Press.

Hossler, D., & Gallagher, K. S. (1987). Studying student college choice: A three-phase model and the implications for policymakers. *College and University, 62*(3), 207–221.

Hossler, D., & Stage, F. K. (1992). Family and high school experience influences on the postsecondary educational plans of ninth-grade students. *American Educational Research Journal, 29*(2), 425–451.

Pope, L. (2012). *Colleges that change lives: 40 schools that will change the way you think about colleges* (Rev. ed., H. M.Oswald). New York, NY: Penguin Books.

Zipp, Y. (2013, March 10). Kalamazoo College celebrates the 50th anniversary of the K Plan. *MLive*. Retrieved from http://www.mlive.com/news/kalamazoo/index.ssf/2013/03/kalamazoo_college_celebrates_t.html

Antioch College

Scott, C. (1948, April–June). Why I came to college. Reprinted from *Opportunity: Journal of Negro Life, 26*(2), pp. 1–2. New York, NY: The National Urban League. File 2: Race Relations-General historical info. Antiochiana, Olive Kettering Library, Antioch College, Yellow Springs, OH.

CHAPTER 5

Arriving on Campus

Kenyon College

Stan Jackson, 1948–1952

I don't recall visiting. I did well on the college entrance exam and got this scholarship offer. At that time, my recollection is there was a Black funeral director in Steubenville who knew a Black family in Mount Vernon, Ohio. The funeral director offered his vehicle to drive my family to Kenyon and he introduced me to this family in Mount Vernon. When I first saw Kenyon? My recollection is, well, I'm in a sea of White students. At that time, this was post-World War II. Freshmen students were housed in barracks. There was a V-12 unit there, right.[1] They had barracks, and this is where they housed the incoming students. The barracks were constructed in some way that there were two people in each unit, individual unit, with bunk beds. My roommate was a gentleman from New England. I think I was in the lower bunk and he was, no, he was in the lower bunk. I was in the upper bunk. For my first semester there, I resided in the barracks. Since I was athletically inclined, I did join the soccer team as a freshman. I joined the band, little band unit that they had. One of the other ways to supplement the scholarship was as a waiter in the dining room. I got a

The 11 narratives in this chapter are organized by participants' years in college, the earliest in 1948 and latest in 1964, then by institution from 8 colleges.

© The Author(s) 2017

D.-L. Stewart, *Black Collegians' Experiences in US Northern Private Colleges*, DOI 10.1057/978-1-137-59077-0_5

job as a waiter in the dining room. Also, there was a coffee shop, which provided opportunities for evening snacks. I got a job washing dishes, helping the cook in the coffee shop, for additional supplementary income. I spent a lot of time, in my first semester, in the library, in the stacks. I found a table in the library. Every moment I had not working and in class, I was in the stacks in the library. I was isolated. I isolated myself. It was not required, but I spent every spare moment I had in the library. I wanted to do well.

Earlham College

Janet Williams, 1951–1953

You know, you go visit the college that you might be going to? They had a luncheon or something.[2] *[Beauford[3]: I think we were there a week before.]* Well, I ended up living on campus, but it was interesting. I didn't have a roommate because there wasn't but two other Black kids in our class that I can remember. They were from Jamaica. They were roommates, but there wasn't another Black one. There wasn't a Black girl.[4] There wasn't anybody to be my roommate. Hear me? I got a room all to myself, and it didn't bother me at all. Now, that might have bothered some people, but I thought, gee, isn't that nice? I get a room all to myself. Didn't have to pay any more than the rest of them for it either, you know. No, I had no realization that it might have been because none of the White girls wanted to room with me. I'm aware of prejudice. I can see it. I can sense it. I can feel it. I can look at it. I had awareness, but I always know, if I sense that in you, I will make a special effort to win you with kindness and love. It doesn't take long before people will forget what color you are. I think they actually forgot what color I was, because I was really friendly.[5] I'm going to just go into your little conversations. I'm going to integrate you real quick. That was the only thing I can say about it.

Sybil Jordan Hampton, 1962–1966

I went to Earlham after never having gone to the campus. We drove there. My father had a convention in Cincinnati, and so then we came over after that. It was so cool. One of the things about Earlham—I will never forget arriving at Earlham. We drive up and they have this system, and all the cars line up. Someone came to open the door for my mother, and as I stepped out, the person said, "Welcome, Sybil Jordan." We're kind of going, "Oh," but they have what they call the Wolf Book. What people did is that they went through the book very quickly to see who was coming. My parents were very impressed that someone—without us introducing ourselves—came up and introduced themselves. That was cool. They unpacked the car. I didn't come with much; my trunks were mailed. Then my parents were sent on their way. They didn't have any parents' orientation or whatever.[6] My brother, my mother, and my father gave me big hugs and they drove right off, and that was it. Oh, Richmond was like being Up South,[7] honey, because when we were driving there, we saw a big billboard of the Ku Klux Klan about Martin Luther King because the Klan was having a resurgence in Southern Indiana. I really was very focused on the campus. I loved the campus. I thought it was so—it seemed to be something I could negotiate. It was very lovely. I stayed in Earlham Hall, which was really very lovely. I was surrounded immediately by people who were talking to me.[8] I felt so much as if I had made the right decision and that I was going to be okay here. Then I discovered that you couldn't go to the movie theater unless you sat upstairs, and the place that everybody went to drink beer—I didn't drink beer—but this place, Connie's, you had to go to the back door. Then, *Richmond*—the newspaper—didn't capitalize "United Nations," and they always referred to Earlham as a "pinko commie college," and that there were these—Richmond was this—jumping-off places for these people coming up from Kentucky. There would be these raids where these guys would try and attack Earlham students in the town. I realized that I had moved Up South and that I needed to keep in mind what I knew about living in Little Rock to be able to negotiate between the Earlham campus and Richmond, Indiana. There was really not much reason for me to leave the campus to do anything, remember? I was one of those people who I didn't feel constrained by being on a small campus. I felt protected, frankly. When we had freshman tests, it was really very funny because I was identified as a student whose writing skills were not strong, and so I was assigned for one year to a faculty tutor. It never phased me. This woman was like such a mothering person, almost dithering. She was wonderful, and she just gave me great feedback. I've always loved to write, and I didn't feel that I had been identified as being less. It was a wonderful testimony to my parents who always told me that correction was just something to make you stronger. It's not a statement about your lack of worth. I know there were two of us women, and there was only one other woman on campus, so during my freshman year, there were three Black women on campus.[9] There must have been 30 Black guys because they played basketball and football and they ran track and played soccer, so there were a lot more guys because they were in athletic programs.[10] We knew each other and we talked to each other, but we were not sitting together. First of all, they have served meals. That was wonderful. They had served meals and you were assigned to your table for your served meal. My job to my shock and horror was to work in the food service. I called my parents and I thought [*gasps*] I'm one of the few Black students out of only three Black girls and I'm going to be serving meals? My parents said, "You know what? It's good to learn to be a waitress because you may be able to earn some money in a really good restaurant sometime. You need to pull yourself together and understand that yes, indeed, this is a little awkward, but guess what, you'll get to know everybody and everybody will get to know you." They were right!

Ohio Wesleyan University

Denise Baisden, 1954–1959

I got accepted to both Western Reserve[11] and Ohio Wesleyan, but I got a scholarship to Ohio Wesleyan. That kind of sealed the deal because I didn't have to try to beg my father to help with it.[12] It was all paid for. If a Black person in the South applied to a school outside the South, you could get money. They would provide scholarships, and so I got one of those grants to go to college outside the South.[13] Then I had a grant from Ohio Wesleyan. That's how I happened to end up there, sight unseen. I didn't know anybody there; had never seen the campus except in pictures. My parents drove me up, and I think two of my aunts drove up, too. I had some uncles and aunts, who came down from Cleveland and we had like a mini-reunion there at the time that I started college there. I wasn't too happy the first year. It was just very, very different, and we had to take some kind of exams—placement exams—when we got there. I did not do well on those exams. The person who interviewed me about that was quite concerned as to whether or not I could make it with my test scores. She just didn't see how I could manage it. There was such a difference in the quality of the education for Blacks and Whites in Atlanta that even though I had high grades, my grades probably would not have been as high if I had been competing with the White students there. We didn't have the books that they had. Our background, we were just not as well prepared. The good thing was that I studied hard and I made it, and I did well.

Allegheny College

John Herbert Niles, 1955–1959

What did I find about Allegheny that was so compelling?[14] Well, first of all, it was the landscape of the campus. If you have an idyllic impression of what college life should be like, what a campus should be like—if you think about the ivy cover, federalist-type buildings. There was just lots of grass, very quiet, in a small town. I felt that this would be a place where I wouldn't have any distractions. We had a schedule. We sat in on classes. They gave us the typical tour of the buildings: this is the chemistry building, this is the history building, this and that. What was very interesting to me was that they had a dance that night. I stayed in the dorm with—I've forgotten who it was—shared a room with someone who was already a student. Everyone was getting ready to go to this dance. I had been hanging around with these folks all day, so this was the second day. Suddenly, when the time comes for the dance, they all disappeared. Nobody said, "Come on, Herb, let's go to the dance." They were gone. So I walked into the dance all by myself and just walked around and it was just very eerie that the folks that I had been socializing with before sort of went off on their own. No one came and said, "Herb, how you doing?" It was very different. Then I ran into a Black student and her date. We talked for a long time. Then I went on back to the room, because there was nothing for me to do there. So I recognized the—I would call it maybe—social ostracism, to a degree, that I was going to experience but, frankly, that didn't matter. I wanted to be a doctor. It mattered that this school purported itself to be one of the leading liberal arts schools for getting people into medical school. That's all I needed to know. I think part of disappointment is expectation. If you don't expect anything, you're not disappointed. If you're expecting someone to glad-hand you and pat you on the back and it doesn't happen, then you're upset. If you don't expect that, then you're not upset because you didn't expect it in the first place.

DePauw University

Willis "Bing" Davis, 1955–1959

I was sent off by my church. I remember my church on that last Sunday saying, "We have one of our members who's going to get a chance to go to college, so this collection is for him." It was the church on the street that I grew up on and across the street from the community center where I learned to draw, and paint, and play sports, and across the street from the playground where I played football, and basketball, and all that. My mother and my sister—my older sister, who was a beautician in town—and her boyfriend drove me over. [*Chuckles*] That was strange too. I didn't know about the time change.[15] I got there and was late for my first job. Part of my job was waiting tables in the dorm where I stayed, and my boss was a Black student on the campus. So I had to report an hour late to this guy, and first thing he says, "You're late. This is the last time you can be late on my crew." [*Laughs*] Yeah, my parents drove me over. They were excited, and the church sent me off with a bang. I will never forget that, because when things were tough that first quarter before I could make the adjustment, I was going to drop out. I said, "But I can't go home, because my church, my neighborhood, all of them expected me to do something. Maybe I can join the Army from here." [*Chuckles*] After work, that was on Monday, I met the person who would be one of the most important people for my academic and social survival. My other job besides waiting tables for my meals was assisting a custodian in the gym where I'd be playing ball. They took me over to meet him, and I had a job that averaged over a couple days a week and just helped him. That's where I got my spending money for the incidentals, and washing clothes, and things of that nature.

Oscar Brookins, 1961–1965

Visit? The visit I did was on the bus when I got there to enroll in school. That was the visit. In those days, you went and you took advantage of the opportunity. The idea of going and scouting around? No no. It wasn't done. Very limited by anyone, White or Black, in those days. Now, what had happened after high school, there was—probably through the National Scholarship Service Fund[16]—a notion that one should be prepped going to a White school, other than as you said, just landing there. There was a school located in Monteagle, Tennessee. Have you ever heard of it? Highlander Folk School.[17] You ever heard of it? Highlander

Folk School was running a summer program in—I guess we could call it—the humanities. Music, theater, writing. I was invited to apply and I got accepted. The only summer program that I ever went to was there in Tennessee. Now, there were White counselors and there were White students. It was a laboratory for getting high school-aged Blacks and Whites to interact socially. Then, of course, it was an academic program. It was essentially an academic program.

Wabash College

Robert Wedgeworth, 1955–1959

I had a high school classmate who went to DePauw, and so we traveled to college together.[18] Crawfordsville was the most rural place I had ever been in my life, but in Indiana, if you are a basketball player, it's like you're on a different planet. When I walked downtown in Crawfordsville the first week I was on campus, I walked into this little convenience store that they called the Bank Cigar Store. One of the guys said, "Are you Bob Wedgeworth?" I said, "Yes." They already knew all about me because I was a basketball player. That set up a conflict for me because shortly after I got to Crawfordsville, I got to know a man who worked as the cook in the Beta house, one of our fraternities. Mark and his wife invited me over and befriended me when I first got there and briefed me on the lay of the land for African Americans in Crawfordsville. I was aware that African Americans could buy wine and liquor from the bars, but they were not allowed in the bars. They really weren't welcome in a lot of the downtown stores. They lived kind of a fringe existence there, although a number of them were employed by—the largest employer—Donnelly's printing plant. A number of them were employed there, but there wasn't much going on. I made a decision very early when I was there that I would not set myself apart from the people in the Black community. I pretty much confined myself to the campus, and I didn't try to break any barriers in Crawfordsville or anything like that. I know I would've been able to as a star athlete. Yeah. I would go downtown and have coffee with my college mates. I would go to the Dairy Queen or what was equivalent—Velvet Freeze, I think it was—to have ice cream and sit at the counter and do that. I would go to the local movie theater. Since I was a Roman Catholic, I would go to mass at St. Bernard's, but other than that, I really didn't have regular contact with the town of Crawfordsville.

Oberlin College

Adine Ray Usher, 1957–1961

I came in feeling very comfortable. I realized that Whites had a ways to go, and Oberlin was really trying and I gave them an A for effort. The year before, my Oberlin friend who, not encouraged, but, well, facilitated my interest in the college—she said that while she was at Oberlin from about '53 to '57, or '52 to '56, whatever, that Oberlin was trying to get interracial rooming. They had sent a letter to some of the White students saying, "Do you mind having a Black roommate?" When the Black students found out about it, they went to the president and said, "We need to get a letter saying, 'Do you mind having a White one?'" Oberlin said, "Woops, sorry." By the time I got there, everyone got the same letter saying, "Are you interested in an intercultural or international experience in roommates?" Everybody got the same page.

Kirston Brick, 1964–1968

At that time, Oberlin had just received a huge grant from the Rockefeller Foundation for African American students.[19] It was in the paper. The purpose was to recruit more minority students, but it was after April when they've already made their decisions. Anyway, I called them and I said, "You have enough money to give me more because of how much Rockefeller gave you." [*Laughter*] I just called the admissions office and told them that I was interested, but I needed more money because my mother had just died. Anyway, they said, "We don't have any more rooms, since you didn't accept." I said, "You must have some kind of room." They called back and they said, "We found some space, but I don't know if it's going to be enough for you." I said, "We'll work it out." Because I needed to be near home. That was the main thing. I ended up going to Oberlin on the bus by myself. Everybody else's parents were taking them in and whatever. It was a very lonely situation. My father didn't take me or anything. Oberlin really was my happenstance based on all of these experiences with my mother dying, knowing I couldn't afford—I really was planning to go to be with my best friend,[20] but I thought, oh no, I can't afford that. After I'd had that really awful experience in Columbus,[21] I thought I don't want to be there. Then when I saw that Rockefeller had given Oberlin money—I mean I really just negotiated my way in—I'm actually a very good negotiator. I just negotiated my way in. I ended up being in a storage closet.

Kalamazoo College

Tanya Summers, 1963–1967

I think my mother took me. Maybe we went on a train. We didn't have a car. We were from New York. Nobody had a car. Maybe we took a train or rented a car. I just don't remember, but somehow or other I ended up in Kalamazoo. Well, I was a New York snob, of course. It was like, "Oh God, this place"—I mean the campus is beautiful. You can't knock that. The facilities are very nice and fortunately we had good food. As colleges go, Kalamazoo was pretty good. I think they introduce you to your roommate. You exchange information with your roommate. I have a vague recollection that we met. We went to Evanston, Illinois. We had some family members in Evanston and my roommate was from there. Anyway, I think I vaguely remember, and maybe my mother was with me because it seems like we may have gone to Evanston to visit these family members, and we met my roommate, and we met her parents. Somewhere along the line we all met. They were White. She was very, very nice, and very nice family, so we had a great relationship. My first year I lived on the first floor of Trowbridge Hall. It was a very short corridor and then there was another kind of lobby on the other side. I don't know how we got the name "Poverty Row." For the girls on that floor, they were kind of—somehow we got the name Poverty Row and had this little identity.[22] I thought we had good relationships.

***

(Dis)Comfort in a Different World

For many of the participants, they arrived to their college sight unseen. There were a few with the economic means to visit, or who had connections and activities that brought them to the campus. Whether during a visit in their senior year or when they came for the beginning of classes in the fall, the common response upon seeing their campus for the first time was to emphasize the beauty of the campus and its idyllic nature. Their college looked like what they had pictured a college should look like. As John Niles, who went by his middle name "Herb" as a young man, noted, the architecture of the buildings and the ivy growing up the walls communicated a reposed, studious environment. The participants' first impressions of the physical campus of their institution were uniformly positive. Yet, the physical campus is only one feature of a campus environment. The human aggregate, organized environment, and constructed environment of norms and values are also important campus environment features (Strange & Banning, 2015). Although the physical environment sent uniformly positive signals, the other features sent somewhat mixed messages to these participants to inform their first impressions of their new schools.

Human Aggregate

The human aggregate of a college consists of the people who are members of the campus community, including faculty, staff, and students (Strange & Banning, 2015). Strange and Banning explain that the aggregate can be described in terms of its demographic characteristics or according to typology (e.g., personality, vocational interests, or involvement). As noted in Table 1.1, Black students did not constitute more than 1% of the total campus student population at any of these colleges, and only Oberlin and Ohio Wesleyan would have at least one Black faculty member during the time period of this study. Black staff did work as custodians, housekeepers, and in dining services across the colleges, though still not in large numbers.

As a result, these participants, many of whom came from segregated neighborhoods and schools, were brought into close contact with White people for the first time in their lives. Others were quite comfortable with the whiteness of their campuses because they grew up in or attended integrated neighborhoods and schools. In their experiences, *integrated* always meant that they were in the significant numerical minority of an otherwise heavily predominantly White environment. Therefore, college presented a familiar experience. As Adine said above, "I came in feeling very comfortable." Others would take note of how many other Black students were or were not with them on campus. As noted by Janet and Sybil in their first semesters at Earlham, Black women on campus were very few in number. When Jeane Bounds Williams entered Allegheny in 1951, she remembered that she "was the only African American girl" in the entire college. In fact, she was the first Black woman to matriculate at Allegheny. This was rarely noted by Black men, mostly because they were not typically ever the only Black student on campus. There are just 3 exceptions to this among the 68 participants in this study: Clyde Francis, who began at Allegheny the year before Jeane; Karl Johnson, who was the only Black student at Wabash during his two years there from 1952 to 1954; and Robert Wedgeworth, who was the only Black student on campus in his first year at Wabash, 1955–1956.

Beyond the numerical representation, the human aggregate also communicates whether a new member will find others with whom they can associate and from whom they can find support. For some of these participants, their first days and weeks on campus quickly introduced them to those who would become "their people" so to speak. For Bing Davis, who had very positive interactions and mentoring with DePauw alumni before coming to campus, a Black custodian who was one of his bosses would become an instrumental support person. Janet Williams threw herself into making connections with her White peers, not giving racial prejudice a chance to possibly derail her ability to make others "forget what color [she] was" and get to know her. Sybil was relieved to find, after three years of being deliberately ignored by her White classmates in high school, that her peers at Earlham were exuberantly friendly with her from the minute her family drove onto campus to drop her off. These positive interactions helped set a positive tone going into the academic year and, as Sybil noted, provided reassurance that they had made the "right decision." A few others though received a colder reception that lowered their expectations for how they would be treated, at least by fellow students. During John's prospective student visit to Allegheny, finding himself suddenly abandoned and ignored when it came time for the dance that weekend alerted him to the "social isolation" that was likely to be the norm when he arrived to begin classes in the fall.

Organized Environment

The third feature of the environment discussed by Strange and Banning (2015) is the organized environment. This aspect of the environment includes the institution's policies and practices, the extent of hierarchy and formality, and the relative ease with which institutional change can or cannot be made (Strange & Banning). The narratives here reflect two ways in which this group of participants encountered and formed first impressions of the organized environments of their institutions.

Decision-making in the flat organizational structure and collegial character common to small, liberal arts colleges (Birnbaum, 1988; Hirt, 2006; Strange & Banning, 2015) is typically handled through personal networks and relationships instead of complex bureaucratic systems (Birnbaum,

1988; Hirt, 2006). This was reflected in Bing's account in Chap. 4 of how he gained admission to DePauw. The friendship between his high school coach, a DePauw alumnus, and the admissions director gained Bing admission as well as financial aid, including the two work-study jobs that Bing's narrative in this chapter recounts. Kirston's memory of how she "negotiated [her] way in" to Oberlin demonstrates the same flat organizational structure at work. Kirston called the admissions office, despite not accepting Oberlin's offer of admission, and requested to be admitted and receive increased scholarship aid, and found campus housing. Although Kirston's first-person perspective does not give insight into the institutional processes that were set in motion by her call, the fact that she received admission, more scholarship aid, and housing (albeit in a "storage closet") within several days—not several weeks or months—reflects the simpler decision-making common to small, liberal arts colleges, particularly in the 1950s and 1960s when administrative staffs at these colleges were lean.

Strange and Banning (2015) identified *formality* as one indicator of the nature of an institution's organized environment. In their usage, formality referred to the breadth and specificity of rules and procedures; highly formal environments have specific rules and policies governing how things are done, while less formal environments operate by unwritten codes and rules (Strange & Banning). How roommates were assigned at Earlham, Oberlin, and Kalamazoo indicated three different levels of formality regarding this procedure.

Janet noted that she did not have a roommate because there was no one for her to room with, and that there were only three Black women who matriculated to Earlham that year. Janet had not requested a single room, but was given one regardless and at no extra charge. A pattern of rooming Black women only with other Black women must have been apparent to Janet, thus informing her impression that the reason she did not have a roommate was because there were an odd number of Black women beginning at Earlham that year. The fact that Janet took this as an unrequested favor instead of being indicative of institutional racism does not contradict the apparent unwritten code that governed roommate assignments at Earlham at that time.

Meanwhile, at Oberlin, Adine's narrative recalls how the roommate assignment policy had changed from her friend's tenure as a student, about 1952–1956, by the time Adine began in 1957. There had been a formal policy at one time that banned rooming segregation.[23] Student activism led to its end, but in its place apparently was a procedure by which only White students were queried as to whether they would accept a Black roommate. Again student activism intervened. Adine's friend shared with her that students went to college officials and requested that incoming Black students also be asked if they were willing to have White roommates. By the time Adine was preparing to enter Oberlin, the policy had changed to send all incoming students a letter asking about their interest "in an intercultural or international experience in roommates." Not only had there been a formal policy in place, but there were specific procedures guiding its implementation at each iteration of the policy.

The third example from Kalamazoo College also illustrates formality regarding roommate assignments. At Kalamazoo, roommates were assigned without regard to race. The procedures that accompanied the assignment of roommates included instructions and encouragement for new students to reach out to their roommates and begin the process of getting to know each other. Taking care to add this element to their roommate assignment procedures led to Tanya and her family being able to not only meet her first-year roommate and her family, but also to begin forming a friendship with her before classes began in the fall.

Constructed Climate

The final environmental feature discussed by Strange and Banning (2015) is the constructed environment or climate. This aspect of the environment is communicated through language, norms, values, and tacit assumptions (Strange & Banning). It is often the most difficult feature of the environment to identify, but its effects pervade the campus. During this era, the GLCA colleges espoused values for fostering interracial engagement and support for integration. The intentional recruitment of Black students through alumni networks and their partnerships with the NSSFNS reflected those values in action. Although not sponsored by DePauw, Oscar Brookins' participation in the Highlander Folk School's summer program is also indicative of the desire to see colleges' integrationist efforts succeed. Yet its existence reflects a tacit assumption that the pervasive social segregation of Southern life would leave both Black and White youth unprepared for positive, effective interracial engagement. For Oscar, it was a meaningful experience that informed his impressions for what interactions with White students at DePauw would be like.

On the other hand, the insider conversations that Robert had with a local Black family in Crawfordsville educated him about the racial segregation in public accommodations that was openly practiced just off Wabash's campus. Sybil also would learn through the billboard sponsored by the Ku Klux Klan seen on the drive from Little Rock to Richmond and through conversations with older students that Richmond was "up South," a mirror reflection of the Jim Crow segregation she had already learned how to navigate as a child. Both Robert and Sylvia learned the norms for being Black in their college towns and mostly restricted their activities to the confines of the campus, choosing not to "break any barriers," as Robert shared. Other students also encountered these norms and these will be discussed in greater detail in the next chapter.

The meaning and approach to certain common procedures also communicated insights about the campus climate and attitudes about certain faculty and staff. For the most part, these students' initial, early encounters with faculty and staff were positive and encouraging. These examples pervade the college choice narratives in Chap. 4, as well as the stories about arriving on campus featured here. Placement tests were a ubiquitous feature of their early college experiences, either before classes started in the fall, or upon arriving for orientation. For Sybil, the placement tests indicated that she needed further support to develop her writing and so she was assigned a writing tutor for her first year. Sybil was encouraged by her parents to not see this as a slight, but rather as an opportunity for continued improvement. Moreover, there was nothing about how the tests were handled by the staff who administered them or the attitude of her writing tutor that would dispute that. At Earlham, placement tests were used to ensure that students who needed academic support were connected with resources and people who could help them achieve.

Denise Baisden's experience at Ohio Wesleyan was different. The proctor of the exam openly questioned whether Denise could be successful at Ohio Wesleyan given her low scores. This triggered anxiety in Denise and doubt that her high grades in Atlanta's segregated schools were the best reflection of her academic talents. She concluded, "My grades probably would not have been as high if I had been competing with the White students there." This could have had a potentially devastating effect on Denise's persistence at Ohio Wesleyan. Fortunately, her anxiety that she would not succeed caused her to focus more on her studies and be successful despite this faculty member's doubts. This faculty member tacitly assumed that a student's low scores on placement exams were a sign that the student did not belong at Ohio Wesleyan. Tacit assumptions communicated through the words and actions of an institutional representative shape a student's perception of the institution as a whole for good or ill (Strange & Banning, 2015).

The four features of the campus environments of these institutions encouraged either the participants' comfort or discomfort in their new environments. It is important to note the inconsistency of the messages sent by these different features of the campus environment. There were apparent contradictions and conflicts. How these messages affected the students and their impressions of their colleges on the whole depended on their personal characteristics and resilience. For the most part, these participants demonstrated a high degree of resilience, positive regard, and—in Adine's words later in her interview—understanding for the "effort" being made by these colleges to embrace integration on campus.

These early impressions would be confirmed, expanded, or contradicted as the participants moved through their college careers. Chapter 6 now explores the narratives of their academic and social engagement as college students.

Notes

1. The War Department established these Navy College Training Programs to provide a liberal arts education to their recruits and refresh the supply of commissioned officers during the war; the program ran at 131 colleges from 1943 to 1946 (Herge, 1996). Review of the GLCA yearbooks found notations of either Naval College Training (V-12) or Naval Aviation Cadets (V-5) units, at five of the six Ohio colleges (Kenyon, Ohio Wesleyan, Wooster, Oberlin, and Denison), as well as at DePauw (both V-12 and V-5 units) and Wabash in Indiana. These units had typically left all of these campuses by 1946. The 1946 edition of *The Wabash* noted that their V-12 unit numbered 677 men, who left campus in November 1945 and had kept the 7 fraternities on campus alive. According to the 1947 edition of Kenyon's yearbook, *The Reveille*, civilian enrollment on campus went down to just 50 men during World War II. One thousand Kenyon men had served in the war; 41 were killed in action. It is likely that the V-12 unit helped the men's colleges to remain open during the war years. Since Kenyon's

V-12 unit had already left campus, the college must have maintained the barracks for use as new student housing.

2. It seems that this was not a prospective student campus visit, but rather a type of new student orientation program.
3. Beauford and Janet Williams met at Earlham and later married. They did their interview with me together.
4. In the 1952 edition of Earlham's yearbook, *The Sargasso*, I identified nine Black students who started at Earlham in the fall of 1951, including Janet and Beauford. Other than Janet, there were only two other Black women, who would graduate in 1955. In that yearbook, only one is specifically noted as being from Jamaica, but they were both members of the Foreign Students Club. As Janet noted, she was the only other Black woman to begin at Earlham in 1951.
5. In fact, in the 1952 *Sargasso*, Janet is pictured with her elbow in the lap of another student, a White man, who has his arm around her shoulder at the Frosh Talent Show.
6. As in any kind of parent orientation session or activities.
7. A colloquialism used to describe the pervasive Jim Crow character of some parts of the North.
8. Readers will recall from Sybil's narrative in Chap. 4 that she endured three years at her high school, Central High in Little Rock, AR, with none of the White students speaking to her.
9. The 1963 *Sargasso* does not entirely confirm Sybil's memory. There were three other Black women on campus other than Sybil and the other woman who began with her (Elizabeth). Two of them were "Day Dodgers," meaning they were from Richmond and commuted to campus; one graduated in 1963, the other in 1964. It is unlikely that Sybil would have had much opportunity to see either of them. The third was a sophomore from Dayton, Ohio, during the 1962–1963 academic year and therefore living on campus. This is likely the other woman that Sybil is remembering. In terms of just the Black women living on campus, Sybil's memory is correct.
10. My count of Black students on campus for the 1962–1963 year numbered 22 Black men. Sybil's offhand estimate was not that far off.
11. Western Reserve College was founded in 1826 in Hudson, Ohio and would later form a federation with Case School of Applied Science in 1967 and become Case Western Reserve University (Case Western Reserve University, 2014).

12. Denise's father had only agreed to pay for a college in Atlanta, so she was left to find funding completely on her own to go out of state.
13. This is likely a reference to the NSSFNS.
14. John is recalling an overnight campus visit to Allegheny that he participated in during his senior year of high school.
15. In 1918, the Standard Time Act placed the state of Indiana in the Central Time Zone. This was not changed until 1961 when the Interstate Commerce Commission divided the state between the Eastern and Central time zones (Time & Date, 2016).
16. NSSFNS.
17. Highlander Folk School was founded in 1932 in Monteagle, TN, initially to organize those who were unemployed and working on behalf of the Congress of Industrial Organizations (Highlander Center, 2012). In the 1950s and 1960s, its anti-segregation stance brought it into the Civil Rights Movement and Citizenship Schools were begun (Highlander Center, 2012). These schools were an adult education program that was later turned over to the Southern Christian Leadership Conference in 1961 (Levine, 2004). The Citizenship Schools offered basic literacy and political education classes and helped to increase Black participation in civic life, including voting (Levine, 2004). It is unlikely that Oscar's summer program at Highlander Folk School was in one of these Citizenship Schools, but I could not find any information about Highlander running a college bridge program of the nature that Oscar is describing here.
18. Robert is referring to Melba Zachery, who was the first Black woman to attend DePauw.
19. According to Baumann's (2010) documentary history of Black education at Oberlin, the college participated in a coalition with other liberal arts colleges (Antioch was the only other GLCA college involved in this effort) to submit a proposal to the Rockefeller Foundation for "an inter-college effort to achieve improvements in education and educational opportunity for American Negro students" (Document 20). The foundation authorized the grants and funded the six institutions individually; Oberlin received two grant awards in 1964 and 1967 of $275,000 each, of which Oberlin directed $240,000 to support scholarships in 1964 (Baumann, 2010). The Rockefeller Foundation expected the colleges to give special emphasis in their initiatives to the "discovery of talented

Negro and other minority group students" and to "further focus on the education of Black males" to rectify the lower proportion of Black men who were seeking college education (Baumann, 2010, Document 20).

20. Kirston had also been admitted to Sarah Lawrence and this was her preferred choice, but they did not offer enough financial aid. Kirston remarked that it was "the most expensive school in the country."
21. During a visit to Ohio State University in Columbus, Kirston and her friend were heckled and called "niggers" by a group of young White men passing by in a car.
22. Tanya's family was lower-middle class.
23. In the 1950 *Hi-O-Hi*, Oberlin's yearbook, there is a picture of the Oberlin Interracial Committee with the caption that the group's focus was on "altering admissions policies and ending freshman [*sic*] rooming segregation."

References

Baumann, R. M. (2010). *Constructing Black education at Oberlin College: A documentary history*. Athens: Ohio University Press.

Birnbaum, R. (1988). *How colleges work: The cybernetics of academic organization and leadership*. San Francisco, CA: Jossey-Bass.

Case Western Reserve University. (2014). *Our history*. Retrieved from http://case.edu/about/history.html

Herge, H. C. (1996). *Navy V-12* (Vol. 12). Paducah, KY: Turner Publishing Co.

Highlander Center. (2012). *Timeline*. Highlander Research and Education Center. Retrieved from http://highlandercenter.org/media/timeline/

Hirt, J. B. (2006). *Where you work matters: Student affairs administration at different types of institutions*. Washington, DC: University Press of America.

Levine, D. P. (2004). The birth of the Citizenship Schools: Entwining the struggles for literacy and freedom. *History of Education Quarterly, 44*(3), 388–414.

Strange, C. C., & Banning, J. H. (2015). *Designing for learning: Creating campus environments for student success* (2nded ed.). San Francisco, CA: Jossey-Bass.

Time and Date. (2016). *Indiana's time zones and Daylight Savings Time*. Retrieved from http://www.timeanddate.com/time/us/indiana-time.html

CHAPTER 6

College Life

Women's Voices

Laura Simms Wiltz

Oberlin College, 1953–1957

I do remember being very active on the yearbook committee my senior year. I worked real hard on that with a group of kids. Let me tell you this. I got a letter, I think around 1999 or 2000, from the editor of the yearbook that I worked with back in 1957, '56–'57, really lamenting his insensitivity to me during that period. It was a really lovely letter. He just did not realize how I must have felt when I could not go to Cincinnati with them to review, to do the final edit, because there was no place for me to stay. He said he just didn't know what that really meant. He just felt so bad. He offered to take me to lunch whenever I was in DC. I never answered that letter because I really never knew what to say. I just never knew what to say about that. The fact that I couldn't go, I guess, for me was just a foregone conclusion that was to be expected.

The six narratives in this chapter reflect the typical academic, extracurricular, and social lives of the participants and the issues which they confronted and are shared at greater length because of the number and depth of issues covered and the participants' own insights into their experiences.

© The Author(s) 2017

D.-L. Stewart, *Black Collegians' Experiences in US Northern Private Colleges*, DOI 10.1057/978-1-137-59077-0_6

Jeannette Phillips

Ohio Wesleyan University, 1958–1962

I met Rose[1] the second or third day I was there. They had some kind of reception or something during orientation. I came in and across the room I saw one spot of color. [*Chuckles*] I think, from her perspective, it was similar. We found our way to each other sooner or later. We hit it off immediately, we really did. Both Rose and I had looked around, and we had found a woman on the other side of the tracks who did hair.[2] I guess that's an issue also. She happened to be a very nice woman who introduced us to some folks and so forth. Not of a dating kind of nature, but just socialization. We visited her church a few times.

Some of the classes I felt the reception was better than others. It depended upon what the class was. One of the classes where I felt most ill at ease—my freshman year I'm talking about now—was philosophy. I think that had to do with the professor. He seemed to work very hard at ignoring me. I don't think I was paranoid. [*Chuckles*] Because of that, I never got a sense of getting to know anybody else in the class very well. I think that atmosphere just wasn't conducive to it. Plus, it was the first class after lunch. [*Chuckles*] That can be difficult anyway. People are sleeping. There are all kinds of things. He did not make his subject matter interesting. All of those factors came into play. There were other classes, though. I had a history class where the professor was fantastic. Everybody in there was involved in part of the discussion and so forth. As a consequence, I got a sense of getting to know some of the students in there, because they were contributing to conversation and it was back and forth. My most positive memory, hmm. Academically, it would revolve around two or three professors whom I think affected what I became. One was the only Black professor on campus at that time. He was fantastic. That was my department, because I was a sociology major. I didn't get to have him for any classes my freshman year, but my sophomore year, I finally got to take a course with him that I wanted in my major. He was demanding, took no less than your best, and opened my eyes to how you really observe. I always thought I was pretty attentive and knew how to look at things. The very first test we had—he announced we were going to have a test and so forth and so on. We came in, and we had this pop quiz. We had all studied diligently. I felt I was all up on the social theories and so forth that were in that chapter. The very first question on the test was, "What is the full name of your textbook?" [*Chuckles*] The second was, "Name the authors." Third one was, "What is the copyright date?" I can't remember what some of the others were, because by that time, I was in shock, because I did all the studying but I didn't pay any attention to that stuff. His point was anything you're doing, you've got to put it in context. If you're reading a textbook that's 20 years old, things may be very different than what it's saying there. Also, the importance of setting the framework. To this day, even when I'm reading a "for fun" novel, I do not begin to read it until I have looked at the copyright date and all the other things that go into setting the framework. I learned so much from that man. The first course I had with him I ended up getting a B and I worked my tail off. When I finally got an A-minus from him [*chuckles*] my junior year, I felt as if I had really arrived.

Yes, I was in extracurriculars. By the way, I got a job too. I was working at the library. I had been active with the Red Cross in high school and they had a Red Cross student group at Ohio Wesleyan. I took part in that. I had also been active in the YWCA, so I also joined that. Community service was very important to me. I found it very satisfying.

Well, there weren't a whole lot of folks that were going to be asking me for dates. [*Chuckles*] That wasn't that important to me, but it would've been nice if there had been some. Well, I went out on a date one night with a White man. He happened to be Jewish. We went to one of the local restaurants for dinner. There were people at two of the tables in there who spent a lot of time looking at us and twittering and that kind of thing. When one of the groups got up to leave, I distinctly heard the N-word as they passed by. That was a definite memory in a negative way. Then another time when Rose and I were walking back to the dorm from class, there was a row of rooming houses that were connected to the fraternities in that area. My friend, as a matter of fact, she was a roommate—she happened to be White. She was rooming with me and Rose, which drove her father crazy because he was from the hills of Kentucky. We're walking down the street, and from the second floor in one of those rooming houses, somebody tossed water out on us. That created quite a furor. I had always considered myself meek and mild, but somewhere along the line, I developed some backbone, because I complained about that one all the way up the line to the point that they required that the guys publicly apologize and also include it in the newspaper. The friend that invited me down before I decided to go to Wesleyan, she was by this time editor of the newspaper. She had been in a sorority, but because of the things she was observing and the fact that I did not have that option—I, along with other friends of hers—she eventually dropped out of her sorority. The guys had to apologize, and it was in the newspaper. Then she wrote an editorial, too, about maturity and how people get treated, and that kind of thing. I don't remember experiencing the sororities and fraternities doing shows in blackface, but I heard about them.[3] It made me angry and frustrated because there wasn't a whole lot I could do about it. Or at least I didn't feel there was. There may have been more that I could do. Also, I had a sense of helplessness, like "When are we going to ever get past this part?"

Something had occurred that took a friend of ours to the admissions office to protest.[4] I don't recall what that issue was, but during the course of it, that's when he was told, "Well, we only let in X number of Blacks. You barely made it." By the way, he's a federal judge now. [*Chuckles*]

Sybil Jordan Hampton

Earlham College, 1962–1966

I got to know lots of people. The two other Black women on campus, we all knew each other, but we were all so different, and it was interesting. I was not dated when I was at Earlham by any of the Black guys. I really never took that as they were discriminating against me. My parents said, "It's a small number of Black students. It's quite possible that there's just not somebody there who's for you. Don't get discombobulated by that. Don't be distracted. Concentrate on your studies. You went there to get a degree." We were all friends. There was no kind of infighting. We were friends. In fact, when the guys' parents would come, they'd take me out to dinner with them. There was one guy who was from town. He would take me over to his aunt's house to study with him. People would ask, "Is he hitting on you?" "No, not at all," I said, "I think I'm his beard.[5] He doesn't want his aunt to really know who he's talking to." I looked presentable enough.

Yeah, I got involved in the choir because I had done that before,[6] and then I got involved with the student newspaper. Then I was working. Studying. The academics were really a challenge for me. When I graduated, I was a C-plus student. It was a challenge. Earlham really attracted a lot of kids who had not only gone to George School in Westtown, but Mount Hermon in Northfield. There were a lot of East Coast, private school kids there.

My life really was on the campus. People who came to the campus—they were Black kids who came from the town, who hung around. There were people who were children of people who worked on the campus, who we go to know. We had a very dynamic interaction with some young people from Richmond. Somebody in the community did my hair, who I was able to find. I knew nothing about doing my own hair.

I had such a wonderful group of friends there. I knew such a rich and diverse group of people. I loved the things that we did. I played Bridge. Just kind of generally hung out but just that quality of being on a campus where you literally could know people from all kinds of different friendship groups. I had a great group of friends that I hung with, but I really moved in and out of all kinds of groups of people. Some people you knew because of class, some people I knew because of being the copyeditor of the newspaper.

I went to Japan actually. I was selected by what was then called the Experiment in International Living. They got my name from the National Scholarship Service. They invited me to go at the end of my freshman year summer to be an experiment to Japan in 1963. After I came back, I studied Japanese because Earlham, of course, is the center of Japanese language and cultural studies, and so I studied Japanese as my language in college. There was a Japanese artist and there was a Japanese teacher. That was really a wonderful, wonderful, wonderful immersion in another culture. I'm sure I was there like eight weeks. It was just a summer. I had no language ability. I lived in Nagano, which everybody knows now because the Winter Games were there. It was once again, there would be all these little ladies hunkering down at the bus stop, pointing. People in that part of Japan—people in Japan had not in 1963 seen Black women. They had seen men. People would want to touch me and they would want to touch my hair. The kids who were with me, because I was the only Black student in the group, they were all kind of freaked out. They said, "Does this make you crazy?" I said, "No, I understand where they're coming from, and I'm here as someone to learn, but they're also to learn about me."

Tanya Summers

Kalamazoo College, 1963–1967

Let's start out with I wasn't all that interested in doing any work. I was definitely not studious. I mean it was okay. I don't remember it being particularly difficult. I don't remember thinking, "Oh my God, this is so hard." I don't have that recollection. I just wasn't that interested in it I think. I could do the work. I was busy socializing, hanging out on the quad. I was a radio DJ. I remember having a lot of fun. The first six weeks you had hazing. You had a little beanie you had to wear as a freshman.[7] Then you had a big sister. I had a really nice big sister. You were assigned a big sister, who would check on you and make sure you were doing your homework. I think we had forced study halls. That's probably why the transition wasn't as difficult. You had to be in your room. No TV, no radio. You were supposed to be studying. There was one woman, who was a straight-A student. I remember saying, "Bertha, now tell me how much do you study? What do you do to get As?" She told me she studied about six hours a day. I wasn't trying to do all that. I pledged one of those societies.[8] I'm describing all these support structures. So it seems like they had a lot of those support structures, like big sisters, the mandatory admission to one of the societies. Because you had to be admitted at that time. If you wanted to be in one of those societies, you had to be admitted to one of them. I guess you had a structure where you could become part of different things whether people liked you or not. The faculty seemed to be friendly and supportive. That was my experience.

I went to Sierra Leone. Oh, it was phenomenal. It was phenomenal. We had the opportunity, which is phenomenal. We had two weeks before we got to Sierra Leone to travel. We went to Europe first and then we went to Sierra Leone. I liked the idea of staying in one place rather than kind of traveling throughout Europe, so some of the students traveled throughout and I chose one week in Paris and one week in London. It was fabulous. It was fantastic. Well, Sierra Leone was really fabulous, because it was the first time I had been in a majority Black environment, majority Black as in not just my neighborhood. I just blended in with the crowd. It altered my worldview in some way. I was never the same after I left there. Having the experience of being in the majority altered my view of life, altered my worldview, altered my view of people, and just my experience of myself. First of all, Sierra Leone is an absolutely gorgeous country. When we got there, we took the ferry across, and it was awesome just seeing the hillsides and the lush green and just the beauty of the country. Then Fourah Bay College is a very nice campus. We were on a hillside and we had a room that overlooked the hill, so you can see out to the sea and you can see the city beneath. It was just like, "Wow. This is so incredible." Yeah, it was great.

Men's Voices

Willis "Bing" Davis

DePauw University, 1955–1959

One of my favorite teachers at DePauw who I always talk about was a custodian, Mr. Simms.[9] People thought he was just a custodian, but he was a really brilliant Black man. Really, people don't know that I would take my schedule to him after I talked with my advisor, because he would tell me, "Oh, don't take that section. You got another section left? Because that teacher is bad. He won't give you any help and support. This one is better." I would do a double check with Mr. Simms, because he knew the people. They didn't know he knew, but see, he'd hear the fraternity guys talking about who was good and who was bad, who could teach—he was smart. He knew that school. He'd been there most of his life. He knew that school, knew the teachers, knew the administrators, and ran a good ship. Made sure I didn't work too hard, made sure I had things that I needed. That I studied a little bit more. As a matter of fact, most schools don't serve evening meals on Sunday, so the three of us there got our meals from members of the Black community on Sunday. I remember in the snow, first time I found out about it, I looked out the door and I see these footprints leading through the campus and going toward the Black community, so I just followed those footsteps, and we'd end up just at dinner time at somebody's house. [*Laughs*] Mr. Simms and several other families sort of nurtured us. Yeah, I had two or three families who I could go to. Sometimes they had children of my age or just a bit younger, or either I met them another way. There were three or four families that I knew I could go to for a meal anytime I needed. If I just needed to get away and just relax. My mama, she said, "Now, I want you to find yourself a church there. I want you to find yourself a community." That was a saving grace. Matter of fact, to this day, to this very day—and the last few years—I've been very conscious to make sure it's continued, I never go to Greencastle without stopping at a couple houses before I get to the campus. We used to sit at the feet of the other alumni who would come back and talk with us how they survived. Yeah, it was vital. When we used to sit and listen to them, that was how most of the Blacks survived.

Yeah, there was only one Black woman on campus. I remember seeing her across campus that first day I arrived. I said, "Oh, I see that spot!" and

I walk over there to speak. "Hi! How are you? I'm Bing Davis. I'm a new student." I'm talking very excitedly. She said, "Don't you think because I'm the only one you're going to date me." Yeah, it was very, very small, and very few in the community of our age. Many of them would leave as soon as they could graduate and get a job.

Then the closest city was Indianapolis, 42 miles away, so some of your social life had to be there. Barbershop, shopping for clothes that you like. [*Chuckles*] Yeah, if you wanted a real haircut you went out to Indianapolis. Otherwise, you'd do it yourself, or you'd do each other's hair on the campus. As a matter of fact, the year before I came, another Black student told us about marching on the barbershop because they wouldn't cut Black hair, and it was a Black barber. But yeah, those kind of things we knew—I knew going in. Because when I checked, the Black community would take me around and show me all the places where I could and could not go. I would ask them, "What do I do for this?" They'll say, "You'll have to go there." "What do I do for this?" "You'll have to go there." You learned it.

Oh, my academic transition was rough. Not having had college on my mind, and not having taken any college prep classes, not taken any entrance exams, I was going in cold. I went there because of the support and nurturing from my coach, and his family, and other family members in trying to get me to do something positive. I knew I wasn't academically prepared—I was aware of that old system, particularly for Black males, of putting you in the general track, so you don't take any college prep classes. Just assumed you're getting ready for a job. Going to a place like DePauw, and I think my personality in being able to get along with most people helped, because I knew I needed, and I appreciated those tutorial courses: the speed reading, how to study, and how to take notes. I had to do it on the fly. I knew I had to—"Hey, I am not going back home. I've got to learn this." I knew I had to do some of those extra things to make up for what I had not been prepared for.

My first roommate, who was a saving grace, was one of the Black athletes who was a junior that I just admired, right to this day. Lenny[10] took some rough edges off me. That first boss I had did too. They told me, "You're uncouth, man. You're street. You're street all the way." Lenny had a wonderful air about him. Very classic guy. Very smart too, because he'd remind me, "Man, you aren't studying, man." He'd be studying, I'd come in, and he'd look over his glasses and I knew to get quiet, he's studying. You better pretend you're studying, or you go back out. He took some rough edges off of me, in a nice way. He was a star athlete. Actually, almost Olympic material. I still count him as one of the most important people for me surviving there. Just observing him as a peer, as an upperclassman, even letting a freshman room with him. He took me in and he would talk with me, work with me, point me out. Academically, it was tough, particularly at the beginning until I got the hang of it and realized I had to put in some time, because I didn't do much studying in high school. Yeah, I made all A's and B's, but I wasn't taking challenging courses.

Oh, there were some faculty that made life difficult but there were a lot of good positive faculty, even outside the arts. In the arts in particular, I had the good fortune of having an advisor, who was a ceramics and art educator, and he was not only a mentor but he also was my academic advisor. He really was very very very very positive. Matter of fact, he was from Indianapolis, a good craftsman, and a down-to-earth Hoosier. I mean, he was just one of those old, slow-talking, easygoing kind of persons that took a liking to me. Matter of fact, I had a lot of meals in his home, out in the country. As my academic advisor, I was with him, and he nurtured me and encouraged me quite a bit, to the point where we became good friends, matter of fact. I had that kind of a nurturing environment that allowed me to survive there. That would have been a lot rougher without that.

Yeah, the social life was very rough because there was such a small enclave of Blacks, and the fact that most of them that would've been our age, as quickly as they could get a job in Indianapolis or someplace else, they would leave and only come back to visit. The social life in the area—I remember one large event I went to socially, like a big dance—I had to call back to Dayton and encourage the young lady I graduated from high school with to come over and attend an event that I wanted to go to, because I really hadn't even developed a lot of relationships in Indianapolis, which is 40 miles away. Having a social life required that extra effort, if you needed it—if you wanted it.

Oh, not at all, there was no dating among the White community. You would go across to get a Coke at the student union, but it was really still frowned upon. There's a couple people I'm still in touch with now that probably had it been different, it may have been a different situation. Sometime you'd be in an environment, and you could almost see who's with who, even though they may not be saying it. You could get a sense of it if they're leaving together, they're leaving five minutes apart. You know? [*Laughs*] Yes, I remember there were several people in my arts circle that I'm sure, had it been a different situation, we would've dated.

Robert Wedgeworth

Wabash College, 1955–1959

I was fully engaged on campus. I was the only African American student in the whole college my freshman year. I was so actively engaged in the college academically and athletically, I didn't really have time to think about what was going to affect that. I had no dates. Every now and then somebody was going to DePauw and would give me a ride, and I'd drop my friend who was there a note and say, "I'm coming down to see you." I'd go down and we'd either go for a meal or just have coffee or something like that, just to visit because we'd grown up together. I got to know some of the guys at DePauw. Of course, they were all curious about my friend, so they were cultivating me to find out how to get to her. It was strange because there must've been about 20 Black guys at DePauw, and there were two Black women. I used to tease them about that. I said, "At least when I go back to Wabash, I know I'm in the same boat with every other guy at Wabash. Here, you guys, you sit here, looking at the candy in the jar, and you can't touch it." Interracial dating was a no-no in those days. I told them I wouldn't tolerate that. "You're there doing all these things for the college, and they treat you like this. At least they could recruit more Black women."

The basketball trips in terms of my actual experience were uneventful with a couple of exceptions. What I found out later was that my coach and a couple of the players went out of their way to be sure that there would be no incidents with my traveling with them, but there were a couple of exceptions. When I was a freshman, Wabash had a contract to play the University of the South, Sewanee. They had a contract to play another team in Memphis, and I can't remember the name of that other team. They had these games over the semester break. My coach said to me that they had city ordinances in Memphis that prohibited interracial athletic contests, so I couldn't play there. They didn't see any point in my going. He asked me to stay at the college and practice while they were going to Tennessee. [*Laughter*] I told him that it was semester break and I was going home. We had this running conversation for about a week. Semester break came. They went to Tennessee and I went home to Kansas City for semester break. The first game after break, he benched me just to prove he was in charge, you know. We had settled the issue with those games though. I told him that if they continued those contracts, that I wouldn't play basketball. So they discontinued those contracts after my freshman year. We were completely in accord about that. I always knew that he had my back in terms of race. So that was one incident that occurred. The other incident occurred when I was a senior and we went to Washington University in St. Louis. I had a very good friend who was a year behind me in high school who was attending there. I knew her family in Kansas City and I knew her family in St. Louis. She was living with her grandmother. They invited me to dinner when the team came to St. Louis. They came and picked me up at the hotel, and took me to their house for dinner, and brought me back to the hotel after I'd visited after dinner. When I got back to the hotel that evening, the bellboy said that the manager had asked him to tell me that they wanted me to use the freight elevator. I told him to take me up to the sixth floor where my coach was staying. I told Coach about this. I've never seen him get so mad as he did at that moment. His face got flaming red. He said, "Come with me," and he stormed out of the room. We went down. The manager wouldn't come out of his office. He hid in his office and wouldn't come out. [*Chuckles*] The coach said to me in front of the bellboy, "You use the same elevator that everybody else uses." That was the end of that. What I found out later, after I graduated, was there were a couple of other things that came up. When I was a freshman, we went to play in a Marine tournament at Quantico, Virginia. Before the tournament started, we were just in town, just walking around, seeing what it was like. We went into this coffee shop, convenience store. We'd only been in there five minutes or so. A couple of the seniors said, "Come on. Let's go. There's nothing in here for us." I found out later that the owner of the place told them that he wouldn't serve me, so they just said, "We're not going to be here," so we left. I didn't find out about that until years later when they told me. The other thing that happened was there was a big crossroads restaurant near Columbus, Indiana. One of my classmates was from Columbus. Once when we were coming through there, on the way back from a trip—we may've been to Evansville or someplace—we stopped there for dinner. Sam got off the bus. I thought he was just going to check on the reservations, but actually he went in and cleared it with the manager that we would have no trouble with my coming in to have dinner with the team. That passed without incident, but, here again, Sam didn't tell me that story until years later that that's what the coach had asked him to do because he was from Columbus and knew the manager. I had no incidents on the playing field and really had no incidents in any other athletic endeavors.

Fraternities dominated social life at Wabash, but during the years that I was there, the Independent Men's Association was very strong. I was active in the Independent Men's Association. In fact, I was the president when I was a senior. Since I had turned down two fraternities when I was in high school, that wasn't an issue for me. It surprised a number of people because they told me that they expected me to make fraternities an issue because in those days not only were Blacks not allowed in the national fraternities but Jews weren't allowed either.[11] The result of that was we had a rich mix of students who were independents, and we competed successfully with the fraternities on academics, athletics, whatever. Even though the fraternities dominated social life at Wabash, I never felt deprived as a result of a not being a member of a fraternity. For example, the Independent Men's Association sponsored the fall dance on campus that was at homecoming. Then the fraternities had the interfraternity panhell dance in the spring. Those were the two big social events on campus during the academic year, and so we split those. Fraternities—I never made an issue of fraternities because I wasn't interested in fraternities. Maybe that was copping out a little bit, but it was never an issue for me.

The only problem was it was a men's school. There were no women around. A lot of their guys were in the same position I was, so I didn't feel I was left out. A lot of guys—we had one guy who came—one African American guy who came to the college from Cleveland who really felt—he would hitch rides to Purdue and to Butler on weekends and all, but he wasn't an athlete. He didn't have anything else to do but study. Then one other guy came from Kansas City to Wabash two years after I did, and he was just so lovesick that he couldn't stay and ended dropping out of the college and going back to Kansas City.

The academic transition for me was not terribly difficult. I had a good year my freshman year, even though I had a very tough biology course and I had a very tough freshman English course. What else did I have when I was a freshman? I started studying Spanish as a freshman. My freshman year was solid. I think I had probably a B-minus average when I was a freshman, even though I was playing basketball. My sophomore year was disastrous. For one thing, and I tried not to make this an excuse, but I think I didn't really start to grieve for my parents until after my freshman year.[12] I was so excited about being in college my freshman year and I was so excited about doing well that I repressed everything else, but when I went home for Christmas and then when I went home for the summer, I realized my life had changed forever and it would never be the same because my parents weren't there. I came back and I made a disastrous mistake, which my academic advisor didn't—he was very tolerant. He let me do pretty much what I wanted to do. I was too ambitious because I knew I was going to be a starter for the full year for the first time, but I was taking physics, chemistry, economics, calculus—because I thought I was going to be a math major—and religion, plus my English courses and Spanish courses. I ended up taking 22 hours the first semester of my sophomore year. As you can guess, it just killed me. I got about halfway through the term, and I realized that I was failing calculus. I was not doing well in economics because I couldn't devote as much time to them as I should have. Instead of going in to the calculus instructor and asking for additional assistance, I just stayed away. I ended up taking a Withdrawal F from the course. I could've probably stayed with it and gotten some extra help and gotten a D or a C-minus out of it, but I just tightened up and I said, "I got to get control of what I'm doing." I got passing grades out of physics and chemistry. I got a barely passing grade out of economics and I did pretty well overall. That sophomore first semester, I got an A, three B's, a C, a D, and an F. It was just disastrous for me, but I bounced back in the second semester and I did well. I would say from the second semester of my sophomore year throughout my junior and senior years, I probably had a B-plus average, but that one semester. The other thing was since nobody in my family had ever gone to college, and I wasn't a person who would ask advice a lot, I had no idea what Phi Beta Kappa[13] was. My objective was to do well, but I didn't necessarily want to be the best, and so I didn't try as hard as I could have as long as I was doing well. What helped me in the transition was I had worked in the library all those years from the age of 14, and there wasn't any academic problem that I felt that I couldn't solve. The first class I ever attended was Contemporary Civilization, which was a broad-based history course. The faculty member teaching the course was just talking about politics. He was a political science professor, but a number of different faculty members taught this basic course in contemporary civilization. They were talking about this senator who was creating a lot of problems because of his obsession in searching for Communists. I didn't know what they were talking about. I barely knew what communism was. I didn't know what they were talking about. I was sitting there praying that he wouldn't ask me a question. [*Laughter*] The period was over and I made a beeline for the library. The next class was two days later. Two days later, I came in, I knew all about Senator McCarthy. I knew all about communism. [*Chuckles*] But the textbooks arrived and we started studying ancient Egypt. [*Laughter*] I say that as an illustration that I felt that I had the tools that I needed to be successful in college. I also felt I could do it on my own, which was a mistake. I should've asked for more advice than I did, but I was never in academic trouble. The only thing that happened was that I had one dean of students who was on to me and he kept after me about doing better. He knew I could do better, and he was after me about doing better, but he left after my freshman year, and the others never pushed me.

***

(A)Part of Us

The tasks that confronted each of these students varied, some common to most college students, while some diverged and reflected the unique challenge of being Black in an overwhelmingly White environment. Common to many first-time college students, these Black collegians had to resolve tasks related to academic, social, and instrumental competence (Chickering & Reisser, 1993). In other words, they learned what it meant to be a college student, making friends and becoming involved in organizations, and how to navigate taking care of basic needs and desires for self-care and wellness. However, these tasks were typically complicated by their racial distinctiveness and the intersections of race with other structures of injustice. Moreover, gender marked and differentiated the experiences of these Black students. Academic transitions are discussed first, then social transitions, and finally, navigating the local community.

Academics

For students who attended segregated public education, in schools that were typically underfunded and overcrowded (Anderson, 1988; Harding, 1981), racism and classism intersected to underprepare them for the academic demands of the college environment. As noted in Sybil's narrative, they were now in classrooms that included White peers who had attended elite boarding schools due to the academic status of their colleges. Therefore, they were not only in class with White students, but perhaps many of those White students' families were comparatively wealthier and able to provide an enhanced education. The disparity in preparation most often showed up in participants' references to their reading and writing skills. Like Bing, others spoke of taking advantage of tutorial classes in speed reading, note taking, and other study skills. Other students, like Vivian Hopkins Jackson at Oberlin, feared that the standards would be different: "An A at my high school felt like a C here [at Oberlin]," she commented. Not all students were invested in their academic achievement. Although both Robert and Tanya wanted to do well at Wabash and Kalamazoo, respectively, they were not primarily motivated by academic success.

Overall, the participants were also able to point to various support structures that helped to ease their academic transition. At Kalamazoo, Tanya referenced being assigned a "big sister" whose role was to ensure she was studying as well as mandatory study halls as factors that helped her to transition academically from New York City's public schools. At DePauw, Bing referenced the supportive role that a custodian played, one of his campus job supervisors, in helping to augment—or correct—the advice he was getting from his official academic advisor. This gentleman proved to be a vital anchor in Bing's transition, both academically and socially. Faculty were also instrumental in supporting these students' success. Jeannette, Robert, and Bing all speak in their narratives here about academic advisors and classroom instructors, who helped them with study skills, stoked their excitement for learning, and became mentors and lifelong friends. Larry Browning had been advised by the Dean of Men to withdraw from Earlham late in his tenure there, because he was about to fail out of the college. However, his new faculty advisor gave permission for him to return on probation and worked with him to teach him a new study technique that Larry would use throughout the rest of his academic career.[14] This faculty member "saw [his] potential" and not only helped Larry to raise his grades but also recommended that he go on to graduate school. Even for those who did struggle during their first year of college, the differences in writing skills, academic achievement, and confidence largely disappeared by the time they reached upper division courses, either through their own persistence and resilience or with the support of peers and faculty advisors.

Career Internships and International Study

Career internships and international study were unique features of the curricula at Antioch, Kalamazoo, and Oberlin. At Antioch, their co-op program was nationally known and highly regarded. In this system, students took classes for eight-week periods alternated by three- to six-month internships intended to be in the students' field of study. Across all the colleges, students majoring in education had to complete at least one student teaching experience. Kalamazoo initiated career internships and international study for all students as a part of its "K-Plan" just as Tanya was matriculating to the college (see endnote 9 in Chap. 4). While at Oberlin, the Conservatory had a required international study program in Austria for students majoring in performance studies and those in the College of Liberal Arts could also participate in the program. Sybil's summer study abroad in Japan was connected to the college's Near East Studies program. International experiences were not commonly pursued by students generally before the 1960s and were especially rare for Black collegians. The fact that these students took advantage of these opportunities speaks admirably to their willingness to step out of their comfort zone.

Career Internships

The co-op program was a mandatory feature of Antioch's curriculum and each student referenced their co-op experiences in their Senior Paper.[15] The Personnel Department was referred to repeatedly as the unit responsible for helping to place students with employers. However, Black students commonly referenced either their own or fellow students' experiences with discrimination. A senior woman's 1949 paper asserted that "Negro students should be forewarned" of the difficulties they might face as education or sociology majors with obtaining co-op placements because of racial discrimination and segregation. More than one student referenced Coretta Scott's experience of being unable to obtain a student teaching placement in the Yellow Springs public school system and their disappointment in what they saw as the college administration's refusal to act. Coretta wrote about this herself in her autobiography:

> I was the first black to major in elementary education. This required that I teach a year in the Antioch private elementary school and a year in the Ohio public schools.... However, the Yellow Springs School Board was very reactionary, and the supervisor of practice teaching at Antioch would not allow me to push the matter when I was turned down. She was the type who openly said, "God did not intend the races to mix." The Yellow Spring schools were integrated, but the faculty was all white,[16] and she told me that if I forced the issue it would imperil the whole Antioch practice-teaching program.... I appealed to the president of Antioch.[17] He was quite new to the school and was no pioneer in race relations.... But, on the teaching supervisor's advice, he refused to act. (King, 1993, p. 41)

Two men writing in 1951 extended these concerns to those majoring in business fields. One wrote forcefully that he was "thoroughly disgusted with Antioch and its supposed liberal stand on race relations and doubted the sincerity of the whole program" after having a co-op position fall through in Cleveland when the prospective supervisor expressed concern that the student would not be positively received by the community in which he would have been living. He credited his persistence, "bitching" in fact, with getting the Personnel Department finally to use the alumni network to locate positions for this student. A few of the men wrote about being the "first Negro" to be employed at their co-op site; one man described his experience with this at an organization in New York City in this way:

> I was placed on the proverbial spot. It was not only a challenging situation, but one which gave me an opportunity to discover at first hand what there is in a job situation which has created the illusion that some minority group representatives will never be capable of handling certain duties or will never be capable of becoming an integral part of the organization. I did not feel duty bound to prove my worth, but I wanted to do so in order that I could enlighten others. (Senior Paper, 1951)

A 1947 memorandum from the Race Relations Committee reached the conclusion that although the work of the Personnel Department had been "generally satisfactory," a complete survey of placements of Black students had not occurred and it was felt that the department needed to work to place more "minority groups" in the future.[18] Although a woman writing in 1950 noted that after speaking with the director, she had "seen more jobs become open to minority students," students after that, including the two men referenced earlier in 1951 and a woman writing in 1955, complained of losing co-op positions due to employers' racial discrimination. Alternative positions were typically found and substituted in such cases, but they were usually unrelated to their majors or intended career fields.

International Study

Without exception, each student who completed study abroad as part of their college curricula at Kalamazoo and Oberlin (all women except for Ronald Spann) reported having, as Tanya described it, "phenomenal" experiences. For Tanya, who went to Sierra Leone in West Africa, her time abroad in a predominantly Black nation was indescribably transformative. Others, who went to European countries, reported an unprecedented level of social freedom as Black women. Brenda Root, who studied abroad in Salzburg for her junior year, was encouraged to get a German boyfriend to help her learn the language. She reported having no problems doing so, unlike her experience on campus at Oberlin where she never dated at all. Her "most memorable experience" at Oberlin happened in another country. For those who were able to go abroad, their international experiences, though part of their academic studies, often positively supplemented their social engagement on campus.

Making Friends

Social life on campus consisted of several components, including forming new friendships and dating, as well as involvement in athletics, clubs, and fraternal organizations. It is in this realm that gender played the largest role in differentiating students' experiences. Although Jeannette and Rose gravitated toward each other at Ohio Wesleyan and Bing referenced the peer mentoring role that his Black roommate, a junior student-athlete, and some Black alumni played in his development, for the most part, these collegians did not seek out associations with other Black students. As Sybil shared, they all knew each other but they had not come to college for that purpose. Another participant quipped, if they were going to do that, they might as well have gone to Black colleges. Therefore, in their conversations with me or those at Antioch writing in their Senior Papers, they focused most on their fellow White students.

Many of these 68 collegians had little to no contact with White peers prior to college, either as co-learners in the classroom or as friends engaged in socializing outside of school. Among the Senior Papers of Black students at Antioch College, there was mention of the awkwardness and tentative approach to socializing with their White peers. One man who submitted his Senior Paper in 1950 wrote, "I approached it first with timidity. My first two weeks were full of fears and uncertainty. Things soon became free and easy in the hall unit and I saw none of the old color restrictions I had known." Other students embraced their new living situations eagerly as Janet Williams' narrative from Chap. 3 illustrated. A Black African student, from the Gold Coast,[19] wrote in 1955 that "the Antioch community deserves to be called a very friendly community" and that although he has been "abused and insulted elsewhere in the United States on account of the pigmentation of [his] skin," at Antioch he found that he was "accepted and loved just as anyone else." As Robert's narrative illustrates, these peers sometimes even intervened to prevent or challenge racial segregation and bias.

Black women also spoke of developing warm friendships with White women, despite the fact that they may have been prohibited by official campus policy or unofficial social custom from rooming with White women. When Denise Baisden was on the verge of leaving Ohio Wesleyan, a non-traditional housing arrangement in an off-campus house she shared with two White women proved to help her to persist at the college. Whether it was Denise going back over lunch with her housemates or groups of students hanging out in someone's room, card games were typically featured, particularly Bridge. Many of the Black women in this study had not played Bridge before coming to college. As Lesley Aranha shared at Allegheny, "I learned how to play Bridge. Now I played Pinochle before and I played Bid Whist before, but I never played Bridge. Well, Bridge was the card game of choice, so I learned to play Bridge." Vivian suggested a racial difference in what card games were played when she noted that after dinner at Oberlin, the scene would be "White students playing Bridge and the Black students playing [Bid] Whist." None of the participants talked about teaching their White peers to play Bid Whist, but rather several noted that they learned to play Bridge.

Black students did not always perceive their interracial friendships to be very deep or to reflect more than superficial commitments to race relations, however. One man at Antioch wondered in his 1951 Senior Paper, "Students look forward to vacations as periods in which they can exchange visits and become familiar with the families and home towns of their friends. I wonder how many Negro students have enjoyed this kind of friendship." When I asked across the 68 participants in this study whether they had ever been invited to visit one of their White friends over the holidays or summer break, only one, a man, replied that they had done so. Another participant, a woman, dismissed my question as something she would not have expected to be able to do. Another woman at Antioch writing in 1950 raised the point that there were three places in Yellow Springs that were "<u>known</u> to discriminate against minority groups or rather against Negroes," yet they were "frequented by students who advocate[d] verbally racial equality" (emphasis in original). An African Kikuyu[20] student discussed in his 1952 paper that he chose to discontinue his involvement in the Race Relations Committee so that he could engage with his White peers as friends first instead of being confronted by the inconsistencies of their racial attitudes. Public places, like soda shops and restaurants, helped new friendships to germinate and solidify, and therefore segregation disrupted opportunities for interracial engagement and friendships.

Dating as college students revealed deep fissures between men's and women's experiences. Since interracial dating was officially discouraged at some institutions,[21] social customs often found Black students without dates most weekends. Only one woman, who was at Allegheny, shared that she dated White men and one of the men at Antioch wrote in 1950 that he had dated interracially "often and with enthusiasm." For other Black men, interracial dating was done cautiously and not typically out in the open. As Bing suggests in his narrative, paying attention might reveal who was with whom. There were White women who were willing to date Black men, as an Antioch man wrote in his 1948 Senior Paper. However, as an Antioch woman in 1952 wrote in her essay, "The Negro girl who comes to a school which is predominately [*sic*] white is consciously or unconsciously sacrificing her chances for marriage until a much later time." Some Black women, like Sybil, noted that they had not come to college looking for husbands so it did not matter, "though it would have been nice" as Jeannette noted.

Campus Involvement

For the men to whom I spoke, the initial brokering of interracial friendships typically happened through their residence hall roommate assignments. From these beginnings, athletics and study partnerships helped to form lasting friendships. A few men at Kenyon and Wabash, each eventually having one integrated fraternity chapter during the period,[22] also had access to fraternity life as a means of cultivating friendships with White peers. Although, as Robert mentions at Wabash, the Independent Men's Association was active and vibrant on the campus and is where he fulfilled his social engagement needs. Black women, however, had much narrower options. Intercollegiate athletics did not exist for women at these colleges at the time, and none of the women to whom I spoke participated in the limited intramural activities available for women, which included modern dance. In the archival data across all the institutions and the entire 20-year span, I only noted one woman who participated in the modern dance club. At the time, none of the institutions that had fraternities and sororities had chapters that admitted Black women. Most of the women with whom I spoke claimed to care little for sorority life, however. Independent women's groups were not active in campus life and the fraternities and sororities often dominated social involvement on campus.[23] Campus involvement for these women was mainly through academic department clubs and organizations.

On the whole, both Black women and men were heavily involved in academic clubs, civic organizations, and religious life groups. The Black students at Antioch were often involved in the Community Government's Race Relations or Interracial Committees. At the other campuses, a diverse array of language clubs, academic clubs related to their majors, and civic groups were listed in their yearbook senior profiles. As noted in Laura's narrative, however, these engagements were not necessarily free from reminders of their second-class status as Black people. Unlike Robert's experience on the Wabash basketball team, Laura did not have peers or a faculty advisor for the yearbook at Oberlin, who intervened on her behalf to make sure she was included in all aspects of the group's activities despite racial segregation.

Local Community

The towns in which these colleges were located were typically small and rural. The Ohio colleges were also relatively isolated; none of them was adjacent to a major state highway. The Michigan, Indiana, and Pennsylvania colleges, however, were all in cities that had exits along a major thoroughfare.[24] The local towns were unavoidable since most entertainment and shopping options were located off campus. Although not located in the South, segregation was prevalent and commonly practiced at primary and secondary schools, residential areas, as well as movie theaters and barbershops. In most instances, the only integrated place in town was the GLCA college campus (inspired by their religious values) with the exception of the fraternities and sororities that also generally prohibited racial integration.

Most of these Black collegians reported very limited engagement with the towns beyond their campuses. When they did go into the town, they were usually in interracial groups and sometimes did experience being refused service at a local soda shop or restaurant. Both Black men and Black women shared stories like this. One Black woman at Allegheny in 1955, Jeane Bounds Williams, shared that she had been warned to make sure she was wearing her "freshman beanie"[25] whenever she went off campus alone so that she would be recognized as an Allegheny student and therefore not be harassed by local White citizens. Sybil shared later that she passed as Mexican, using her lighter complexion and her limited Spanish-speaking skills when she rode the city bus in Richmond to avoid racial harassment. These Black collegians either avoided being alone or publicized their college affiliation to deflect racial harassment in the local communities at the time.

However, some students found enriching and nurturing second-families among the Black communities in town. Bing's narrative is just one example of this, as is Robert's from the previous chapter and this one. Sybil and Jeannette both spoke to being able to find hairstylists who could do their hair among the Black community off campus. For students who had access to these community-based resources, they were able to find a place to relax and escape the pressures of being Black on their predominantly White campus.

Interpreting Campus Involvement and Engagement

As Harper and Quaye (2009) have written, a culturally relevant model of student engagement is necessary for properly situating collegiate involvement among students of color. Despite the invisibility and presumed isolation of Black women in the college records, their own stories suggest quite the opposite. Although they were definitely few in number in most of the GLCA colleges, they did not spend their college years hiding in the shadows. Neither was their involvement predicated merely on self-selection or the number of activities available. Rather, their involvement was mediated by racism, limiting access and belonging for Black women. Scholars have identified the institutional factors and types of student involvement that significantly contribute to student success (Kuh, Kinzie, Schuh, & Whitt, 2010). Among these "high-impact practices" were involvement in civic and social action and academically enriching activities, as well as interracial engagement (Kuh et al., 2010). These women tended to be engaged in exactly those sorts of activities leading to application of learning beyond the classroom, meaningful relationships with faculty, and engaging in quality cross-racial interactions.

Yet, a colorblind reading of these Black women's college experiences does little to dismantle the endemic racism that is proliferated by dominant models of student success based on predominantly White, middle-class student samples (Patton, Harper, & Harris, 2015; Patton, Ranero, & Everett, 2011). Assuming that Black women merely self-selected out of certain student involvement experiences belies the racism that limited their choice sets, as well as elides the ways that whiteness is centered in determining what activities should be promoted for student engagement (Stewart, in press). From residence halls to athletic clubs to sorority spaces, racism delimited Black women's visibility and integration on campus to only academic and religious spaces. In this way, as Patton et al. (2015) point out, racism arguably had as much to teach these Black women as any of the departmental clubs or civic activities in which they were able to engage. Issues of exclusion, access, and belonging are fundamental for understanding Black women's college experiences in the GLCA colleges. Ignoring the climate and intergroup behavioral dimensions (Hurtado, Milem, Clayton-Pedersen, & Allen, 1999; Chang, Milem, & antonio, 2011) informed by systemic exclusion and racial discrimination will result in efforts that are only partially effective and which do not address access to student engagement.

Notes

1. "Rose" in Jeannette's narrative is another participant in this study. By Rose's request, she is only identified by her pseudonym, Rose Jackson Enco.
2. As described by all the participants who attended Ohio Wesleyan, Delaware's Black population all lived on the same side of the tracks across from the university.
3. While Jeannette was at Ohio Wesleyan, the 1959 *Le Bijou* included a picture of Winter Homecoming with fraternity men in an "ugliest of the ugly" contest that included one man in a black painted face wearing an animal print top (p. 161).
4. Rose had made it very clear in her interview with me that she believed that Ohio Wesleyan had practiced a quota system for the admission of Black students, particularly Black women. I asked Jeannette her impressions of this and this was what she shared with me. Over the course of this period, an estimated 113 Black students matriculated to Ohio Wesleyan. Of that total, there were 76 men and 37 women, nearly a 2:1 ratio.
5. A "beard" is now commonly used to refer to a heterosexual woman that a gay man pretends to be dating to maintain a heterosexual façade. However, Sybil's usage of this term was meant to recognize the similar desire that some people have regardless of sexuality to keep private the intimate details of their lives. She did not think that her friend was a closeted gay man.
6. Recall from Sybil's narrative in Chap. 3 that she was banned by law from participating in any extracurricular activities during high school at Little Rock's Central High to maintain racial segregation.

Sybil had been highly involved in her segregated Black junior high school in choir and other activities.

7. Allegheny also required first-year students to wear a beanie on campus. Other colleges had different kinds of rituals to initiate the first-year class.
8. At Kalamazoo College, there were no local or national fraternities and sororities. The faculty had banned them because they considered them to be elitist and exclusivist. The societies, although gender-segregated, were required to accept any student who was interested without regard to race, religion, nationality, or any other factor.
9. "Mr. Simms" is a pseudonym.
10. "Lenny" refers to Leonard Yorke, who is a participant in this study.
11. The exclusion clauses prohibited fraternities and sororities from initiating anyone who was Black, Jewish, or Catholic. This was common to all the GLCA colleges that had national fraternal groups: Wabash, Kenyon, Ohio Wesleyan, DePauw, Hope, Albion, Denison, and Allegheny. The social clubs at Kalamazoo and Wooster were local to those campuses and were not racially exclusive. Antioch, Earlham, and Oberlin did not have similar societies or social clubs.
12. Robert's parents died during his senior year in high school as shared in his narrative from Chap. 4.
13. Phi Beta Kappa is a national academic honorary society and is the nation's oldest Greek-letter organization (Thelin, 2011).
14. Chapter 9 includes a portion of Larry Browning's narrative that shares more about this new advisor and the transformation in his study habits.
15. The Senior Paper was required of all graduates at Antioch College prior to 1960 and submitted in the fall of their senior year. According to the syllabus for the 1958–1959 academic year, the nature of the assignment was described as follows:

    > As a Senior [sic] at Antioch, then, you have reached a point where it should prove valuable to you and to Antioch for you to take stock of yourself, the world around you, and your relation to it. As you approach the end of your undergraduate experience here, it is especially important that you should assess once more your development and the influence of Antioch as you have felt it in your own life and as you have observed it in the lives of others. (Antioch College, 1958–1959, p. 1)

The paper was to be organized into two sections: the first focused on the students' individual development and how they got to this point in their education and life, including career interests, values development, and understanding of the world around them. The second section was to share their critical assessment of the Antioch College curriculum and any suggestions for its improvement. The file copy of the Senior Paper became part of the student's permanent college record and is a confidential document accessible only by those with permission to review it. Students are assured of the following: "Unidentified excerpts may be quoted without your permission; publication, as a whole or in part, when attributed to you will not be done without your consent" (Antioch College, 1958–1959, p. 4). In compliance with this restriction, my quotes from the 24 Senior Papers that I was able to review are masked and shared completely anonymously using only the author's gender and the paper's year of submission, making it impossible to match definitively with the list of these papers in the primary sources included in this book.

16. As noted by both a senior woman in 1951 and Murray's (1951\1997) compilation, employment discrimination was illegal in the state of Ohio, but this prohibition was not necessarily enforced.
17. Douglas McGregor, who succeeded Algo Henderson in 1948.
18. Treichler, J., Hollister, H., & Lemcke. (1947, May 13). *Memorandum from Race Relations Committee.* File: Race Relations – Jessie Treichler's File 2/14/1951. Antiochiana, Yellow Springs, OH.
19. Before liberation from British colonialism, the Gold Coast was the name of the country now known as Ghana.
20. The Kikiyu are an ethnic group in what is now the independent nation of Kenya, previously colonized by the British.
21. Discussions at Earlham about how forcefully they should discourage interracial dating are noted in the faculty minutes from the late 1940s to 1952. At Antioch, a man's 1950 Senior Paper criticizes President McGregor's 1949 statement confining interracial dating to the campus. At Ohio Wesleyan and Oberlin, students shared stories of Black students, usually men, being called into the Dean's office about White women they were dating and the women being sent home.

22. Iota Chi Theta which became Beta Sigma Tau at Kenyon and Tau Kappa Epsilon (TKE) at Wabash.
23. The 1949 *Le Bijou* at Ohio Wesleyan noted that 85% of men and 70% of women belonged to Greek-lettered organizations and these groups were the "mainstays of campus social life" (p. 13).
24. The interstate freeway system was mostly nonexistent at this time in the Midwest. As the federal interstate freeways developed, still only the colleges in Michigan, Indiana, and Pennsylvania would be in towns that had a freeway exit.
25. A common practice among these institutions during this era but would now be regarded as hazing of the first-year class. One consistent element of these rituals was the requirement to always have one's beanie on as a first-year student while on campus. At Allegheny and other GLCA colleges, this requirement did not customarily extend to off-campus visits.

References

Anderson, J. D. (1988). *The education of Blacks in the south, 1860–1935*. Raleigh: University of North Carolina Press.

Chang, M. J., Milem, J. F., & Antonio, A. L. (2011). Campus climate and diversity. In J. H. Schuh, S. R. Jones, & S. R. Harper (Eds.), *Student services: A handbook for the profession* (pp. 43–58). San Francisco, CA: Jossey-Bass.

Chickering, A., & Reisser, L. (1993). *Education and identity* (2nd ed.). San Francisco, CA: Jossey-Bass.

Harding, V. (1981). *There is a river: The Black struggle for freedom in America*. San Diego, CA: Harcourt Brace & Company.

Harper, S. R., & Quaye, S. J. (2009). Beyond sameness, with engagement and outcomes for all: An introduction. In S. R. Harper & S. J. Quaye (Eds.), *Student engagement in higher education* (pp. 1–16). New York, NY: Routledge.

Hurtado, S., Milem, J. F., Clayton-Pedersen, A. R, &Allen, W. R. (1999). *Enacting diverse learning environments: Improving the climate for racial/ethnic diversity in higher education*. ASHE-ERIC Higher Education Report, *26*(8). Washington, DC: The George Washington University, Graduate School of Education and Human Development.

King, C. S. (1993). *My life with Martin Luther King, Jr* (Rev. ed.). New York, NY: Henry Holt & Co.

Kuh, G. D., Kinzie, J., Schuh, J. H., & Whitt, E. J. (2010). *Student success in college: Creating conditions that matter*. San Francisco, CA: Jossey-Bass.

Murray, P. (1997). *States' laws on race and color*. Athens: University of Georgia Press. Retrieved from https://books.google.com. (Originally published in 1951).

Patton, L. D., Harper, S. R., & Harris, J. (2015). Using critical race theory to (re) interpret widely studied topics related to students in US higher education. In A. M. Martinez-Aleman, B. Pusser, & E. M. Bensimon (Eds.), *Critical approaches to the study of higher education: A practical introduction* (pp. 193–219). Baltimore, MD: Johns Hopkins University.

Patton, L. D., Ranero, J., & Everett, K. (2011). Engaging race in multicultural student services. In D. L. Stewart (Ed.), *Multicultural student services on campus: Building bridges, re-visioning community, ACPA Books and Media* (pp. 63–80). Sterling, VA: Stylus.

Stewart, D.-L. (in press). (In)Visibility, involvement, and success: A counter-narrative of Black women in predominantly White liberal arts colleges, 1945–1965. In L. D. Patton Davis & N. N. Croom (Eds.), *Critical perspectives on Black women and college success.* New York, NY: Routledge.

Thelin, J. R. (2011). *A history of American higher education* (2nd ed.). Baltimore, MD: Johns Hopkins University Press.

Treichler, J., Hollister, H., & Lemcke. (1947, May 13). *Memorandum from race relations committee. Race relations – Jessie Treichler's File 2/14/1951.* Antiochiana, Olive Kettering Library, Antioch College, Yellow Springs, OH.

Antioch College

Antioch College. (1958–1959). *Syllabus: Senior paper X 389.* Antiochiana, Olive Kettering Library, Antioch College, Yellow Springs, OH.

CHAPTER 7

Roadblocks and Detours

Beauford and Janet Williams[1]

Earlham College, 1951–1953

B: We were just going to get married and not tell anybody, but the lady, my Spanish teacher, she saw the license. We went to another town to get the license because we didn't want anybody to know.

J: I was in the dorm, and he was in another dorm. We were just going to stay where we were, and everything was going to be cool.

B: She told. She squealed on us. There was a notice on—they used to have call boards. When someone wanted to get in contact with you, they put a little note on the bulletin board. It was called the call board. There was a note there and it said, "See me immediately," from the Dean of Men, and Janet got one on hers.

J: My note was from the Dean of Women: "See me immediately," because we could have been expelled! See, because you're not supposed to be involved with someone like that. You didn't do that at Earlham.

B: When we went to Earlham, there was no drinking or smoking on campus.

These five narratives from six participants are organized by years of attendance, beginning with the earliest matriculates.

© The Author(s) 2017

D.-L. Stewart, *Black Collegians' Experiences in US Northern Private Colleges*, DOI 10.1057/978-1-137-59077-0_7

J: Now, most kids, they'd just shack up. Well, they didn't know we were married!

B: See, we would go on the weekend to her sister's, who knew about us. We were going to keep it a secret. Then we found out in March or April or something that she was pregnant, but we still didn't tell anybody that we were married. We were already married in January. Well, anyway, I'm standing at the call board and I've read my note. This other lady was standing at the call board. She said, "Well, how's Janet?" I said, "Well, she's fine." She says, "Well, I'm from Winchester. I'm from Winchester." We got the license in Winchester, because we didn't know anybody [*laughter*] in Winchester. She was from Winchester, but, see, she had kept it a secret for a couple—about a month probably. Well, now, then the whole thing was exposed.

J: See, really, we were so well liked. I think we would have been expelled, but everybody liked us, though.

B: Plus, Momma and Daddy knew we were going to get married. We had already made the arrangements, because I had to go to the Army.

J: We hadn't made arrangements. I just didn't want them to know!

B: Well, we didn't want them to know because you were going to go back to school without anybody knowing it. Well, they made arrangements for us. They gave us an apartment in Vetville.[2] Right after they found out we were married, just before the end of our sophomore year. Two months, three months? The kids all got together and gave us a shower and rerouted the traffic from National Road and into Vetville. They were tooting horns and stopping. You remember that?

J: Mm-hmm. We stayed in the extra bedroom that some friends of ours had until the end of that spring semester.

B: The Army gave me a deferment until after the baby was born, and that was probably the second deferment. They gave me a deferment to finish school that semester. Then they gave me a deferment because the baby was due in October. That was my third and last deferment. I couldn't defer any more. They gave me until November. Margo was less than a month old; I went to the Army the second of November. Margo was born the fifth of October.

J: I had to stay with his parents to have the baby. I had no choice. I was being a wife and obeying my husband. [*Eye roll*]

B: I knew that the only survival that we had, because I was going to be gone for two years, was going to be with Janet staying with my parents. That's what happened, but then after Margo was born, then she moved out to Colorado with me where I was stationed. I never got sent overseas. Therefore, then we started making our lives together. Yeah, we left Earlham, never did go back and finish anything. No, no, because by then I started a career. I had a career in music after the Army. Thirty-five years on the road.

J: He was on the road 50 out of 52 weeks of the year at times. I wanted children. I raised our family and managed the finances. We still have great friends from Earlham. We go back nearly every year.

Mary Barksdale

Earlham College, 1952–1953

I got married in April of my freshman year. I needed to move to Fort Wayne because that's where my husband lived. So, I finished out the year and then the people I was working for asked me if I'd stay till August until they could get somebody to take my place. I thought that I was just a low-level clerk, but I was all they had entering records and that kind of thing. I stayed till August and then I moved to Fort Wayne. We got married when I was 19. I didn't finish my bachelor's degree. I got up to 60 hours, my dear. One class at a time. I never had time. You saw everything I was doing,[3] and I had three children, and I was a Parent-Teacher Association (PTA) member.

Karl Johnson

Wabash College, 1952–1954

It was country. It was Indiana country. In spite of the fact that the education was good, there just wasn't a whole lot to talk about. I spent a year at Western Reserve then I dropped out of school because I had to pay. The Major Work Program involved in elementary school and in junior high summer courses in French at Western Reserve. I'd been there many, many times. I can point out the building where we studied. I was tired of going to school. I worked for a while as a taxicab driver. Then I went into the US Air Force for four years. I became a Korean-language specialist for the Air Force and spent a year in postwar Korea. Studied at the Army Language

School, which is now the Defense Department Language School, in Monterey, California.

Mildred Denby Green

Oberlin College, 1955–1957

Oh, I didn't make my grade. At the end of my sophomore year, I didn't do well in a theory class. I didn't really flunk out, but I didn't do—yes, I did, I guess, if you don't make the grade. I went home and started at Hampton, but I couldn't keep up with all the partying there. Then the daughter of one of my dad's friends was talking about Ohio State and I was telling her about Hampton. I said, "I don't think I really want to go there. I was thinking about maybe I'd go try Virginia State or some place." She said, "Why don't you come to Ohio State?" I said to myself, "If I go back to Ohio, I'm going to try to go back to Oberlin." They had told me I could appeal to come back. I said, "Okay, I'm going to go to Ohio State if they accept me. Then I'll transfer back to Oberlin." I went over to Hampton and asked and begged them to let me send my transcript for the summer. They had—what did they call it—special delivery then, kind of stuff. So I knew how some of those schools were slow and I said, "Please let me—you can seal it, but let me put it in the mail." The lady did. I happened to call just to make sure that Ohio State had gotten it. The guy said, "Yeah, you've been accepted." I said, "Really? I can come?" He sent me all this stuff. I had to stay in what they call university housing, Ohio State Dormitories, or something. So I went on the train again, this time to Columbus, by myself and got enrolled. I started liking it. I kept thinking I was going to leave there, but I enjoyed it and—I don't know. It was a different experience, much, much larger, of course. I knew a couple of people, that girl from my home, and I met some people in the transfer class. I just stayed. I would visit Oberlin, you know, to see the guy I was dating. We got married when we both graduated. But it was an experience. I really was torn because I kind of really wanted to go back to Oberlin. You know, I really respected that school, but I had, by the end of my year at Ohio State—in fact, at the end of the first quarter—I had really bonded with those instructors. Even though there was a lot of prejudice there, I still had a good experience at Oberlin. It kind of got me ready for that at Ohio State, you know.

Chauncey Mann

Allegheny College, 1956–1959

I didn't *decide* not to finish there. It was that whole monetary thing coming up and it hit me in the head. I couldn't afford it. The guy tried to give me a break by more scholarships. At that time they did not have student loans. They didn't have the government aid and all those things.[4] I utilized the GI Bill. I also utilized one year when I went back to high school. Yes, the high school was free. I signed up and they paid with the GI Bill that one year. Had I known that there was a choice, I would have had all the four years. I did my three years at Allegheny and then I ran out of money. I ended up going to a correspondence school at the University of the Pacific and then I worked for the post office for two years and then I went into the ministry.

***

Attrition at the GLCA Colleges

Of the Black collegians in this study, there were 12 who did not complete their degrees at the GLCA college to which they matriculated. Although they are a minority of this group, rates of attrition among Black students at the GLCA colleges seem to be much higher. Unfortunately, it is impossible to report exact numbers of graduates and nongraduates based only on the alumni office records and institutional yearbooks. It is less likely that those who do not graduate from an institution would be inclined to want to receive communication; moreover, relocations, marriage, and other changes in life circumstances can make maintaining contact difficult. Tracking enrollment and graduation through the yearbooks is also unreliable because students who did not live on campus, were not involved in fraternities, sororities, or athletics, and/or who could not afford to pay for individual profile pictures[5] were often not included in the yearbook. Also, the inclusion of student directories and indexes varied considerably across these colleges, with most typically not including such information. Although most graduating seniors did appear in the yearbook in their final year, it should not be assumed that students not in the yearbook in their presumptive final year did not graduate.

Nevertheless, cross-referencing alumni database information with names of Black students appearing in the yearbooks at these colleges reveals that attrition of Black students before graduation was more common than not.[6] Wabash had the highest estimated attrition rate among its Black men of 78%; 18 of the 23 matriculates did not graduate from the college. Kalamazoo also had a relatively high estimated attrition rate of 61%, with 23 of 38 matriculates not persisting to graduation. Excluding these outliers, average estimated attrition for the remaining ten institutions was 33%. With only 18 of 133 matriculates not persisting to graduation, Antioch had the lowest estimated attrition rate (14%). Four of the colleges (Albion, Allegheny, DePauw, and Hope) had higher estimated attrition rates for women matriculates than for men, which was opposite the trend at the other eight institutions. These are also the four co-educational colleges whose enrollment of Black women was far below that of Black men (see Fig. A.1).

Among the 12 participants in this study who did not persist to graduation were 5 men and 7 women. Their reasons for leaving spanned six areas: academics, marriage and pregnancy, finances, climate, military enlistment, and college choice. Four participants had to leave due to low grades and did not have the benefit of the kind of support that Larry Browning received at Earlham that enabled him to stay and graduate. Mildred's narrative in this chapter illustrates this. Although she could have appealed her dismissal, she had made strong connections with faculty and peers at Ohio State University and decided to remain there to finish her degree.

Marriage and pregnancy were the next most common reason for students to leave college before graduation. There were three participants who cited this reason. This was not isolated to women and it was typically not marriage alone that forced participants out of school. Ralph Jones shared that he had gotten married in 1968 early in his final semester at DePauw, but it was the fact that his new wife was already pregnant with their first child that required him to leave school to support his family. As he said, "the shotgun was loaded when we got married….Had the shotgun not been loaded, I would have finished." For Janet Williams, she wanted to finish her studies at Earlham regardless of her marriage to Beauford, but it was her pregnancy that required her to leave school because Beauford wanted her to live with his parents in Fort Wayne to have the baby. Traditional customs that encouraged women to defer to their husband's authority, as Janet noted "to obey," interrupted her college studies. Similarly, Mary Barksdale also left Earlham after marriage because her husband lived in another city and she needed to relocate to join him. The social custom of the "trailing spouse" that privileged men in heteronormative marital relationships interrupted these women's studies.

Finances only affected 2 of these 12 participants. Chauncey Mann had served in the military prior to enrolling at Allegheny but had exhausted his GI Bill tuition benefits because the first year was credited to his high school completion. Although an administrator at the college offered more scholarship money, it was not enough to help Chauncey stay enrolled for his last year. Richard Hammond also faced financial challenges midway through his tenure at Ohio Wesleyan. He had joined a fraternity, Beta Sigma Tau, and was living in the fraternity house. In order to afford to stay there, he would have had to "help the cook and…do the cleaning, the bathrooms." Ultimately, Richard decided that he could do better by leaving college and working full-time since he assumed his major, sociology, would lead to a low-paying and hazardous job as a social worker. He wished he had "a mentor or someone to say, 'Hey, you can be what you want to be.'"

The military, preferred college choices, and climate issues were the reasons the remaining three nongraduates left their colleges. Although Janet had to leave Earlham because she was pregnant, Beauford left Earlham because he had been drafted into the military. Again, their marriage was not the principal reason for his attrition. For Mamie Cavell Adderly, who readers were first introduced to in Chap. 2, Swarthmore was always her first choice for college and Earlham was more of a way to fill the time while she waited for the fall term to begin. Her parents were not going to allow her to just "sit out for this year." After two years, she would transfer from Swarthmore to Temple because the academic adjustment was too rough. She shared, "In retrospect, you know, I really should have stayed all four years at Earlham." Finally, Karl Johnson's narrative in this chapter cites the "country" climate of Crawfordsville and Wabash as his reason for leaving. Basically, Karl was bored and not engaged with the campus. At this time, there was not an integrated social fraternity on campus[7] and the Independent Men's Association that helped Robert Wedgeworth find his place on campus the year after Karl left apparently was not serving this purpose for Karl, who was also not an athlete.

Excluding pregnancy, the issues that these students faced and that prompted their departures were not unique. Other participants shared that they faced academic difficulties, ran out of money, were drafted into the military, had lackluster social lives, or were attending the institution that was not their first choice. However, in these other cases, faculty or administrators at their colleges stepped in to make it possible for them to persist through to graduation. These interventions were not structural safeguards, but rather reflected personal investments in these students made by individual staff. If Larry Browning's initial academic advisor had not gone on sabbatical and been replaced by the faculty member who would transform his study habits, he would also have had to leave Earlham because of his poor grades. College attrition was not inevitable, but neither was persistence solely a reflection of individual resilience. Instead, their persistence was a product of their individual resilience and the personal support of (usually White) faculty and staff. Chapter 8 illustrates the ways that these individual, personal investments in Black students did not necessarily reflect an institutional ethos committed to racial equity and justice.

Notes

1. Beauford and Janet Williams married while in college, as they discuss in this narrative, and conducted their interview together. The narrative shows how they helped each other to tell their story.
2. Pictures and notices about campus housing for veterans and married students were included in the yearbooks for DePauw, Earlham, Kalamazoo, and Ohio Wesleyan. Albion's 1947 *Albionian* noted that the college had increased enrollment and that "married vets and families [were] a familiar sight." In 1946, *The Milestone* at Hope noted a Veteran's Institute for those who were beginning at a "sub-college level."
3. Despite never finishing college, Mary spent a career in public service, serving on the local school board as well as the boards of several nonprofit organizations in Fort Wayne.
4. Following the GI Bill, the next federal financial aid program would not be passed until 1958, the NDEA. The NDEA created the National Defense Student Loan Program based on financial need for students studying in the sciences, math, or languages (Long, 2013). Allocations did not begin until February 1959 and over 24,831 students at 1188 institutions borrowed funds for college through this program in its first year (Flattau et al., 2006, p. II-3). Chauncey had been pursuing a math major and was highly interested in military service. Unfortunately, Chauncey never learned about the NDEA loan program that could have helped him return to Allegheny to finish his degree.

5. For example, an announcement on page 1 of the October 30, 1947, issue of *The Anchor* at Hope College noted that individual pictures for "underclassmen" were 50 cents each.
6. Oberlin College had a very thorough database of alumni, but their records did not indicate the graduation status of each alum and both graduates and nongraduates were included.
7. Wabash's first integrated fraternity, Tau Kappa Epsilon (TKE), was reestablished in 1962 after a 40-year absence (*The Wabash*, 1962).

References

Flattau, P. E., Bracken, J., Van Atta, R., Bandeh-Ahmadi, A., de laCruz, R., & Sullivan, K. (2006). *The national defense education act of 1958: Selected outcomes.* IDA Document D-3306. Washington, DC: Institute for Defense Analyses. Science & Technology Policy Institute. Retrieved from https://www.ida.org/idamedia/Corporate/Files/Publications/STPIPubs/ida-d-3306.ashx

Long, B. T. (2013). Supporting access to higher education. In M. J. Bailey & S. Danziger (Eds.), *Legacies of the war on poverty, The national poverty center series on poverty and public policy* (pp. 93–120). New York, NY: Russell Sage Foundation.

The Wabash [yearbook]. (1962). *Archives and special collections*, Roy O. West Library, DePauw University, Greencastle, IN.

CHAPTER 8

Integration and the Movement

1945–1949

April 1947: *Jackie Robinson desegregates Major League Baseball in his debut with the Brooklyn Dodgers.*[1]

July 1948: *President Harry Truman signs Executive Order 9981 desegregating the armed forces.*

The participants' narratives in this chapter are set against the backdrop of some of the most significant events of the CRM. Many other events and actions were taking place around the country as Lewis noted in his memoir (Lewis & D'Orso, 1998). However, the events recorded here were particularly noteworthy in the history of the movement. The five-year time spans are introduced by the list of key events in the CRM and then followed by one to three participant narratives across the 11 institutions for which student perspectives of campus activities were available (including Antioch College). The concluding essay introduces the archival data and how they amplify or diverge from students' reflections, drawing conclusions about student and institutional responses to local and national activism.

© The Author(s) 2017

D.-L. Stewart, *Black Collegians' Experiences in US Northern Private Colleges*, DOI 10.1057/978-1-137-59077-0_8

R. Edd Lee

Earlham College, 1946–1950

Race and segregation were hot topics. The most amazing thing to me about Richmond, Indiana, was the fact that Black and White children went to the same schools. Black children play on the athletic teams. They participate in all of the school activities, but the restaurants are segregated. I found that difficult to understand that you could ride on the same buses, no segregation, but to sit down and have a meal in a restaurant was virtually impossible at that time. There was a great deal of discrimination in the factories around Richmond not only against Blacks but even Jews and sometimes Catholics and sometimes foreigners, Europeans or people who had accents who had come into the community. The college was right in the thick of it all and couldn't manage to get themselves to take as active a role in stopping those kinds of things. Maybe they thought they couldn't stop them anyhow. Anyway, that was the situation in Richmond when I got there, and it remained that way pretty much until after I left.

Sam Lewis

Hope College, 1947–1951

The only conversations that I heard about segregation and civil rights were students saying that they were hoping that Truman was able to do what he was trying to do. They were not opposed to that. As a matter of fact, they were in line with it.

Allan Ballard

Kenyon College, 1948–1952

I was learning in this White environment to use academic tools to examine my own and my people's past. I wrote papers in my classes, in psychology, in political science, and then I think another paper in constitutional law, where I wrote a paper on certain Supreme Court cases that concerned Black adolescents and the death penalty and similar issues. I did a lot of that kind of exploration. No one stopped me from doing it.

Everyone—my faculty—encouraged me to go ahead and do it if that's what I wanted to do, but I had to do it like everybody else did. In other words, write the same kind of research paper everybody else is going to write.

1950–1954

May 1954: *US Supreme Court decision in* Brown v. Board of Education of Topeka, Kansas, *declares segregated public education unconstitutional.*

Clyde Francis

Allegheny College, 1950–1954

There were no conversations about race relations in class. Not in class. The only conversation I had pertaining to race was with some Jewish guys on campus and it was never anything in depth. Mostly, it was along the lines of them acknowledging that both Blacks and Jews had been discriminated against. To that degree, there might have been a bit of camaraderie. Then they would say, "Well, it's going to change," and they were right to a degree, but they had this thing about patience; it's going to take time and education.

William Allison

DePauw University, 1950–1954

There were never any conversations about race and this is the period of the 1954 desegregation decision by the courts. You would have people come and speak at these lectures they had, the Gobin lectures in the chapel. I don't think I initiated conversation and I don't think there was much conversation. We kind of lived in a little bubble of college life.

1955–1959

August 1955: *Emmett Till is murdered on a visit from Chicago to relatives in Money, Mississippi.*

September 1955: Jet *magazine publishes the gruesome photos of Till's mutilated body in an open-casket funeral at his mother's request.*

December 1955: *The Montgomery Bus Boycott begins after NAACP chapter secretary and civil rights worker Rosa Parks is arrested in a planned action refusing to give up her seat to a White man on a public bus.*

February 1956: *Autherine Lucy attempts to enroll at the University of Alabama, but is forced to leave the campus after mob violence erupts.*

June 1956: *Paul Robeson testifies before the House Un-American Activities Committee.*

November 1956: *US Supreme Court upholds federal district court ruling in* Browder v. Gayle *that segregated seating on public busses is unconstitutional.*

December 1956: *Martin Luther King calls an end to the Montgomery Bus Boycott.*

September 1957: *The "Little Rock 9" desegregate Central High School in Arkansas under escort by federal marshals and the National Guard.*

Earl M. White

Ohio Wesleyan University, 1955–1959

Fifty-five to fifty-nine, you know, we didn't have very much conversation about it. Nothing major on campus, not even in our classes. I think I was in sociology and we didn't talk about that very much. I was taking sociology a few different years there and I can't remember that much discussion about those matters even in those classes. I don't know if we had our heads in the sand or not, but even in the fraternity, we didn't talk about it very much. This was an interracial fraternity. I don't remember much conversation about it at all.

William Bright and Winfred Bowen[2]

Albion College, 1956–1960

Winfred: Discussions in class? Never.

Bill: Where I got any of that kind of conversation was in the Methodist Student Movement. That's where any of the discussions around these issues occurred, for me.

Winfred: I guess it's because we were in the sciences, and didn't take too many liberal arts courses, that those topics were never brought up in that context. It made me feel good that there were kids, students on campus, that were interested in my life, and what was going on—particularly in the fraternity. I remember this one guy; he would sit down and talk to me about what it was like being a Black person. Yeah, there were not a lot of conversations in TKE, but there was nothing that was structured. It didn't happen a lot in spite of all of the events that were going on.

Bill: I didn't have any conversations with anybody there about that. My conversations were outside of class in the Methodist Student Movement events, primarily.

Lesley Aranha

Allegheny College, 1956–1960

Not in class, but if you're sitting in the coffee shop talking to somebody, it might be something that would be talked about, because it was in the news. Kind of like, "Did you see it," kind of conversations, and "What do you think?" Matter of fact, a couple of people were going to Florida. I have relatives in Miami. "Come go with us to Florida," they said. I said, "You realize if we were to pass through the South, you all will be pulled over to the side and locked up for bringing me down there. So no, that's not a good idea." They told me, "No, that wouldn't happen." I said, "Okay, you haven't been where I've been." That was not the time for an interracial group of people to be traveling south. At the time, they were saying, "No, it wouldn't happen." They saw it in the news, but it's happening to these other people. It's not going to happen to us, they thought.

1960–1964

February 1960: *Woolworth lunch counter sit-ins in Greensboro, North Carolina, by students from North Carolina A&T and Bennett College.*

April 1960: *Student Non-Violent Coordinating Committee (SNCC) is founded at Shaw University in Raleigh, North Carolina.*

December 1960: *US Supreme Court decision in* Boynton v. Virginia *declares segregated interstate transportation unconstitutional.*

January 1961: *Hamilton Holmes and Charlayne Hunter desegregate the University of Georgia after successfully suing the university in a federal district court.*

May–November 1961: *Freedom Rides initiated to register voters in Mississippi.*

September 1962: *James Meredith desegregates Ole Miss escorted by federal marshals.*

June 11, 1963: *Vivian Malone and James Hood successfully desegregate the University of Alabama escorted by federal marshals.*

June 12, 1963: *NAACP civil rights worker Medgar Evers is assassinated on his front lawn in Jackson, Mississippi.*

August 1963: *March on Washington for Jobs and Freedom is held, organized by Bayard Rustin; Rev. Dr. Martin Luther King Jr. delivers his "I Have a Dream" speech.*

September 1963: *16th Street Church Bombing and murders of Addie Mae Collins, Denise McNair, Carole Robertson, and Cynthia Wesley in Atlanta, Georgia.*

November 1963: *President John F. Kennedy is assassinated in Dallas, Texas.*

June–August 1964: *Congress on Racial Equality (CORE) and SNCC coordinate voter registration efforts in Mississippi, known as "Freedom Summer."*

June 1964: *Civil rights workers James Chaney, Andrew Goodman, and Michael Schwerner are assassinated in Nashoba County, Mississippi.*

July 1964: *President Lyndon Johnson signs the Civil Rights Act.*

January–March 1965: *Protests and marches for voting rights in Selma, Alabama.*

February 1965: *Malcolm X is assassinated in New York City.*

March 7, 1965: *March for voting rights from Selma to Montgomery across the Edmund Pettus Bridge, known as "Bloody Sunday."*

August 1965: *President Lyndon Johnson signs the Voting Rights Act removing restrictions from voting that had been granted by the 15th and 19th Amendments to the US Constitution.*

Marylyn Harrison

Oberlin College, 1958–1962

Yes, there was a lot going on at Oberlin. I found that Oberlin was very liberal at that time. Even the kids were liberal, the students were liberal. What we ended up doing, my girlfriends and I, we went to Cleveland and did a sympathy sit-in at a Woolworth's in Cleveland. That was the best we could do at the time. I so admire the people who sacrificed their education and went south and sacrificed their lives and their health and their well-being to go south and sit-in. We were emotionally very much involved and had very strong feelings about integration and the CRM, but I think that I—and maybe some of the others—felt that the best thing that we could do would be to get our education and then go back to the community. We'd be of more use to the community with an education.

Kyle McGee

DePauw University, 1959–1963

I don't remember much activity or conversations. We rarely watched television. A lot of what was going down just never filtered into us. None of us ever even talked about going south to participate in anything. The only time in sort of a public arena that I can remember was my senior year which would be spring of '63. I took a one-hour current events course. The faculty member there raised the issue of what was going on in the

South. I was the only Black student in the class and I was the only one who had any knowledge of what was going on at the time. I think by our junior year, we began to raise some fuss about segregation in the Greek organizations. We also made some contact to try to get townspeople treated better in terms of barbershops and dining facilities and stuff. When the girls were killed in Birmingham, a small group of students at the campus organized a silent march from the homecoming game. You had about 25 people marching in the street and all this whole mob scene on the sidewalks with folks wondering what was going on. I mean, life just did not affect the campus at all. As I say, outside of that one class, I can't remember anything being brought up about racial problems or anything like that.

Anonymous

Earlham College, Early 1960s

Civil rights marches were happening over the years that we were there: freshmen, sophomore, and junior year. The protests against the House Un-American Committee were happening. Lot of new unrest about how it is that we see our world in terms of social politics and humanitarian politics and the context for both rejecting communism, as well as acceptance of some of the ideas which were popularly known as socialist ideas. One of the things that happened in 1961 was that a new Earlham political group called the Earlham Political Issues Committee, EPIC, was formed. The purpose of this group of people who stayed up all night and talked was to try to bring these transformative issues—that were happening in the world away from Earlham and sometimes at Earlham—to bring these issues to the campus through writing and meetings and inviting speakers. As a part of the student government, EPIC talked about and organized for marches and bus rides and other activities and wrote articles for the newspaper. Then we had the famous opinion board, which is a place where you post your ideas and thoughts and complaints and concerns for the whole community to see and respond to. The violence, the killings, the bombings—I would say that, maybe for reasons that are natural or maybe just because of the fact that they're so desperately alienating in terms of what do you do when somebody that you know or a group of people whose activities that you affirm have been hurt or killed? How do you find the appropriate response to that? Especially when you're at a Quaker school where nonviolence is supposedly the guiding principle, how do you respond to that? In that context, I think that what EPIC tried to do was to have deep conversations to find out more about how bad things can happen when we live unexamined lives—unexamined with respect to privilege; unexamined with respect to how it is that we will relate to one another; unexamined with respect to the meaning and the purposes of the laws that we have; unexamined with respect to what we do with the stereotypes and codes for interpreting our everyday lives. What is the meaning of Medgar Evers being shot or any of the other great leaders that were being shot and killed during the time that I was in school? Sometimes I feel that the Quaker practice which can allow you to be still for a while and think and pray and be contemplative is a good start. I don't know that there's a perfect response, but I think it's a good start.

Daniel Boggan

Albion College, 1963–1967

I was a commuter student, and on the weekends, I was a civil rights worker. I did a lot of organizing of youth chapters and college chapters while I was at Albion. The first couple years I think I spent more time doing work for the NAACP than I did anywhere else. I had a job, as well. So, I had to manage my job, I was doing organizing work, and I was a student. My sophomore year, between that and my junior year, we had gotten the Voting Rights Act passed. I figured now I could focus on being a student. My grades went up the last two years significantly. I took a hit my freshman and sophomore years because of the other activities I was involved in. One of the issues that always came up was "What's it like to be Black," you know, from the White kids, basically. Many of them had never gone to school with, back then, a Negro. I got tired of answering that question. You're a human being first. You just happen to be born a particular color. A lot of folks just didn't get that. This is not about anything other than how you treat another human being. I led a demonstration at Albion against the governor of Mississippi, Ross Barnett was his name, speaking at Albion College. You see, I was also the president of my freshman class, because I knew everybody. The chaplain wanted to make sure that he introduced me to Ross Barnett. Barnett didn't know that the president of the freshman class was Black. I'm sure he assumed that he was White. When the chaplain introduced me, Ross Barnett says, "Boy, you are in tall cotton."[3] He knew he was being offensive, but he didn't care.

It was a way of putting me down. Yeah, '63–'67. Like I said, the first two years were just hectic. You get that sense at some point, well, I can't fail. I can't allow myself to fail. The urgency, in terms of that, is that you don't want to let a whole bunch of folks down, including yourself, because of the fear of failure.

***

The Archives Speak

Although this book is driven by the oral history narratives of the 68 participants in this study, these are not the only available perspectives on issues of race and the effect of the CRM on these institutions. While some institutions were hotly debating issues of fraternity segregation and the lack of Black student enrollment as Christian duties and reflections of the national scene, other colleges were more inward focused and silent on issues of race, even when Black students became more visible on campus. This chapter introduces the "voices" of the institutional archival records at these 13 colleges in five-year spans to broaden and amplify the participant narratives that opened this chapter.

Postwar Engagement (1945–1949)

Immediately following World War II until the onset of the Korean conflict, 13 colleges in this study were varied in terms of student reflections about campus engagement with issues of race, segregation, and race relations and institutional actions related to these issues, including the presence of Black students on campus. A range of engagement is featured, from silence to limited awareness to more vocal and active engagement with campus or local issues.

The student publications of 3 of the 13 GLCA colleges—Albion, Ohio Wesleyan, and Wabash—did not include any significant discussion of race relations on campus or nationally. For example, although there were five Black students at Albion and one Black man at Wabash during this time, there were no announcements of visits by Black speakers or performers. However, 1948 witnessed contradictory images in the yearbook and newspaper files at Wabash. In the yearbook, the fraternity men of Phi Delta Theta are pictured in blackface and drag while a letter to the editor in *The Bachelor* calls upon Wabash men to "meet the challenge" and refuse to patronize local businesses practicing discrimination, illustrated by a sign in one of the local restaurants that read, "We do not cater to colored trade."[4]

Others of the GLCA colleges would be better described during this period as having limited engagement with racial issues, but greater representation of Black students in campus publications along with more contradictory messages of racist motifs. For example, at Allegheny, only one Black student was enrolled between 1945 and 1949, David Johnson, who graduated in 1947 and appeared regularly in the yearbooks while enrolled in multiple roles. Yet, a candid shot of first-year student hazing introduced the winter section of the 1948 *Kaldron* yearbook with the caption, "Aren't we all slaves?" Allegheny's student newspaper, *The Campus*, mostly featured articles about Black artists and speakers coming to campus or whose works were reviewed in the paper. There was evidence of White campus speakers who lauded the necessity of "lack of race prejudice" for future careers and side-by-side letters to the editor, one asking for less political discussion and the other advocating for the ending of segregationist practices such as poll taxes and the terrorist violence of the Ku Klux Klan (KKK).[5]

Also, at Earlham with 23 Black students, including Jamaican internationals and African Americans, students were featured across many activities, including men in athletics and men and women students in departmental clubs. Although not featured in *The Post*, faculty meeting minutes from 1947 and 1948 included the drafting and approval of the Race Relations Policy that prohibited students from taking direct action to end segregationist practices in Richmond through groups affiliated with the college and requiring minors to file written parental consent with the dean to participate in any boycotts. Instead, students were admonished to "work in the community to develop Christian social attitudes and values by means of education, rather than by requirement."

During this time, there was only one Black student at Denison University, Robert Anderson, who graduated in 1947 and is in *The Adytum* for both 1945 and 1947. Though an exchange program with Hampton University approved in November 1948[6] would bring more Black students to campus in the following period, only one other Black person was featured, an unnamed "visiting dignitary" in 1948. Native American caricatures were prevalent in the yearbooks with cartoon images of "Chief Ady-tum-tum" and "Little Chiefs" in 1946 and a large painted wooden cutout of "Big Red" with a tomahawk and football in hand and several White students posing with it in 1948. The 1949 *Adytum*, however, opens with the following statement: "To be one world, a campus must know fellowship with all races," and this edition featured the women's Shepardson Club collaboration with the men's American Commons Club—both open to Black students though neither had any at this time—to "work with an interracial group of children in Newark" (*Adytum*, 1949, p. 114), a nearby town. In *The Denisonian* student newspaper, there were three editorials specifically on racial issues and particularly how they affected Denison: (1) supporting the exchange programs with Black colleges[7]; (2) decrying the existence of prejudice on campus as a threat to Denison's ideals as a Christian college[8]; (3) asserting the possibility for a Christian college like Denison to "wage war against intolerance and misunderstanding" but only if the campus community was racially diverse.[9]

A fourth example of this pattern was Wooster, whose yearbook *The Index* highlighted the contradictions of this period. Among the Black students featured across these five years was a Black woman, Delores Fish, who was a junior in 1947 and served on the editorial staff for *The Voice*, the campus newspaper. The next year's *Index* included a picture of a women's social club's initiation ritual captioned "Master vs. Slave." That year's issue also featured the "Stage Negro Church Program" with a racial fellowship theme sponsored by the Westminster Fellowship Group held at two of the local Black churches in Wooster. Then, in 1949, the yearbook included pictures from "Hell Week" of the "Third pledges' prize blackface show" (p. 151). This ping-ponging contradiction was also evident in the campus newspaper. There was an editorial in October 1945 critical of Gary, Indiana students protesting a Black student in their school. Yet, another issue in October 1945 included an article about the end of the "girls' club" pledge period titled, "Slave masters put away whips at midnight." A December 12, 1947, cartoon showed Black African foreign exchange students cooking a White student in a large kettle, but a February 13, 1948, opinion article compared Christian proselytizing to racial supremacy doctrines and a week later Delores Fish was featured addressing the Wooster Rotary Club on racial discrimination.

At Antioch, Kenyon, and Oberlin colleges, students seemed more actively engaged with issues of segregation, discrimination, and racial prejudice, including criticizing their fellow students. Antioch did not publish a yearbook during this period and evidence of the following sentiments was not noted in the campus newspapers. However, two of the three Black students whose Senior Papers were available during this period (one each for 1946, 1948, and 1949) noted the hypocrisy of White students at Antioch.

A senior woman in 1946 had this to say about White student participation in the Race Relations Committee and NAACP chapter meetings:

> When a person says "Yes, I believe everything you say" in a meeting, and the next day calls the Negro help in the dorms by their first name or nickname and the White help by their surname in a respectable manner, I have a feeling that the meeting can't go much beyond the intellectual acceptance.

Nevertheless, Jessie Treichler and other administrators and faculty were discussing in the Admissions Committee how well racial integration was going on campus since the college redoubled its efforts to matriculate Black students. However, the authors acknowledged that social integration was "not satisfactory" due to the near absence of interracial dating among students (Treichler et al., 1947). The committee also noted that the Student Counseling office should inform incoming Black students that there were businesses in town that "do not serve Negro patrons." However, neither in these minutes nor in the other documents related to the Race Relations Committee does the college commit itself to advocating for the end of segregation in the local community. In fact, as noted in a 1950 Senior Paper, the president published a statement discouraging students from taking their interracial dating activities off campus.

At Kenyon, the 1947 *Reveille* yearbook noted that the Philomathesians, a campus literary society, who were described as "race conscious" decided to "put the Negro problem into intellectual mothballs" to focus on Buddha in April. Yet, several articles from *The Kenyon Collegian* during this span are noteworthy. An article published in late 1945 about the fraternity system suggested three reforms, the last of which was to "eliminate all feeling of social exclusiveness and racial intolerance."[10] In April 1948, a recent alumnus wrote about the brutality of the KKK in Georgia,[11] and the next month, the paper published an article announcing the "first Negro men to enter Kenyon" the following semester, referring to Allan Ballard and Stan Jackson.[12] Then in December 1948,[13] a report of the Interfraternity Council discussions noted that while 46% of chapter representatives opposed eliminating discriminatory membership clauses, over 60% of fraternity members supported such actions; the council tabled the discussion of the issue for one year. Finally, a fall 1949 editorial informed fellow students of the significant barriers that race and religion posed for prospective college students based on data that had been published by the

ACE.[14] Prior to Al's arrival on campus, Kenyon men seemed to be greatly engaged in conversation and debate about how to deal with issues of race and segregation on campus.

While Kenyon men were debating fraternity racial discrimination, segregation in local establishments, particularly barbershops, was the topic of debate at Oberlin. Baumann noted that by the early 1940s, the college was "less integrated than it had been a century before" with most of the Black and other racially minoritized students enrolled in the Graduate School of Theology and that "Jim Crowism existed in the town of Oberlin" (2010, p. 116). The *Oberlin Review* (college) and the *News-Tribune* (local) both included articles, concentrated in May 1944, about a barbershop segregation controversy concerning Vic's establishment which ended up closing in late May over the insistence that he service Black men in the shop. Vic's would reopen under new management headed by an Oberlin faculty member who intended to operate it on an interracial basis.[15] Following this controversy, students took the lead in asserting the continued relevance of Oberlin's democratic ideals. The student senate formed an Interracial Committee to pressure college administration to admit more Black students and end any discrimination against hiring Black faculty, and the campus chapter of the NAACP took on the local lunch parlors to end racial discrimination there (Baumann, 2010).

During this period, most of the GLCA colleges had at least limited engagement in conversations about racial issues through their student newspapers, clubs, campus committees, and sponsored lectures. However, talk did not always result in action and some students chided their peers and their institutions for not living up to their espoused values. Moreover, at several colleges, campus discussions supporting integration and student activities using racist motifs presented contradictory impressions.

Turning Inward (1950–1954)

The next five years contained few national highlights. In fact, the *Brown* decision is not announced until the middle of the final year in this span. From the participants' reflections on this period, including those graduating between 1952 and 1956, it seems that little was discussed on campus concerning race, integration, or civil rights. In light of this, the publication of blackface and other racist motifs without any counterpoints suggests several colleges were potentially hostile places.

In spite of this general characterization, there were two colleges that seemed to simply move along steadily with advocacy for changes in institutional policy or greater integration of Black students in campus activities. The 1950 *Hi-O-Hi* at Oberlin noted that the college's Interracial Committee was focused on altering admissions policies to increase the numbers of Black students on campus and ending first-year student rooming segregation.[16] Also, Fisk and Talladega were added to the institution's Black college semester exchange program.[17] Down state at Ohio Wesleyan, Black students were represented increasingly in music and drama, honorary societies, a social fraternity (Beta Sigma Tau, "founded on principles of racial equality," 1953 *Le Bijou*), and the Century Club that helped recruit new students. The 1952 *Le Bijou* included a "problem play," *Deep Are the Roots*, that was presented by the Wesleyan Players that dealt "realistically" with racial prejudice in the Deep South; three Black students were actors in leading roles. A Black woman was a candidate for homecoming queen that year and other Black women were also included in the women's glee club, intramural track and tennis teams, the modern dance organization, and Cosmodelphia (the Independent Women's Association). A Black man, Butler A. Jones, joined the sociology faculty, and is featured in *Le Bijou* in both 1953 and 1954, first as a visiting faculty member and then as an associate professor.

While limited in the previous period, these five years saw much greater representation of celebrations by White students in blackface, usually with limited or total absence of discussion of any issues related to race, integration, minstrelsy, or blackface. The introductory pages of the 1951 *Albionian* includes a choir of White men in blackface. There were at least six Black students on the campus that year. *The Pleiad* did print two advance notices[18] of the upcoming second annual performance by the Albion a capella choir, promising in its first article that it would be "a minstrel show with all the trimmings."

The Denison *Adytum* editions from 1950 to 1954 span the years of enrollment for the first Black woman to graduate from Denison, Florida Fisher, who came to Denison in the fall of 1949 from Durham, North Carolina. Joining Florida in the 1950 *Adytum* is a photograph of a blackface performance on campus. There is no other blackface during these years, but the 1951 *Adytum* does feature the return of Native American imagery related to the campus mascot, Big Red, including tomahawks, peace pipes, and teepees. At Hope, both White men and women performers in blackface were included in the 1950 *Milestone* on the Omicron

Kappa Epsilon page and the 1953 edition on the Kappa Beta Phi page from their masquerade event. Although Denison's newspaper does take up fraternity racial exclusion during this period (see discussion below), Hope's student newspaper includes no coverage at all of critical issues from March 1949 through October 1957.

For the remaining two colleges, Kalamazoo and Wooster, blackface minstrel shows appear nestled among other features of racial diversity and messages against racial prejudice. At Kalamazoo, more racially minoritized students, including international students from Asia, Latin America, and Africa, are noted in the campus yearbooks and an Asian American faculty member has joined the political science department in the 1951 *Boiling Pot*. Black and White students are pictured together in comfortable poses with arms draped on each other's shoulders in 1952. Yet that year also begins the annual inclusion through 1955 of the Century Jamboree[19] minstrel show. Singers, including whole choirs of White men in blackface, are prominently displayed. In an article from 1953,[20] the Century minstrel show is included as one of the examples of the ways that "society life" benefits the entire college by providing "apportunities [*sic*] for members to show their talent."

Meanwhile, at The College of Wooster, Black students were exceedingly few in number, no more than three in any given year, and there were no Black faculty or staff. Wooster's fraternities and sororities were local organizations, unaffiliated with a national group, but strongly represented on campus.[21] In the 1950 *Index*, the groups commonly adopted racialized rhetoric: pledges who "slave for their master" (p. 37); "Indian blankets" and "war paint" (p. 40); dressing in "real Egyptian style" (p. 45); and "dressed as darkies for a skit in the Union" (p. 46). Dr. Howard Thurman visited in the 1951–1952 academic year, and the 1952 *Index* featured his visit and noted that "a great majority of the students felt the presence of a sincere and devoted Christian … who aided many to make a new commitment" (p. 133), yet, the following year, "three blackfaced Bowman girls polish boots at the YWCA carnival to earn money for their dorm" (*Index*, 1953, p. 175). The only discussion of racial issues in *The Voice* during this period is an editorial published after the *Brown* decision that argues that "segregation is an evil that should be rectified as soon as possible," but disputes that it is unconstitutional, upholding the philosophical argument that legal separation by race is not inherently an assertion of inferiority.[22]

Three of the colleges were dealing with fraternity racial exclusion policies during this period. At Denison, this was occurring contemporaneously with the use of blackface by its fraternal groups as noted above. Consistent with a new editorial policy,[23] in place of discussion of national issues were opinions and perspectives on college racial segregation and the HBCU exchange program. A March 1950 article reported that two-thirds of the Denison student body, numbered at 891, wanted the "White clause" repealed from the constitutions of college fraternities and sororities.[24]

Similarly at Allegheny, newspaper coverage mostly related to discrimination in fraternities. Early in 1950, a magazine article is reported as having attacked fraternities for religious discrimination.[25] In 1951, the Dean of Students said that discrimination in fraternities was "bad" and supported local autonomy from national membership directives, but resisted making policy for the campus.[26] Later that fall, an editorial urged local fraternity chapters to purge their discriminatory practices.[27] The campus falls silent about this issue for three years until November 1954, when an earnest editorial rejects the continued discrimination against Black men in six of seven fraternities and against Jewish students in two of seven.[28] This editorial is followed in the succeeding weeks by letters to the editor from faculty[29] and a student[30] in support of the editorial. Only one letter to the editor is published defending the fraternities, saying that students should have the right to choose their friends without being dictated to by others.[31]

Like Allegheny, there were very few Black men on Kenyon's campus and featured in *The Reveille* between 1950 and 1953. These men were active in athletics and other student clubs and organizations on campus, but not fraternities at this time. *The Collegian* again published debates concerning racial and religious exclusion in the fraternities, but not until 1954. Perhaps inspired by the *Brown* decision and using the term "discrimination" on this topic for the first time, a straw vote was scheduled to allow fraternity chapters to determine their own membership without consideration of national organizations' exclusion clauses.[32] An editorial by the news editor urged his peers to vote on moral grounds in favor of autonomy. The outcome of the vote was not reported until October[33]; it passed nearly unanimously but no action had been taken on it.

For students at Antioch, DePauw, Earlham, and Wabash, the 1951–1954 period included great disappointment with institutional inaction or regressive actions that undermined progress toward racial justice. These students, particularly Black students at Antioch and DePauw, had harsh words for their college administrations. The disappointment of Antiochian Black students in the failure of their college to practice their ideals continues into this five-year span. A senior man wrote the following in his 1953 Senior Paper:

> I came to Antioch in the hope of seeing an interracial student body, but found that we were represented in name only. I hoped to find a representation of Negroes large enough to afford me an opportunity to choose friends, possibly a wife, and I did not find it. I hoped to find in Antioch a place where I could study and work as an individual, and found that I was once more educating whites to Negroes, and a real curio to many people.

This sentiment was echoed the previous year by a woman in her 1952 paper where she asserted that a Black student's Antioch education "adds more to his [*sic*] marginality than to his personal effectiveness" and concluded that "Antioch is <u>not</u> an inter-racial college" (emphasis in the original).

Robert Smithey, who was president of the Council on Minority Problems, in 1950 wrote the most damning piece coming out of this period in *The DePauw*:

> Negro girls are not admitted to DePauw for lack of housing accommodations. That is, it is not deemed advisable to admit them to residency in the girls' dormitories. Why? Among other things, there is a possibility that Negro boys would call on them, and thus expose themselves to seeing their fairer classmates too often and on a too personal basis. The nightmare of miscegenation hangs like a sword of Damocles over the elimination of this barrier.[34]

According to Smithey's analysis, Black women were excluded from pursuing a college education at DePauw to safeguard White women's purity from the threatening sexual potency of Black men. There is no evidence of an institutional response to this charge and no further commentary about it. The first Black woman would not matriculate to DePauw until 1955, despite a report a year following Smithey's letter of the findings of a poll showing the majority of students would room with a Black student, patronize a local shop that also served Black people, and affirmed the admission of Black students to the institution.[35]

At Earlham and Wabash, alumni and current students challenged institutional policies restricting interracial engagement and nondiscrimination. The Earlham college community—extending to the senior administration and alumni—was embroiled in a debate concerning interracial dating and marriage.[36] College policy discouraged interracial dating due to the "hardships" incurred. As Edd Lee's narrative in Chap. 6 illustrated, along with stories shared by other Earlham participants, that policy was frequently ignored by students. In 1950, two students, who were seemingly prohibited from continuing their studies on campus—a Black man and a White woman[37]—were the subject of many letters between the president and various alumni and fellow students. Two years later, this situation repeats itself, but this time with a Black woman and a White man, who actually married while they were students. Again, the man leaves campus to finish his degree by correspondence and there is a flurry of correspondence from alumni to the president urging him to reconsider his position, asserting the college's policy against interracial relationships is contrary to Quaker principles and "un-Christian." These situations put Earlham in the national news with reporting done in newspapers from Ithaca to San Francisco and throughout Indiana.

Further west, at Wabash, a photo in the 1951 yearbook showed the college welcome entrance decorated with large wooden, painted caricatures of Black people with stereotypically large lips, bones through their noses dressed in top hats, polka dot bow ties, grass skirts, and dress shoes with spats. *The Bachelor* printed a critique in 1954 of the fraternity system, noting racial discrimination as one of "two great defects" but which is "forced" on chapters by national constitutions or alumni pressures.[38] The author suggested that "unfortunately" Wabash college administrators were unlikely to require the college's fraternity chapters to end racial exclusion clauses as had been done at other colleges.[39] There is no other indication of social or political topics being discussed on campus. This is consistent with Karl's narrative in Chap. 7 that there was nothing to talk about and a campus mindset that may not have been attuned to these issues at this time.

Across the colleges, student opinion favored ending segregationist practices, especially within the fraternity and sorority systems, as well as in support of interracial housing and romance. Participant reflections, though, show that these sentiments were not carried out in practice as Black women mostly went without dates and both Black men and women continued to be absent from fraternities and sororities. The appearance of blackface at six colleges,[40] long out of public use by the 1920s and perceived as offensive and racist by Black Americans (Lott, 1993/2013), also represents a contradiction to these espoused values of unity and kinship, albeit perhaps an unconscious one. Finally, some institutions were challenged to set college policy that would serve as an ethical guide for students. At times, it seemed that students and faculty were clearer about what changes needed to occur than senior administrators, who were far more cautious and conservative.

Comfort and Incredulity (1955–1959)

Silence about national issues continued in classrooms and informal student conversations even as the CRM began to spread and strengthen in the aftermath of the *Brown* decision and Black matriculation increased. For instance, at Albion, the number of Black students on campus as reflected in the *Albionian* increases during this time frame. By their senior year, when the full record of student involvement is included in the senior profile pictures, these students have been engaged in a cross section of student activities from civic and religious activities to independent social clubs, academic honoraries, and athletics (among the men). Yet, neither *The Albionian* nor *The Pleiad* note or feature any campus or national issues related to race relations, during this time, despite the increasing visibility of efforts to enforce desegregation across the South. Down in Ohio, even at Oberlin, which continued boasting the largest enrollment of Black students, numbering 44 in the 1955 *Hi-O-Hi*, no significant issues of discrimination, segregation, or civil rights activism among students were apparent in the *Oberlin Review*. The *Kenyon Collegian* also printed nothing of relevance to issues of race relations during this period, other than an article summarizing a speech given by Charles S. Johnson, the president of Fisk University, to the student assembly asserting that desegregation was inevitable, rejecting the "eventualism" philosophy attached to the *Brown* decision, and predicting the likelihood that Black voters would use the fall election as an opportunity to further integration.[41]

At some campuses, this silence was accompanied by continued use of blackface by White fraternity and sorority groups, such as at Denison, Hope, Kalamazoo, and Ohio Wesleyan. For example, the 1956 and 1957 editions of Denison's *Adytum* both included White women, members of Kappa Kappa Gamma, in blackface during rush activities (1956, p. 34; 1957, p. 25). The 1957 *Adytum* contains two other instances of cultural appropriation and mockery: members of Kappa Alpha Theta did a performance in yellowface[42] (p. 77) and the Delta Gamma's Novelty Party included a skit from *Show Boat* performed in blackface (p. 86). The situation at Hope is similar; *The Milestone* included photographs of fraternity and sorority members giving blackface performances in the 1956, 1957, and 1958 editions. Blackface performances bookend the Ohio Wesleyan yearbooks from this time span and are included in the 1955 *Boiling Pot* at Kalamazoo.

The provocative issues raised by some student newspaper editors may not have been taken up in casual conversations between most of the participants and their White peers. For example, desegregating the fraternities and sororities on campus was the topic of much conversation early in 1955 in the student newspaper at Allegheny. In February, *The Campus* reported that the college's Interfraternity Council (IFC) issued a recommendation to its member fraternities to end racial and religious discrimination in membership.[43] Although both support and opposition are expressed, articles from the rest of the period indicate that no action was taken to actually remove racial and religious clauses from fraternal groups until 1959. The next year an editorial from February 1956[44] decried the mob violence that surrounded Autherine Lucy's failed attempt to desegregate the University of Alabama and called for Allegheny students, "the majority of us here believe in Brotherhood," to remove discriminatory clauses from national fraternal organizations and to protest Meadville businesses "where discrimination is practiced." There are no other articles printed in *The Campus* concerning discrimination and segregation until February 1959,[45] reporting the Human Relations Committee's request that students report any instances of discrimination against Allegheny students to be shared with college administrators.

At other colleges, articles reporting student discussion and initiatives to push institutional change also did not necessarily lead to action. At DePauw, articles from December 1955 noted that the Sigma Chi fraternity had been hosting a series of discussions about minority problems in collaboration with the university's Committee on Human Relations and reporting that a petition may be circulated to "show student concern about the discrimination problem of some downtown merchants."[46] The newspaper covered debate about the nondiscrimination resolution that spring with the faculty approval of the statement the top headline for its February 22, 1956, issue.[47] The following academic year saw the student senate pass proposals brought by another Black student to study discrimination at DePauw with the intention of using that information to develop "an enforceable policy, correcting weaknesses now present."[48]

No evidence of the college's adoption of the policy was apparent in the paper. Similarly at Earlham, the Race Relations file in the college archives showed that the college's interracial dating policy, still in the college bulletin, continued to be questioned by those both external[49] and internal to the college.[50] The Earlham *Post*'s articles concerning segregation in this period mainly focused externally and shared reflections and perspectives from others about the situation in the South.

At Wabash, students sought to take action themselves and used the campus newspaper to hold debates. For example, perhaps ignited by the anticipated presence of two Black men on campus (including Robert Wedgeworth)—the first since James Perry graduated in 1947—the fraternity racial exclusion issue is prominently featured throughout the spring 1955 semester at Wabash. Beginning in February 1955, five issues of *The Bachelor* printed campus discussions of this topic, including a report of Senior Council tabling a resolution to take a stand against discriminatory fraternity clauses[51]; a local organization refusing to criticize fraternities for discrimination[52]; an editorial advising caution in overzealously pursuing removing such clauses in the absence of chapter autonomy[53]; and several letters to the editors on both sides of the issue from faculty, students, and an alumnus.[54] The final issue, containing a letter from an alumnus ("an old abhorrer [of discrimination] from way back"[55]) suggesting that alumni opinions be procured before any action is taken, also includes a cartoon[56] of two White men with one pointing with his thumb to a Black man drawn naked in just a loincloth, barefoot, and adorned with a necklace and anklets on each leg. The cartoon's caption reads, "...Ed, this is our new admissions counselor for the Uganda district."[57]

Generally, GLCA students appeared to continue to focus on internal campus issues of challenging the enactment of ideals of integration and equality, mainly concerning fraternal organizations. There was little engagement directly with national issues or even local community issues beyond the immediate confines of the towns in which these institutions were located as an Earlham student shared would be attempted there through EPIC's activities in the 1960s. Only at Allegheny was the student newspaper editor speaking about Black students' efforts to desegregate southern colleges and universities in relation to their own duties as citizens. Moreover, campus discussions of desegregation were taking place at some colleges contemporaneous with White students gleefully performing in blackface and mobilizing other racial caricatures and motifs. Instead of an "illusion of pause" or a "momentary calm between storms" as some asserted to explain the silence of the 1950s (Baumann, 2010, p. 167), colleges like Allegheny, Earlham, Wabash, and Kenyon were deeply engaged in internal storms that pit personal and institutional values of Christian community against confronting social mores and municipal policies.

Activist Students (1960–1965)

The institutional variances that marked the first 15 years disappear in the last 5 years. The civil disobedience of Bennett College and North Carolina A&T students in Greensboro and the founding of SNCC ignited direct action by college students across the country (Anderson, 1995; Carson, 1981; Halberstam, 1998). This activist spirit was reflected among the students, Black and White, at the GLCA colleges as well. As these colleges entered the 1960s, enrollment of Black students begins to swell and these increases are visible in the campus yearbooks across the board, except at Denison, which continued to see single-digit full-time enrollment of Black students. Whether fraternity and sorority blackface performances continued during these years is unknown, but they are no longer featured in any college yearbooks.

Speaking of the fraternal system, the question of racial exclusion clauses begins to be settled in this period at Wabash and Kenyon. In 1961, Wabash's President Trippett announced a new fraternity policy[58] that included forbidding any campus student organization that practices racial discrimination from establishing a chapter at Wabash. Kappa Sigma would "declare war" on its national organization, deciding to pledge whomever they wanted without regard to race in spring 1964.[59] At Kenyon in 1963, *The Collegian* published the Interfraternity Council's decision to approve an anti-bias rule for the campus fraternity chapters.[60] Although there were not suddenly Black students in every fraternity and sorority at these colleges, institutional policy and lack of local autonomy were no longer justifications for racial exclusions.

These colleges also turned their focus outward and began to learn about and reflect on civil rights activism. This often took the form of letters back to campus from White students in the South participating in voting rights initiatives. For example, at Denison, a White student on exchange to Fisk wrote back to his peers about what was happening in Nashville and his involvement in support of civil rights actions.[61] At Kenyon, *The Collegian* published two conflicting reports in the same issue on the second march to Selma, led by Dr. King.[62] One was from two students there to support

Black voting rights; the other was from a student opposing these outside "agitators." Wabash student David Kendall, a participant in Freedom Summer under training with Andrew Goodman, sent a letter about his experience, including being jailed for his activities.[63] A student publication, *The Activist*, began quarterly publication in October 1960 in Oberlin, Ohio, as an independent outlet of the Midwestern Student Coordinating Committee.[64] Member colleges from among the GLCA included Wooster, Ohio Wesleyan, Denison, Antioch, Earlham, and Oberlin.[65]

Support for organizations and individuals engaged in direct action was also evident at many of the colleges. Oberlin student Adine Ray Usher shared in her interview that she was very involved, especially in her last two years, 1959–1961: "I was president of the college NAACP [chapter] for the last two years, that last year was the year of the Greensboro sit-ins. In one week's time, we raised $3000.00." At Wooster, *The Voice* reported that a November 1963 "freedom" drive recruited 60 students as new members in the NAACP.[66] Wabash organized a campus chapter of Congress of Racial Equality (CORE) in May 1963,[67] but after gaining strength and more members that fall,[68] and a plea for broader campus support from its president, Frank Starkey,[69] the group's "obituary" was printed in December of the same year.[70]

Students, Black and White, also participated in direct actions in support of civil rights in their local communities. At Kalamazoo, the *Index* reported in October 1963 that mostly first-year students joined with local citizens in an interracial march for equal employment opportunities sponsored by the NAACP, the Kalamazoo City Council of Churches, and numerous religious, political, and social organizations.[71] The following March, students at Antioch demonstrated against discrimination in Yellow Springs resulting in violent confrontations with police and the arrest of several students.[72] The next month, Albion College took the unusual step of making student attendance voluntary at the convocation talk to be given by Governor Ross Barnett[73] and, as noted in Daniel Boggan's narrative in this chapter, Albion students protested his visit.

Not all campuses would engage in the CRM from a progressive or liberal stance. At Hope College, an editorial in October 1964[74] supported George Romney's write-in presidential bid and noted that *The Anchor* had been "basically conservative and Republican in its political outlook" for the past three years and it would "remain so for at least one more year." Not surprisingly then, there is no student opinion reported in the newspaper about civil rights until 1965, indicating a possible change in editorial leadership.[75] That spring semester, ten articles[76] were printed covering various news reports about voting rights activities, opinion pieces about the effectiveness of protest, and reflections from Talladega students in the semester exchange program. As Faye Hines, at Hope from 1963 to 1967, shared with me, there were no conversations about what was happening in the country related to the CRM. When SNCC leader John Lewis spoke in Grand Rapids, she said there was no announcement on campus; she and a friend left on their own to hear him.

Conclusion

The yearbooks, newspapers, and other archival materials reveal different ways that these nearly totally White student bodies and college administrations shaped institutional racial climates. The yearbooks were generally sites of whiteness as property for White students' use and enjoyment, where Black students were mainly featured only when they happened to be engaged in activities already in use by and for White students. The display of racial caricatures and blackface performances at certain campuses during the 1950s communicated a racial hostility that, whether consciously intended or not, clearly marked fraternity and sorority spaces as "White only."

Through the (dis)engagement with campus, local, and national issues concerning race relations and campus policies governing interracial relationships and participation in local activism, institutions were inclusive and affirming, open but ambivalent, or closed and threatening. At times, institutions were sending deeply conflicting messages, such as at Earlham whose Quaker principles and practice flatly contradicted its prohibition of student involvement in protests against discrimination in Richmond and enacted prohibition of interracial romance between students. Antioch was in a similar situation as Black students clearly saw through the college's progressive rhetoric to the realities of racial prejudices enacted by students and institutional complicity with locally practiced segregation and discrimination. Generally, institutional leaders were caught between customary prejudices and the high ideals of their institution's religious principles. Students seemed eager to offer vocal support to racial equality, but were ill-equipped—and not challenged—to carry out that support in practice.

For their part, many of these Black students felt their presence on these campuses was itself direct action in support of racial equality for the majority of this time period. It was not until the 1960s that Black students began to make demands on their colleges and seek to actively support southern Black resistance for equality.

Notes

1. Robinson was signed by the Dodgers' owner, Branch Rickey, an Ohio Wesleyan alumnus.
2. William (Bill) Bright and Winfred Bowen did their interview together with another student who wished their participation to remain confidential. To preserve their confidentiality, their comments are not included in this portion of the narrative.
3. This colloquialism, being "in tall cotton," refers to being wealthy or well-off; having the best of times.
4. [Letter to the editor], B. L. Vogel, 5/21/1948, *The Bachelor*, p. 2.
5. "Representative of National Nursing Council on campus," 10/12/1944, *The Campus*, p. 1. Cardozo, G. H., & Salitan, L., 3/12/1947, Letters to the editor, *The Campus*, p. 2.
6. Memo dated November 13, 1948. Hampton Exchange Program, 1949–1953 (Folder 12DEx). Denison University Archives.
7. "How about Negroes?," P. Cober, 5/2/1947, *The Denisonian*, p. 2.
8. "Ideals under fire," H. Kavan, 2/20/1948, *The Denisonian*, p. 2.
9. "Our Christian college within a world hampered by prejudice," B. Callaway, 2/18/1949, *The Denisonian*, p. 2.
10. "The fraternity crisis," S. E. Perry, 12/14/1945, *The Collegian*, p. 1.
11. "James Bellows tells of KKK brutality to newspapermen," J. Bellows, 4/16/1948, *The Collegian*, pp. 1, 4.
12. "First Negro men to enter Kenyon next semester," 5/21/1948, *The Collegian*, pp. 1, 3. Ballard and Jackson were actually not the very first men of African descent to matriculate to Kenyon. There are records of an African student, a prince, who was enrolled at Kenyon in the late nineteenth century and died while at the school. He is buried in the campus graveyard.
13. "Poll reveals Kenyon frats more liberal than average," 12/17/1948, *The Collegian*, p. 1.
14. "Race and religion barriers for prospective collegians," 11/11/1949, *The Collegian*.
15. *Oberlin Times*, 6/8/1944.

16. A practice that was not fully ended even when Adine Ray Usher matriculated in 1957. Although asking all incoming students if they would be open to an international or interracial roommate experience, housing assignments were still being made with a race-conscious approach.
17. Baumann (2010), A White student makes his case to participate in Black college exchange program, 1958. Document 19.
18. "College choir to give second minstrel show," 1/5/1951, *The Pleiad*. [No title], 1/12/1951, *The Pleiad.*
19. By 1954 and 1955, this event would be called the Century Showboat.
20. "Society life beneficial to total college," T. Lemon, 2/25/1953, *The Index*, p. 2.
21. The yearbook in 1951 informed readers that "96 of 147 sophomore women pledge" (*Index*, 1951, p. 66).
22. *The Voice*, 5/21/1954, p. 2.
23. Editorial, J. Richards, 1/13/1950, *The Denisonian*, p. 2.
24. "Favor repeal of 'White clause,'" 3/3/1950, *The Denisonian*, p. 1.
25. "Fraternities attacked in magazine article, charge: Un-democratic," 1/19/1950, *The Campus*, p. 3.
26. "McCracken expresses views on fraternities, government," 9/27/1951, *The Campus*, pp. 1, 3.
27. "Toward Men," Editorial, 12/13/1951, *The Campus*, p. 2.
28. "Discrimination," Editorial, 11/14/1954, *The Campus*, p. 2.
29. [Letter to the editor], 11/11/1954, *The Campus*, p. 2.
30. [Letter to the editor], 11/18/1954, *The Campus*, p. 2.
31. [Letter to the editor], 12/9/1954, *The Campus*, p. 2.
32. "Discrimination vote set for Tuesday," 5/21/1954, *The Collegian*, pp. 1, 3; Editorial, P.J.P., 5/21/1954, *The Collegian*, p. 2.
33. "Kenyon College marks time; Williams abolishes discrimination," 10/14/1954, *The Collegian*, p. 2.
34. [Letter to the editor], R. Smithey, 5/1/1950, *The DePauw*, pp. 2, 4.
35. "Council on Religious Life releases Negro poll report," 3/2/1951, *The DePauw*, p. 3.
36. All information about these issues comes out of the Earlham College Race Relations File obtained from the college archives.
37. In the interest of student privacy and because their names were not included in public records, I am choosing to withhold their names in this discussion.

38. “On the defensive,” A. Dewey, 4/23/1954, *The Bachelor*, p. 2.
39. Ibid.
40. Albion, Denison, Hope, Kalamazoo, Wabash, and Wooster.
41. “Integration and the election,” C. S. Johnson [reprint], 3/16/1956, *The Collegian*, p. 3.
42. Yellowface is the mocking impersonation of Asian people.
43. “Non-discrimination policy recommended by IFC,” 2/24/1955, *The Campus*, p. 1.
44. “Beacon of brotherhood,” [Editorial], 2/23/1956, *The Campus*, p. 2.
45. “Committee reports presented at ASG,” 2/27/1959, *The Campus*, p. 1.
46. “Pharr to lead second minority discussion at Sig house Tuesday,” 12/12/1955, *The DePauw*, p. 1. “Minority group committee may circulate petition,” 12/14/1955, *The DePauw*, p. 1.
47. “Campus weighs pros, cons of discrimination resolution,” 2/17/1956, *The DePauw*, p. 1. “Faculty approves proposed statement on discrimination,” 2/22/1956, *The DePauw*, p. 1.
48. “Senate takes action on racial problems,” G. Dodd, 4/19/1957, *The DePauw*, p. 1.
49. R. Huff (1956, January 6). Letter to J. C. Furnas. Race Relations File. Earlham College Archival Collection.
50. Earlham Human Relations Committee. (1957, February 8). Memo to Earlham Board of Trustees. Race Relations File. Earlham College Archival Collection.
51. “Senior Council tables fraternity controversy,” 2/11/1955, *The Bachelor*, p. 1.
52. “Blue Key refuses to hit Greeks on discrimination,” 2/11/1955, *The Bachelor*, p. 1.
53. “In the chapel, precipitation” [Editorial], 2/11/1955, *The Bachelor*, p. 2.
54. Letter to the editor, B. Rogge, 2/25/1955, *The Bachelor*, p. 2. Letter to the editor, R. Caplan, 2/25/1955, *The Bachelor*, pp. 2, 4. Letter to the editor, J. Wendon, 2/25/1955, *The Bachelor*, p. 4. Letter to the editor, R. Caplan, 3/11/1955, *The Bachelor*, pp. 2, 4. Letter to the editor, J. Wendon, 3/11/1955, p. 4. Letter to the editor, J. V. Scott, 26, 4/15/1955, *The Bachelor*, p. 2.
55. Letter to the editor, J. V. Scott, 26, 4/15/1955, *The Bachelor*, p. 2.

56. [Cartoon], 4/15/1955, *The Bachelor*, p. 2.
57. Ibid.
58. "The residential college" [Editor's notes], 5/8/1961, *The Bachelor*, p. 2.
59. "K-Sigs declare war on national organization," 5/8/1964, *The Bachelor*, pp. 1, 4.
60. "IFC approves anti-bias rule," 12/6/1963, *The Collegian*, p. 1.
61. "Nye gives personal account of happenings in Nashville," J. Nye, 3/18/1960, *The Denisonian*, p. 3.
62. "Two conflicting reports on Selma march," J. Allerdrie & N. Levin also W. R. Butt, *The Collegian*, pp. 1, 7.
63. Letter to the editor, D. Kendall, 9/25/1964, *The Bachelor*, p. 2.
64. *The Activist*, vol. 1, no. 1, October 1960.
65. Ibid, p. 3.
66. "'Freedom' drive begins; sixty enroll in NAACP," 11/22/1963, *The Voice*, p. 1.
67. "WCORE approves principles, charter for organization," 5/3/1963, *The Voice*, p. 1.
68. "WCORE gathers force, members," 9/27/1963, *The Voice*, p. 1.
69. "Starkey: WCORE needs more help," 10/5/1963, *The Voice*, p. 2.
70. "Around the big campus," 12/13/1963, *The Voice*, p. 2.
71. "K citizens stage march to urge job equality," 10/10/1963, *Index*, p. 1.
72. Report to the Antioch community from the Student Personnel Committee, 6/9/1964. File 2: Race relations – general historical information. Antiochiana: Antioch College Archives.
73. "Barnett convocation to be voluntary," 4/24/1964, *The Pleiad*, p. 1.
74. [Editorial], 10/16/1964, *The Anchor*, p. 7.
75. At these colleges, the newspaper editor changed over in January in the middle of the academic year.
76. Referencing the following issue dates: 2/19/1965, 3/12/1965, 4/9/1965, 4/16/1965, 4/23/1965 [3 articles], 4/23/1965, 4/30/1965, 5/7/1965 [6 articles], 5/14/1965.

References

Anderson, T. H. (1995). *The movement and the sixties: Protest in America from Greensboro to Wounded Knee.* New York, NY: Oxford University Press.

Baumann, R. M. (2010). *Constructing Black education at Oberlin College: A documentary history*. Athens: Ohio University Press.

Carson, C. (1981). *In struggle: SNCC and the Black awakening of the 1960s*. Cambridge, MA: Harvard University Press.

Earlham Human Relations Committee. (1957, February 8). *Memo to Earlham Board of Trustees. Race Relations File*. Friends Collection and College Archives, Earlham Libraries, Earlham College, Richmond, IN.

Halberstam, D. (1998). *The children*. New York, NY: Fawcett Books.

Huff, R. (1956, January 6). Letter to J. C. Furnas. *Race Relations File*. Friends Collection and College Archives, Earlham Libraries, Earlham College, Richmond, IN.

Lewis, J., & D'Orso, M. (1998). *Walking with the wind: A memoir of the movement*. New York, NY: Harcourt Brace & Co.

Lott, E. (2013). *Love and theft: Blackface minstrelsy and the American working class* (20th anniversary ed.). Oxford, England: Oxford University Press. (Original work published in 1993).

Treichler, J., Hollister, H., & Lemcke. (1947, May 13). *Memorandum from race relations committee. Race relations – Jessie Treichler's File 2/14/1951*. Antiochiana, Olive Kettering Library, Antioch College, Yellow Springs, OH.

CHAPTER 9

The Impact of College

Fern Brown

Albion College, 1956–1960

Let me put it this way. I have no regrets about having gone to school there. The college had, and I guess still has, a very excellent reputation academically. Considering that I moved to a larger Midwestern city, the name Albion College has made a difference in that way, in terms of going further in higher education. I did my master's at the University of Chicago from the school of education. I think it made a difference that I received my bachelor's at Albion.

Betty Johnson

Allegheny College, 1955–1959

I feel that I got an outstanding education. I feel that it helped me to think critically. It was a very, very important part of my life. I'm very happy that I had that experience, with the exception of not being able to be fully a

The ten narratives in this chapter, presented alphabetically by institution, reflect the breadth of responses I received from participants when I asked them what role their college had played in their lives or what difference their college had made in their lives.

© The Author(s) 2017

D.-L. Stewart, *Black Collegians' Experiences in US Northern Private Colleges*, DOI 10.1057/978-1-137-59077-0_9

part of the campus because of the sorority situation. Everything else was great. I was not all that active in high school, but I was certainly active when I got to college. I felt fully accepted by anything that I wanted to do. I didn't feel like I had to fight for anything or struggle about anything.

Willis "Bing" Davis

DePauw University, 1955–1959

I was able to formulate a sensitivity—an African American and Afrocentric sensitivity—in spite of certain kinds of situations that would seemingly not nurture it. By that I mean, I came from a small enclave, attended a school with limited African American experiences in high school, and then went to a place like DePauw. DePauw helped me realize that learning was a lifelong pursuit. I saw a lot of intelligent and highly academically successful students, older and younger, and I saw how they studied. I saw what they did. I saw how they presented information and I was always looking and listening.

Chuck and Ruth Ann Hatcher[1]

Earlham College, 1963–1966 and 1964–1968

C: For me, Earlham made every difference, because I was lost at Ohio State. I gained my footing because of people at Earlham. There were some professors who were very mentoring and supportive. They didn't have much experience with Black people, but they weren't mean. They were a little ignorant, but they weren't mean, and very curious, I think, in some ways.

RA: When you say you went to Earlham, the people who know Earlham have a lot of respect for that. When I got a Danforth fellowship and said I'd gone to Earlham, it was like the door opened. That's really all I needed to say to get the fellowship was that I had gone to Earlham. It makes you a hippie for the rest of your life. I don't know how else to say that, but it does. Quakers are weird and different; it's a nice perspective, even if I'm not a Quaker. It is a grounding experience to be around Quakers. I learned what it really means to govern by consensus. I think that's a real advantage in this world to have that Quaker experience.

Larry Browning

Earlham College, 1962–1966

That man, my advisor, changed and transformed where my life was headed in a way like no one else has. No other human being has impacted me that way. It was only because of my presence at Earlham did that happen to me. My first advisor—I hadn't done well in her classes at all—she wouldn't sign my registration materials to continue as a biology major. I told her I wanted to become a dentist. She told me, "You may be better off getting a degree and being a coach or something." I wanted to be a dentist and I knew I needed to take biology, chemistry, and physics, and all that good stuff. Getting a change of advisors was essential for me and getting the particular advisor I had—it was just the miracle of miracles. I'm probably the only Earlham student, Black or White, who flunked out of Earlham, got back in, and went on to earn two doctorates, a doctorate of education from Harvard and a doctorate of dental medicine from Tufts. I went ahead and became the dentist that I always wanted to be.

Sybil Jordan Hampton

Earlham College, 1962–1966

I would say that Earlham was a pivotal experience where I had the opportunity to develop after that kind of shrinkage during my high school years. I learned an awful lot about lots of different types of people. I had my great stretching academically and intellectually there. Socially, I blossomed there. I learned so much about leadership from the wonderful role models that I had. I had the opportunity to live with faculty families, because during that time students could live during the year with faculty families. It was very important to be in those homes and to have the kinds of nurturing that one would have in a home setting as opposed to being in the dorm. That was very, very important to me to have that nurturing. I think that Earlham tested and reinforced the values that were very important to my family. That was really good. It made me a citizen of the world.

Tanya Summers

Kalamazoo College, 1963–1967

I credit Kalamazoo with having gotten a good education, being able to write well, and to think critically. As I look back, my experience of myself was that I was not a good student. That's evident in my transcript. When I look back at the actual work, the quality is amazing. Especially compared to what I see nowadays with graphic art students. It's shocking. Evidently, whatever the quality of work that we were doing was significant. I have been able to have reasonably good professional positions—administrative positions and faculty positions—with that background. I never thought I could do graduate work because I always had a C average at Kalamazoo College. I never had any problems in graduate school at all. I think when I worked on my master's, I might have earned one B and the same for the doctorate. Evidently, I had a good foundation.

Robert Bennett

Kenyon College, 1950–1954

I think Kenyon was pivotal. The Ivies didn't take me and they did. I learned a lot at Kenyon. It was a small liberal arts college. I had an excellent, sterling education. I had excellent teachers. I was happy with my college life. It was fun. I did all kinds of things and met lots of people. I was quite satisfied with my college education. I learned a lot. I don't know how else to put it.

Edward G. Carroll

Ohio Wesleyan University, 1956–1961

Not much; I didn't gain much from Ohio Wesleyan. [*Laughter*] My education was more certification than education, particularly since, like I said, I wasn't particularly academically aggressive. [*Laughter*] I didn't leave Wesleyan with any memories of outstanding professors or anything, though a couple were memorable. I didn't learn a whole lot from them because I had such a rich education before.

Robert Wedgeworth

Wabash College, 1955–1959

Wabash changed my life. I went to Wabash as an orphan. It was something that I hadn't focused on, but I knew I couldn't go back. I had to go forward and Wabash gave me the tools that I needed to be successful in life. They helped me develop my ability to solve problems, to think critically, helped me to be able to write and speak well. Those basic tools have been important to me throughout my entire adult life. Wabash not only gave me tools, but it gave me a confidence that I could be successful in that wider world.

***

A Toolkit for Life

As the interviews concluded, I invited each of the participants to share what they had done with their lives since leaving college. Collectively, these participants—both graduates and nongraduates—pursued a vast array of careers and several went on to graduate education.[2] This group includes educators in both K-12 and higher education, ministers, civil servants, activists, artists, entrepreneurs, health care professionals, and lawyers. The vast majority of these participants emphasized that their college educations at their GLCA institutions prepared them for competing on equal par in graduate schools and employment. Although their undergraduate experiences were sometimes challenged by the "ignorance" of White students and faculty, those difficult experiences prepared them to successfully face them in the future. As Geraldine Copeland said of her time at Oberlin, "I could get through any other situation because I had made it through Oberlin."

Following college, many of these participants followed career paths that time and again put them in environments where they were the first or the only Black person in an otherwise White space. Their college experiences at these GLCA colleges sharpened their skills in interracial engagement and how to succeed. The importance of tolerance and letting some indignities pass was oft-repeated across the participants. As Ora Dee Fant shared in an interview, "I am very understanding," and this understanding allowed her to recognize the efforts the institution and her college peers were making to do better. A senior woman writing about her Antioch experience in 1956 put it this way: "Five years of living in dormitories, of going to classes, and of taking part in the community activities at Antioch have shown me how well the people here try to carry out their philosophy of democratic education" (p. 41).

This tolerance, patience, and understanding in no way meant that they left college accepting the status quo and second-class status as Black people. Ora also shared, "I mean it just reinforced that sense of social consciousness. Certainly it was very supportive of my intellectual and cultural growth. It was a … great foundation, certainly, and [a] kind of strengthening of character and spirit." A senior man at Antioch said the following in 1948:

> MOST IMPORTANT OF ALL, ANTIOCH HAS HELPED ME TO LOSE MY EARLIER CONSTANT SELF-CONSCIOUS IDENTITY AS A NEGRO…. [I am] no longer on the defensive in race relations. At the same time, I have neither prostituted nor lost my desire to improve race relations. (p. 24, emphasis in original)

Instead, the recognition of their equanimity with White people seemed to galvanize their dedication to continue breaking down walls of discrimination. Bing's narrative also makes it clear that racial temperance was not necessarily an assimilationist orientation either. When he went back to DePauw following graduate school to teach in the art department, he would share the following with Black students:

> Even while you're studying and learning, drop crumbs. Do something that will keep you in touch with yourself. I've found that education, by its very nature in our society, has a tendency to drive you further away from yourself the more degrees you get, if you're not careful … but you don't have to give up who you are in order to excel or contribute.

None of these participants left college with a sense of racial inferiority to Whites. Among the tools that they gained was confidence in themselves and a realistic appraisal of their own abilities and that of others. Henry Deering said that after his time at DePauw, he believed that "if I prepare and do the things, I can win."

The other significant effect of college for these participants was the excellent academic preparation they received. This preparation helped them to rise to the challenge of graduate school with little stress. Tanya's description of her graduate school experience was echoed by several others. For example, Donald Peppers, a Kenyon alumnus, remarked, "I had no problems at Ohio State Law School after I graduated from Kenyon. I went straight through, passed the bar in '62." In addition to easing the academic challenge of graduate school, several spoke of how the recognition from others that their college was academically elite helped to open doors. This is reflected in both Fern's and Sybil's narratives here, from Albion and Earlham, respectively. Geraldine also commented, "I think just the fact that I went to Oberlin played a factor," and she shared that people would be impressed upon learning she had graduated from the college.

Finally, for some, these colleges were a vital lifeline without which their lives would have gone in a very different direction. Richard Dean simply said of his time at DePauw, "Well, number one, the fact that I went to college is a milestone. I'm one of only two people in my entire family that went to college. DePauw was an experience that I'm glad I had." As Chuck says in his narrative, he had been lost at Ohio State and his transfer to Earlham is what helped him gain his "footing." Robert Bennett's narrative above illustrates that these colleges extended the only option for higher education for him; when Ivy League colleges did not accept him, Kenyon offered him admission. Robert Wedgeworth's narrative is perhaps the most wrenching: Orphaned his senior year in high school, Wabash stepped in to become a home when he had none other.

How college affected these participants as reflected in their life histories does not fit neatly in the standard categories of college outcome research (Pascarella & Terenzini, 2005). Beyond verbal and quantitative competence and not quite captured within traditional frameworks of psychosocial development, these participants' experiences speak to another curriculum at work during their time as the only or one of very few Black students on campus during this era. As other research on Black college students has shown (McEwen, Roper, Bryant, & Langa, 1990; Stewart, 2008, 2015), going to college in a predominantly White institution presents additional developmental tasks. Gains in interracial competence, racial identity fortitude, and discernment of the limits of White liberalism were as important to these participants' college experiences as their academic classes and extracurricular involvement.

Notes

1. Chuck and Ruth Ann met at Earlham; Chuck was a year ahead of Ruth Ann and his credits from Ohio State allowed him to finish Earlham in just three years. When Chuck was drafted into the military, Ruth Ann returned to Earlham and finished her degree. This is an example supporting my assertion in Chap. 7 that marriage did not inherently derail women's college completion.
2. See Appendix 1 for a full list of the participants' biographies.

References

McEwen, M. K., Roper, L. D., Bryant, D. R., & Langa, M. J. (1990). Incorporating the development of African-American students into psychosocial theories of student development. *Journal of College Student Development, 31*, 429–436.

Pascarella, E., & Terenzini, P. (2005). *How college affects students: A third decade of research* (Vol. 2). San Francisco, CA: Jossey-Bass.

Stewart, D. L. (2008). Being all of me: Black students negotiating multiple identities. *Journal of Higher Education, 79*(2), 183–207.

Stewart, D.-L. (2015). Know your role: Black college students, racial identity, and performance. *International Journal of Qualitative Studies in Education, 28*(2), 238–258.

CHAPTER 10

Remembering Alma Mater

Willis "Bing" Davis

DePauw University, 1955–1959

When I first got out of DePauw, I would get the alumni magazine and sit down and almost read it cover-to-cover, seeing what my cohorts were doing, and I'd see them giving back just like those first three men I met who were DePauw alumni. Of course, DePauw was a contradictory place. I remember the first time I was called back to speak. I said, "DePauw's on the threshold of greatness. As soon as it deals with the concept of inclusion and diversity, it will be great." [*Laughs*] After that talk I gave, I think the school was a little disenchanted with me and I was disenchanted with the school, but we got over it. We got over it. It wasn't a condemnation of the school. It was just an observation. I appreciate all that I received. I'll use it to the best of my knowledge and I'll share it.

The 14 narratives in this chapter are organized chronologically by college year. I asked participants to describe their involvement with their alma mater, if any, including attendance at reunions, financial giving, and other service activities.

© The Author(s) 2017

D.-L. Stewart, *Black Collegians' Experiences in US Northern Private Colleges*, DOI 10.1057/978-1-137-59077-0_10

Henry Deering

DePauw University, 1959–1963

Like I said, it's like apartheid and I think that has a wearing effect. If you don't have that social cushion and you take a very young person—that is very tough. I'll be honest, when I graduated from DePauw, I was angry with the school. I hated it. It took me some years to think back on some people who had done some very great kindnesses to me out of all that.

Sybil Jordan Hampton

Earlham College, 1962–1966

I think that my service as a trustee was good. I was very pleased to be asked, particularly after I felt that I wasn't really one of Earlham's shining-star students. There is a really vibrant Black alumni association that works not only on issues and policy, but also to raise money to support scholarships. It's really very, very vibrant. I have done some things with them, but I really have not done nearly as much just because I have not had the kind of time it takes with my mother and the volunteering I do here. Also, I have not had an opportunity to meet many students. When I was on the board, I met some students. One of the things that I feel very strongly about is that young people now are different from my time when we were hungry to talk to people who were older, who had experience. When I have been approached, I've really felt the relationships were transactional and I'm not interested in that, you know.

Tanya Summers

Kalamazoo College, 1963–1967

There was nothing that would ever make me want to go back to Kalamazoo College once I left there. My predominant memory is of a place that wasn't all that great. Now when I describe the specific things that I did, it sounds very different. You must understand that I came from New York City, a vibrant environment where you see any and all kinds of things. I mean it was not unusual at all to see people on the subway reading Chinese newspapers, Hebrew newspapers, Spanish-language papers. That wasn't unusual. There was nothing weird about that. That was just part of the mix. You heard all kinds of languages.

You ate all kinds of foods. You went to the East Side. You went to China Town. You went to Little Italy. There's all these ethnic enclaves that were part of the mix. Going to this homogenous, White, mid-western state, it was like, "Oh my God. This place is dull, boring, not stimulating in any shape, form, or fashion." It was that kind of disconnect. Of course, I didn't have words to articulate it that way. I just felt vaguely out of sorts and excluded. Yeah, that's what I'd say now. Those are the kinds of things that left me feeling, "I'm glad to be out of Kalamazoo College." I have no interest in going back. None whatsoever. I would not recommend anyone to go there.

Margaret Ralston Payne

Kalamazoo College, 1964–1968

I have gone back to campus. It was for the first African Studies reunion. I never went to my class reunions until after I went to the African Studies reunion. Then I went to the Black student reunion. I've been to one of my class reunions. I send money every now and then and I read stuff. When Eileen[1] became president, I said, "Well, I have to do better." [*Laughter*] Kalamazoo was very competitive. Very competitive. If you're not sure academically of yourself—in whatever way you got that assurance—it can really mess you up.

James Peters

Kenyon College, 1950–1953 and 1955–1956

I went to every reunion we had. I was on the committee of the last one. I give financially. Hey, I'm thankful. If I got it, I'll give something. What I really think is important about my experience at Kenyon is, well, we could move around and do anything we wanted to and be a part of the body. You would never realize anything. The thing that I can never get over was how they could get everybody on board to be receptive. Knowing the fact that you had some people—Whites—going there who were from the South. This is why it's so remarkable. People came from all over, but yet they still fit into this area where everything seems like it's all right. You fit in and you become a part of that. You get a chance to take advantage of everything that Kenyon has to offer. You knew, normally, this would not happen on the outside.

Geraldine Copeland

Oberlin College, 1953–1957

I think that being Black at Oberlin was probably the best kind of situation I could have had in those days, because I never had a problem with race at Oberlin and I'm sure that wasn't true at other places. I mean obviously I know it wasn't true. I'm not sure how they pulled that off, but that's part of the Oberlin story: a stop on the Underground Railroad and one of the first schools to admit Blacks, to admit women, and all of that. I think that just being at Oberlin probably was one of—I hated it—but I think it was probably one of the best experiences I could have had as far as everything else.

Brenda Root

Oberlin College, 1957–1961

I was disappointed when I went back and I saw this house they had for Black students.[2] That was disappointing to me. I don't want to say it's a form of segregation, because maybe it's voluntary that we're going to have this for this little group. That was very different from what I saw or what I thought Oberlin stood for when I was there. Coming from not even allowing sororities and fraternities to even hold a meeting on campus, let alone get housing—that house, that's going almost all the way in the other direction. Yeah, I didn't go to the 50th reunion. I do still appreciate Oberlin.

Vivian Hopkins Jackson

Oberlin College, 1964–1968

I go back for the reunions, and it's funny, the women that I became closest with were the women that I met my freshman year. It was a small dorm and it actually was two houses that were connected to each other. May Cottage is what it was called. We were May Cottage girls. We stuck together for a while and my best friend was also an African American. One of the things that I was constantly trying to manage was relationships with my own folk and relationships with others. I was very deliberate in not wanting to only have relationships with other Black students. I wanted some cross-cultural relationships and wanted to explore those things, too. I did not want to alienate myself from the Black students, either. Negotiating that piece took a bit of energy.

Ora Dee Fant

Oberlin College, 1964–1968

Yes, I am active with the college. I have been over a period of time to differing degrees. I was on the board from 1994 to 2000. I have, at different times, been involved with the recruiting effort. Right now most of my energy is spent with the ongoing local group that exists.

Patricia Daly

Ohio Wesleyan University, 1952–1956

I will never go back there. I have no longing to see it at all. If I heard that a tornado had come and swept it off the face of the earth, I would notice that for one minute and move on. For a while I did give financially, because they eventually gave me a scholarship and the job in the library. I was grateful for that. I benefited greatly from that. Now that I'm in this transitional period, I tell them, "No, I can't give to you now," and so I don't. Whenever I could, I did. I want to repay. I don't want to remain in their debt.

Edward G. Carroll

Ohio Wesleyan University, 1956–1961

No, I am engaged. I am. I like to send them a little money. Like I said, I went to an alumni event here a couple of weeks ago. When I was working in Columbus, I spent a lot of time back up at Wesleyan. I'd go and visit. I went to our 50th reunion and had the pleasant experience of meeting somebody—now, this was for the class of '60—who I never knew when I was in school. He and his wife and my wife and I really had a wonderful time together. We really enjoyed one another's company. I was just totally oblivious to all that that was going on. [*Laughter*] I get a kick out of seeing Wesleyan people doing well, particularly people that came out of my era.

Robert Wedgeworth

Wabash College, 1955–1959

When I had my 25th class reunion, I complimented my classmates and told them that the thing that made me stronger was they never treated me like a pet and they never taunted me. I was just a member of the class. They treated me like an individual. I think one of the advantages of being the only African American in the class was that they had to treat me as an individual and not as a category, although I was very happy when another Black man showed up when I was a sophomore. [*Chuckles*] After I had developed my career, I became much more actively involved. I attended my tenth class reunion and eventually became the president of the National Association of Wabash Men, which is our alumni association. I also serve on the board of trustees, chairing the academic affairs committee. I recognize that the opportunity that Wabash created for me is something that I wanted to help offer to other young men. African American men have gone to Wabash for many of the same reasons that other men have gone to Wabash. It's pre-professional education. They want to be ministers, doctors, lawyers, businessmen, teachers. That's always going to be true.

Frank D. Starkey

Wabash College, 1962–1966

Although they still send me material, I told them a number of years ago that I wouldn't be engaged with Wabash until they went co-ed. I think it would have improved the education of students at Wabash to be co-ed. So I told them that until they go co-ed, I'm not going to send them money, I'm not going to go back for reunions, and things like that. Although I've talked to fraternity brothers and I've talked to other people. I still run across people who were in college with me, but that was a decision that I made.

***

College Is (Not) the People Who Were There with You

At these colleges, alumni status is not restricted only to those who graduated from the institution. Instead, enrollment for at least one or two semesters was enough to be counted as alumni and part of the college's family. Both graduates and nongraduates received the alumni magazine, invitations to class reunions, and requests to make donations to the annual fund, as long as their contact information was current. Those who did not graduate did not typically remain connected to their college. Beauford and Janet Williams were exceptions to this; they had attended every reunion since they left Earlham and are warmly received by their classmates. Among those who did persist through graduation, some have been very active, while others have not returned to campus since graduation. Three themes describe the engagement patterns of these alumni: actively engaged, distant friends, and heartbreak and estrangement.

Actively Engaged

Those who have been actively engaged have served in leadership roles on campus, as trustees and as invited speakers. These alumni have been to the campus frequently and also frequently give, often in support of scholarships for Black and other racially minoritized students. As noted by Gasman and Bowman (2013), African American alumni are often inspired to give by a "commitment—almost a sense of obligation—to racial uplift" (p. 22). In the narratives that introduced this chapter, Bing, Sybil, Ora, Vivian, Edward, and Robert represent this group. Others included John Herbert Niles, who is a trustee at Allegheny, and Bob Lowry, who has served as a trustee at Kenyon. Also in this group are alumni like James Peters, who give consistently and not only attend reunions, but have helped to plan them as class representatives as well as Ruth Holland Scott, who has returned several times to Albion to give talks to current students. These alumnis' memories of their college years are warm and they were able to readily name faculty, peers, and administrators who played significant roles in making their time in college overwhelmingly positive. Participants in this group also tended to have the most positive experiences with faculty, peers, and administrators. The deep relationships they forged also worked to forge deep relationships with the institution. Negative stories of discrimination or social ostracism were nonexistent. These participants also had the resources, both in finances and time, to give to their college. These factors were also noted by Clotfelter (2003) as instrumental to alumni giving at elite private colleges generally.

Distant Friends

The second pattern of alumni engagement among these participants I labeled "distant friends." These alumni have fond memories of their alma maters, but have either inconsistently attended or been unable to return to campus for reunions or inconsistently donate due to struggles with finances, family commitments, or health challenges. Among this chapter's opening vignettes, Margaret and Geraldine illustrate this form of engagement. Donald Peppers from Kenyon also fell into this group. He shared, "I still would go back to Kenyon again if I had an opportunity. I wanted to go back on the 50th, but for some reason, I think I was sick or something and I couldn't go." Sam Lewis also could no longer travel for reunions from his home on the East Coast back to Hope in western Michigan, but he gave financially.

Frank, whose narrative appears last above, also fits with this group. Although deciding to withhold his financial support and physical presence, he remains connected to other classmates and fraternity brothers. In this way, similar to the others in this category, he maintained relationships with college friends despite having an inconsistent relationship with the institution. Unlike the first group, the college as an institution was a positive tie, but it was not made *more* meaningful because of their social ties. Rather, their social ties stood apart from and independent of the institutional entity. Clotfelter (2003) found the importance of remembering at least one person who took an interest in the alum to be a significant factor in overall giving for alumni.

Moreover, for some, changes in institutional leadership or management would be sufficient to prompt them to move into the actively engaged group. So, as Margaret shared, when Kalamazoo appointed its first Black (or) woman president, Dr. Eileen Wilson-Oyelaran, she had "to do better" in the interest of supporting another Black woman's leadership and what she represented for the (presumably improved) direction the college would be taking. For Frank, if Wabash should decide to begin admitting women, as Kenyon College did in 1971, he would become actively involved again. These distant friends illustrate the significance of Gasman and Bowman's (2013) recommendation for traditionally White institutions to establish trust and demonstrate that Black alumni giving will support positive changes for current and future generations of Black students.

Heartbreak and Estrangement

Finally, some other alumni spoke of their alma mater in terms of either heartbreak or dismissal. Although not necessarily angry with their alma maters (though some certainly were), these alumni did not have special feelings of connection and were strongly disconnected or expressed disappointment in their alma mater. Henry's, Tanya's, Brenda's, and Patricia's narratives here reflect this pattern. This did not mean that they did not give financially, as Patricia's narrative illustrates. Her motivations for giving were more about debt repayment—a "so now we're even" attitude—than support for the institution or current students. Henry and Tanya had feelings of strong *dis*connection from their colleges (DePauw and Kalamazoo, respectively). They were angry and felt bruised by their college experiences to the point that they wanted no contact with the institution. Although some healing has occurred over time, it has brought them closer to individuals, not the institution.

Meanwhile, others simply saw no reason to go back. As Fern shared about Albion, "I guess my attachment to the college was not so great that I have a need to go up and look at the campus." Others had been back to campus since graduation, but what they found there or their interactions with classmates in other spaces wrought disappointment and bitterness. For Brenda, seeing the Afrikan Heritage House during a visit back to Oberlin represented the separationist attitude that she deliberately chose to resist by attending Oberlin. Moreover, its presence seemed to flatly contradict the college's philosophy. Though Brenda seemed to misunderstand the purpose and function of the Afrikan Heritage House, her mistrust of what it might stand for outweighed her faith in the institution. Betty Johnson was once interested in maintaining connection and involvement with Allegheny, but three instances of being ignored by White classmates and fellow alumni in other spaces have completely turned her off to going back for reunions for the last 54 years, as of 2013 when I spoke with her. For these heartbroken and estranged participants, the college was the people who were there with them in a very negative way.

Relationships matter and can bring someone closer to their college or push them farther away. With the ability to maintain contact with friends and significant faculty through phone and e-mail, the institution's reunions are no longer the primary method of maintaining connection. Moreover, the absence of connections to the college and remembrances of a hostile campus climate make "homecoming" laughable, if not an outright farce.

Ironically, the utilitarian motives and gains that informed these participants' college choices (see Chap. 4) undermine the ease with which connections to institutional entities can be made. The institution had served its purpose, and in the absence of substantive, positive relationships with peers and faculty, it would be left behind. These factors have not been addressed in the aforementioned research on alumni giving and engagement (Clotfelter, 2003; Gasman & Bowman, 2013), yet warrant careful attention through empirical study.

Notes

1. President Eileen Wilson-Oyelaran became the first African American and the first woman to be president of Kalamazoo College in 2005; she retired in 2016.
2. Brenda was referencing Oberlin's Afrikan Heritage House, a residential living space for any student, regardless of race, that is interested in an immersive learning experience focused on African and African American cultures.

References

Clotfelter, C. T. (2003). Alumni giving to elite private colleges and universities. *Economics of Education Review, 22*(2), 109–120.

Gasman, M., & Bowman III, N. (2013). *Engaging diverse college alumni: The essential guide to fundraising*. New York, NY: Routledge.

CHAPTER 11

Conclusion

At the end of this journey with these 68 participants, I consider the many lessons I have learned from being in community with these elders—my elders. In many ways, the hours I spent over the phone, in coffee shops, and in living rooms and home offices were cherished and invaluable time. The youngest of these participants were nearly the same age as my own parents; the oldest would have been my grandparents' contemporaries. I saw these interviews as more than data collection—staid, impersonal, and passive. Rather, these interviews were opportunities for intergenerational community-building and for imparting and receiving wisdom. I was gifted to hear stories that many had not yet told to their own children and grandchildren about their youth. The institutional archives, so graciously opened to me, were more than files, clippings, and dusty books. They served as recorded testimony from on-site witnesses, exposing truths and realities both uncomfortable and liberatory. In response, I feel the most appropriate approach to take to this concluding chapter is to speak to the lessons these stories and testimonies taught me, rather than the conclusions I have drawn from them. These seven lessons say as much about me as they do about my teachers here, revealing my questions, my experiences, my hopes, and my frustrations. As such, others with similar questions, experiences, hopes, and frustrations may resonate with these lessons and find relevance for themselves and their institutions today.

© The Author(s) 2017

D.-L. Stewart, *Black Collegians' Experiences in US Northern Private Colleges*, DOI 10.1057/978-1-137-59077-0_11

Lesson 1: On Expectations and Experiences

The first lesson is on the nonlinear relationship between expectations and experience. An old adage instructs that we draw to us what we expect, writing a causal and direct line between the content of our expectations and our life experiences. The intended lesson of the adage is to have positive expectations of people and situations if you want to have positive experiences with those same people and situations. Although some participants in this study did find their positive expectations of these traditionally White colleges met with equally positive experiences within them, this linearity is disrupted by other participants' narratives. Experience shaped expectations for some, like Bing Davis, whose interactions with the compassionate benevolence of three DePauw alumni informed his expectation that DePauw was an institution that would foster such service in all its students. This expectation was met with further confirming experiences. For others, *not* having expectations allowed their experiences to just be lived without a rubric by which to evaluate them. In Robert's case, entering Wabash with no expectations allowed experiences to be read for what they were instead of what they could have been. Some, who had no reason to expect positive interactions with White peers based on past experiences, found themselves pleasantly surprised by the warm reception they received. Still others came in with positive expectations shaped by institutional legacies and histories only to find their lived realities sharply depart from those high hopes. For participants who grew up in de jure southern segregation, expectations of a more hospitable northern racial climate were dashed by encounters with the realities of "up South" segregationist practices in Indiana and Ohio. As Robert shared, experiences create opportunities for disappointment. The best approach for Black students entering traditionally White environments (institutions and local communities) may be to gather as much accurate information as possible, rather than to raise the quality of one's expectations. In this way, indignities and negative and hurtful experiences are rightfully framed as endemic to the environments within which one is living, rather than as personal character flaws.

Lesson 2: On Being Unexpected

The second lesson I learned was about the opportunities and challenges of being unexpected. These institutions sought out these students, specifically for the purposes of broadening the racial diversity of their institutions as a reflection of their espoused religious values and institutional legacies of inclusion. Yet, seeking difference does not prepare one for the arrival of that difference. Institutions prepare for what they expect. In many ways, these participants arrived on their campuses as unexpected inhabitants inasmuch as the colleges had not always given forethought to the gap between institutional commitments to racial diversity and the readiness and competence of their faculty and students. Despite this, being unexpected created opportunities for the presence of these Black collegians to cause White students, faculty, and administrators to ask questions of their colleges that had previously been hidden: What is an institution's responsibility to its students and to the local communities on which it relies? Do racial and religious exclusion clauses in our fraternities and sororities align with institutional espoused values? Who should be invited into conversations about institutional policy and practice related to the academic and social integration of new members into the community?

On the other hand, although being unexpected may prompt necessary campus-wide conversations and reflection, it comes at a cost for those who are unexpected. The stunting or postponement of interpersonal growth and development of mature romantic relationships was one consequence for many of these Black students of being unexpected in an environment not prepared to consider their social and relational needs. Social isolation was unevenly borne by Black women, both shut out of sororities at colleges whose social life was dominated by fraternities and sororities and seen as undesirable and/or unapproachable for interracial, heterosexual dating by White men. The greater expense of needing to travel sometimes off campus to take care of basic grooming (e.g., needing to get from Greencastle to Indianapolis for a decent haircut) or social needs was borne by Black students. However, in these instances, being unexpected also created opportunities for developing strong relationships with local Black residents as some participants followed footprints in the snow for Sunday dinners when campus dining halls were closed and local eateries refused service to Black patrons. Marginalized students bear the burden of institutional failure to prepare for their needs and are "martyred for the cause of race relations" (Antioch Senior Paper, 1952). Being unexpected has material consequences.

Lesson 3: On Institutional Diversity Efforts

Relatedly, the third lesson I gleaned from my participants' oral histories and the archival voices was about the limits and opportunities of institutional diversity efforts. The GLCA colleges were not alone among northern institutions that sought to matriculate their first or a higher number of Black students. They shared key characteristics: they were academically elite and had the financial resources to support scholarships and work-study for financial aid. In specific and intentional ways, these institutions made decisions to recruit (more) Black students, including Oberlin who had seen the size of its Black student population steadily decline to its lowest levels by the 1940s (Baumann, 2010). Relationships with the NSSFNS, establishing pipelines with secondary-level feeder schools in the South, and collaborations with historically Black colleges led to increases in the numbers of Black students enrolled at these colleges. Institutional diversity efforts therefore created opportunities to innovatively support the expansion of compositional student racial diversity on these campuses.

However, this opportunity was consistently challenged and undermined by institutions' failures to look beyond simply adding numbers as the ultimate goal of their diversity efforts. Jessie Treichler's efforts at Antioch stand in sharp contrast to this general approach. Her files reveal that she acknowledged that Black students needed to be both academically and socially integrated at Antioch in order to fulfill the college's intention of offering a truly democratic education. Yet, Treichler's awareness of the need for this was often trumped by other administrators' refusals to act, especially after a new president arrived who was far more conservative than his predecessor. In this way, institutional leadership was consistently related to institutional (in)actions in support of (non)discrimination, campus and community (de)segregation, and expanding the Black student population.

Lesson 4: On the Politics of Integration

The fourth lesson was on the opportunities and limits of integrationist politics as enacted by Black students in these traditionally White colleges. As illustrated in Chap. 4, many of these participants intentionally sought a traditionally White college for their undergraduate education.

They sought to make their own contributions to the effort to confound White supremacist assumptions of Black inferiority from within. They also perceived traditionally White colleges as the places that would equip them with the necessary tools to successfully participate and compete on an equal basis with White people in an anticipated racially integrated future. Their integrationist politics aligned well with the institutional diversity politics of these GLCA colleges. Without Black students willing to arrive as racial pioneers, institutional efforts to increase their compositional racial diversity would have fallen flat. Institutions needed to access and recruit academically capable *and* integrationist-minded Black students, specifically. Although the first criterion was made explicit through the matching of standardized test scores with compatible institutions by NSSFNS, the second was unstated but no less important. Integrationist Black students self-selected to the recruitment pools of these colleges. In so doing, possessing an integrationist politic enabled them to access an academically elite and highly regarded undergraduate education.

On the flip side, the burdens of integration were unevenly distributed across the student body, falling in greatest measure on Black students. It was Black students who had to serve in dual roles, both as students pursuing a college degree and as educators of Black life and culture. It was Black students who were left alone in their residence hall rooms on dance nights. It was Black students who had to resist professors who could not see their potential for the color of their skin. It was Black students who had to decide whether to swallow some indignity to not ruin the experience of their White peers. And, it was sometimes Black students whose race loyalties were questioned by Black peers who could not understand how they could be so comfortable in White spaces. In the best cases, Black students were spared these costs by White faculty, coaches, peers, and teammates who made it possible for them to be seen as just one of the group. However, for some, the wounds were so deep that they dared not revisit their college years, afraid of being scarred as much by remembering as they were when they lived through it. Jeannette Phillips tried to get a friend who had received my letter to participate in this study. He refused her, saying that he did not want to revisit those years; there was too much hurt. How many more were too wounded to revisit the past?

Lesson 5: On Whiteness, Blackness, and Institutional Spaces

This lesson was on whiteness, blackness, and institutional spaces. Specifically, I learned about the invisibility of whiteness and the hypervisibility of shared spaces. In many of my interviews, participants spoke about "integrated colleges" versus "Black colleges." This pairing had two primary effects. First, it marked "Black colleges" as the result of segregationist laws and customs. This is not invalid since it is unclear that such institutions would have been created had existing colleges and universities been commonly open to the higher education of African Americans, both before and following the Civil War, especially across the South where the majority of African Americans lived. However, the extensive racial homogeneity of traditionally White colleges was also the product of segregationist laws, campus policies, and customs.

This pairing had a second effect, to erase the whiteness of so-called integrated colleges and prompt several puzzling questions: How many non-White people does it take to actually be integrated? Is 1 of 500 enough? Maybe two dozen of 1000? Is withholding admission to Black women so as to maintain segregated women's residence halls a mark of integration? If the social groups to which 75–90% of the student body belongs structurally exclude the membership of Blacks and Jews, is the campus integrated? Perhaps espousing rejection of segregationist policies is adequate to be seen as "integrated." Whiteness has always been normalized and centered with the effect of being unmarked and unnamed (Johnson, 2005). One participant admitted to being hesitant to participate in this study because I labeled these colleges as "predominantly White" and they did not want to think of these colleges in racial terms. Yet, the overwhelming majority of the student body, faculty, and staff were often more racially homogenous than that of the "Black colleges" to which they were being compared. The presidents, senior administrators, and pluralities of faculty were White at most historically Black institutions during this era. Moreover, at least a handful participated in semester exchange programs with northern traditionally White colleges at this time. Hampton and Fisk, for instance, had exchange agreements with three different GLCA colleges concurrently: Antioch, Oberlin, and Denison.

These effects also manifested within the GLCA colleges. It was the congregation of Black students and friendships among Black students that would have stood out and been hypervisible to onlookers. Meanwhile, the congregation of White students and their homoracial friendships remained invisible as racialized actions. Uninterrupted whiteness was neutralized of its racial force. These rhetorical practices and their effects were not created by minoritized people, though these Black students were complicit in their enactments. This is evident in White students' defense of homophily to resist desegregating fraternal groups, eliding the role of race in presuming with whom one would have sufficient similarity for bonding.

Lesson 6: On Personal and Social Responsibility

Considering the educational outcomes of undergraduate education provided this lesson. The American Association of Colleges and Universities (AAC&U) developed a framework to guide student learning through college (AAC&U, 2007). One of those outcomes is labeled as "personal and social responsibility" and includes four areas: civic knowledge and engagement that spans local and global communities; intercultural knowledge and competence; ethical reasoning and action; and foundations and skills for lifelong learning (AAC&U, 2007). Lest it is assumed that there was less interest in this area during the time of this study, I point readers to the second writing of the *Student Personnel Point of View* (American Council on Education, 1949). This foundational philosophical treatise written by the Committee on Student Personnel Work (what would later become known as "student affairs") within the ACE explicitly centers what AAC&U 58 years later would term "personal and social responsibility." The ACE called for student personnel workers to support college student learning about civic responsibilities in a democratic society, about others different from themselves, ethics and values, and encouraging a lifelong attitude toward learning.

Listening to the stories of the Black collegians with whom I worked and the printed reflections of Antiochian Black students and the 20 years of White student newspaper editors and letter writers across nearly 13 campuses has revealed the superficiality with which this outcome was pursued. Although international relations clubs were present at each institution throughout the span of this study, interracial or human relations or minority relations clubs were not ubiquitous, emerging at several campuses not until the late 1950s or early 1960s. Discussions of European and US interests in Africa, Asia, and Latin America were common but there was almost total silence in classrooms across institutions for much of this period about the problem of the color line in the USA. Moreover,

White students were generally not challenged by faculty in structured forums, such as compulsory chapel attendance, to consider the contradictions inherent in regularly attending meetings of the NAACP but continuing to support local businesses that refused the patronage of their Black hallmates and classmates. Instead, some institutions explicitly forbade students from organizing direct actions to resist segregation in the local communities and did not aggressively seek to challenge discriminatory practices that harmed Black students' learning experiences. Often among these institutions were the most liberal and racially progressive colleges in this group—Antioch, Earlham, and Oberlin. Seemingly taking a live-and-let-live approach, institutional leaders urged their students to restrict their engagement around these issues only to palatable dialogues that respected the strongly held personal viewpoints of the local citizens. It is worth considering the extent to which alignment of institutional values, formal curricula, and educational outcomes remain subject to the reliance of small, private colleges on sustaining cooperative arrangements with their host communities. The realities of these colleges reveal the porousness of arguments that overemphasize the autonomy and freedom of private colleges over state-controlled institutions.

Lesson 7: On Transhistorical Research

The final lesson I am taking with me from this work is about what it means to do transhistorical research. By *transhistorical* research, I mean to refer to the act of researching across histories, as well as Fields' (1982) usage of the term to refer to constructs that exist statically across time and space. In this study, transhistoricity took three forms: (1) I, located in the twenty-first century, conducted research on mid-twentieth-century events, people, and places. (2) From their perspectives in the second decade of the twenty-first century, I collaborated with 68 participants to look backward in their lives some 50–60 years to when they were young adults on the way to becoming who they were when they talked to me. (3) I researched across the personal histories of 68 individuals and the institutional histories of 13 colleges. Through all of this, race was the focus of my inquiry, specifically as reflected in the lives of Black people. Inasmuch as Fields (1982) argued that race was not transhistorical, but rather the construction of a particular set of historical and societal circumstances, neither are individuals and institutions transhistorical. Like race, both personhoods and institutions (composed of individuals with personhoods) are shaped by the historical and societal circumstances in which persons and institutions find themselves. People as they were 50–60 years ago are not necessarily who they are now and may not see the world in the same way as they did then. The same can be said for institutions, occupied by different persons than they were 50–60 years ago: they have evolved, changed, and forgotten perspectives, actions, and beliefs they once held. Consequently, it is inherently dangerous to fix a person or an institution either to the past or as they exist now. This destabilizing of identity consistency is a definitively queer theoretical notion. This does not mean that the past should be left in the past. The project of history is to learn from the past and to understand how the past has shaped the present and is shaping the future. Without institutional memory and remembering, the pernicious repetition of toxic patterns is unabated.

Summary

History calls and the present must attend to its message. The lessons I have discussed here can provoke transformative institutional change that better prepares for the diversity that many higher education institutions seek. Yet the reality is that minoritized populations continue to show up as "unexpected" on college campuses that pursued their arrival but had not laid the groundwork. Minoritized students continue to provide unpaid labor to colleges and universities as both students and educators on a mission to prove they are capable and that they are worthy of dignity and opportunity. Minoritized students also continue to succeed in spite of it all. Some are even fortunate to have found and been found by advocates and accomplices that were ready to support their empowerment, resilience, and enthusiasm. Until this latter reality for some becomes the common reality for all, institutions of higher education will continue to experience limited effectiveness in becoming more socially just.

References

American Association of Colleges & Universities. (2007). *College learning for the new global century*. Washington, DC: Author.

American Council on Education. (1949). *The student personnel point of view* (Rev. ed.). Washington, DC: Author.

Baumann, R. M. (2010). *Constructing Black education at Oberlin College: A documentary history*. Athens: Ohio University Press.
Fields, B. J. (1982). Ideology and race in American history. In J. M. Kousser & J. M. McPherson (Eds.), *Region, race, and reconstruction: Essays in honor of C. Vann Woodward* (pp. 143–177). New York, NY: Oxford University Press.
Johnson, A. G. (2005). *Privilege, power, and difference* (2nd ed.). New York, NY: McGraw Hill.

Epilogue

We've Come a Long Way to Be Not So Different

Many of the participants would ask me questions about my own background and college experiences. For some, there was shock at how little had changed, especially since I had attended a GLCA college as well, Kalamazoo College. My experiences deeply informed my interest in this topic. I share my narrative here and encourage readers to consider the ways my story relates to and departs from the participants' narratives shared throughout this book.

I was assigned female at birth in December 1973 and raised as a Black girl in the Village of Harlem in New York City as my mother's only child and father's firstborn. My parents were unmarried, and my father left New York when I was about three years old to return to his family roots in North Carolina. I don't remember seeing him again until I was 15 years old. Of course, by the time I came along, Harlem was open, predominantly Black, and full of cultural life and vitality. I attended a parochial school run by Catholic nuns from first grade through eighth grade at St. Charles Borromeo in Harlem. I loved school and was good at it. I read voraciously, quickly tiring of the readers we had in my grade school; competed in spelling bees; and memorized speeches to deliver. I was teased for being a nerd, for wearing glasses, for daring to be a smart Black girl. My mother counseled me to ignore the taunts and let my excellence be my

© The Author(s) 2017

D.-L. Stewart, *Black Collegians' Experiences in US Northern Private Colleges*, DOI 10.1057/978-1-137-59077-0

revenge. So, I did. I was my eighth-grade class valedictorian by a single point.

I took the city's standardized test to go to the Bronx High School of Science but it was too far to travel alone by subway being nearly two hours each way. Instead, I wrote an essay that won me a scholarship to attend Convent of the Sacred Heart on Manhattan's Upper East Side just a half-hour bus ride down Fifth Avenue from where I lived. I had an admissions interview with the headmistress, a White Irish nun, who asked me whether I knew any classical music. I answered Chopin because we had just learned about him that week. I told her that I was an "Anglophile" and she was impressed I knew how to use that word correctly.

Sacred Heart was Catholic too, like St. Charles, but it was very, very different. I had traded my predominantly Black classrooms and mix of Black laywomen and White nuns as teachers for an actual mansion filled with mostly middle- to upper-class White girls from two-parent homes with houses they owned and international vacations they took and taught by nearly all-White teachers in the Upper School, comprising grades 9 through 12. There was no cafeteria then at Sacred Heart like there had been at St. Charles and we Upper School girls went out to buy lunch. I had an allowance of $5 a week that I budgeted like a hawk, buying a toasted bagel with butter from the corner deli for $1.25 and drinking water from the fountain at school to stretch my lunch money through the week. Some Fridays I didn't eat lunch because I had run out of money. My senior year, after pleading for a raise without really fully explaining why, my mom gave me $10 a week, which meant I could add a soda a couple of days a week to drink with my bagel. I never told anyone why I ate so little; I just had a small appetite. I would go home and "eat like a football player," as my mother said. I never told her why I was always so hungry because I didn't want to add to the financial pressure I knew we were under. I continued to excel academically, though tenth grade was rough and I worked incredibly hard for every A I got, which just seemed to put me scholastically on par with most of my class. Teachers were incredibly supportive for the most part and did not doubt my potential.

When it came time to choose colleges, I was unsure where to start. My mother only had the opportunity to spend half a semester at Hunter College. Although my father had earned a master's degree, the social capital that typically would have conferred wasn't genetically inherited. My guidance counselor at school was a very kind woman whose experience with other girls at the school was limited largely to the Ivies and the Seven Sisters. I had no interest in attending that kind of school. I wanted to be farther than a train ride from home and not in the kind of academic pressure cooker that those schools represented. College viewbooks informed my search, which got narrowed to predominantly small, liberal arts schools in the Midwest which emphasized writing, offered Russian language, and an international studies major as I intended to usurp Condoleezza Rice and become the first Black woman ambassador to Russia. The South was too hot, the West Coast was too far, I had no concept of what was between California and the Mississippi River, and had never been west of the Allegheny Mountains. I considered a Black college, but had heard from a former babysitter that hers was class conscious and geographically cliquish. I wanted none of that, plus I was suspicious that the minimum SAT score needed to get in was only 1000. The other schools I was considering wanted at least 1200. I was at 1270.

The only college I ever visited was West Point. I didn't make it in because my eyesight would have made me non-commissionable as an officer by the time I graduated. The other three colleges I applied to were Kalamazoo College, Kenyon College, and Grinnell College. They had the best viewbooks and pleasant admissions officers. Kalamazoo won out because it gave me the most financial aid that included a campus work-study job at the library, the Black student I talked to on the phone actually sounded excited to be there and kind of flirted with me which made me blush, a faculty member in political science was impressed with the essay I wrote, and the admissions officer, a Black man, was sincerely invested in me. I had to explain what and where Kalamazoo was numerous times to people back home in Harlem. "Oh, like the song?" Depending on their age, they were referencing either the Beatles or New Edition. "Yes, like the song," became my rehearsed response.

So, one day in September 1991, my mom and I flew with six bags between us to Kalamazoo the night before freshman (that's what it was called then) orientation began. We stayed at a bed and breakfast and took a cab up the hill two blocks with my possessions and were met by the football players who were helping to unload vehicles. My mom's flight back to New York left in just a few hours, so she got back in the cab, kissed me on the cheek, and left me. I found myself standing in the parking lot, all my bags gone somewhere in Trowbridge Hall, knowing no one. Just as I was about to completely dissolve into a raging sob, an older student, who was a resident assistant and must have sensed my distress, came up suddenly brightly smiling, put her arm around me, and ushered me into the building. I met my roommate Mary and her parents, who were in her room, and began settling in.

Academically, I noticed no difference from Sacred Heart, except I didn't *feel* like I was working as hard to get high grades. I don't think K was easier, but I had gotten so used to the expectations that the transition was smooth as silk. Yet, White students snickered at me as I walked across campus. I was defiantly resistant to confirming people's expectations of me: I was a Celtics fan, a Republican, and listened to Def Leppard and Guns N' Roses more than Public Enemy and Run DMC. I cofounded a student organization called Conservatives in Action (CIA) with another first-year Black student and looked longingly at the Black students, afraid I wouldn't fit in because I never had. I took up smoking cigarettes, which helped me "look cool," and the nicotine helped me pull all-nighters. I kept to myself my utter mystification with White people who had literally never known a Black person before, with the absence of hearing 15 different languages spoken around me, with the disappearance of the aromas of the international mecca that was New York City, with the odd reduction of race to just Black and White, with how much I missed Harlem's unapologetic and beautiful blackness. But at the Martin Luther King Chapel program that the Black Student Organization (BSO) sponsored that year, I recited a poem I had written called *The Nazareth Myth* before the college community about being underestimated by others just because I was Black.

Then, spring came and the trial of the four officers who beat Rodney King, and the not-guilty verdicts at Simi Valley, and then Los Angeles erupted. The White students in CIA were defending the cops in ways that I knew not to be true. I knew police brutality and excessive force against Black people were real. I knew these White students didn't know what the hell they were talking about. I left CIA and sheepishly found myself at a BSO meeting, where I was received like a lost sheep finally come home. Thus began my increasingly more militant political consciousness.

That summer I was part of a small delegation selected from across the country to spend three weeks in South Korea as part of a youth exchange program. I instantly bonded with the only other people of color on the trip, both women. I learned so much that summer about global racism and US neocolonialism, and reveled in being mistaken as African instead of American. I spent my sophomore year as a resident assistant but quit after that year because it reduced my financial aid too much and took too much time from being in fellowship with other Black students and the BSO. I did my internship my sophomore spring at the US Agency for International Development, read Malcolm X's autobiography with Alex Haley while riding the metro to the State Department building, cut off my long hair and fully immersed myself in Afrocentric thinking. I changed my major from the "irrelevance" of International and Russian/Soviet Studies to sociology and planned to become a teacher. I skipped going on study abroad so that I could still graduate on time with my class. I participated in first-generation Internet chat rooms with names like "blacklife" and adopted a pen name, Nzingha Black, to write poetry. I openly argued down racist fallacies spoken by White faculty in my sociology classes. I would serve three times as president of BSO. I moved into the Umoja House, a residential living community, for my senior year after coming back to campus following my student teaching experience.

I was initially all set up to go back to Sacred Heart to teach but I wanted to be somewhere "relevant" so I abandoned that plan mid-summer and arranged instead to go to Forest Hills High School in Queens. Forest Hills was a large public school that had more students than K and a mix of two dozen different immigrant ethnic groups. I taught four sections of tenth-grade global history to a total of 120 students, graded on the subway between Harlem and Queens and my part-time retail job, and intervened to prevent one of my students from being badly beaten up by bullies after school. It was the most exhausting and fulfilling experience I had had in my life up to that point.

When I graduated from K in 1995, I was angry and hurt and frustrated by the constant racial stress I was under. There was never any break from White students' presumptions that I did not belong there, that I wasn't good enough. Their ignorance of other cultures that were basic facts of life that I had learned seemingly by osmosis in New York was draining. I educated others as much as I was educated. For nearly the next decade, the only words I would use to describe my college experience were "anger" and "struggle." It took years to allow the positive memories to take up more space than the negative ones: of going to church in town and getting Sunday dinner at the pastor and first lady's home; of having fun developing performances for the Cultural Awareness Troupe which I helped to found; of going over to parties with Black students at Western Michigan University; of writing for the student newspaper; of acting in a theater production; of my faculty advisor who was incredibly supportive; of the times spent just hanging out in the offices of Black staff on campus.

K taught me the value of Black community and that I never needed to allow anyone to define my capacity or potential. K taught me that I was not accidentally smart; I was smart on purpose. When I tell people now that I am a graduate of K College, those who know higher education know and respect the strength of my academic preparation. K prepared me to take on graduate school and a doctorate with relative ease. Between Sacred Heart and Kalamazoo, I knew what it meant to write well and I recognized that I could. It was feedback from teachers at Sacred Heart and Kalamazoo that steeled my ego against the assaults I received at the hands of some faculty in graduate school.

When Eileen Wilson-Oyelaran became president in 2005, I decided I needed to step up my involvement, so she would have Black alumni support. I accepted an invitation to join the Alumni Association Executive Board and served a four-year term. I went to homecoming every year, helped plan our second Black Alumni reunion[1] where I first met Margaret Ralston Payne, and started giving financially. I went from declaring before I even became a parent that no child of mine would go to K to now begging that same child to at least take a tour of the campus. I have moved from heartbreak and estrangement to being actively engaged, because I have seen K finally deal with the issue of diversity and inclusion. It is not perfect and its work is not done, but it is better than it was. I want to help it keep getting better.

Note

1. The first actually having occurred during my undergraduate years, organized by the BSO during a quarter I was serving as president.

Appendix 1

Participant Biographies

There were 68 Black matriculates who participated in this study. They generously shared the details of their lives and, particularly, their experiences in the GLCA colleges. Each person's story was vivid and powerful and contributed to the vibrant tapestry that has been woven together in this text. I encourage readers to use the index to locate the portions of each individual's narratives that appear throughout the book; some portion of each person's story was used at least once in Chaps. 2, 3, 4, 5, 6, 7, 8, 9, and 10. In these brief biographies, I have recorded their date and place of birth and upbringing, the college they attended and major, and postcollege career achievements and further education, where applicable. The participants are listed in alphabetical order by last name and those participants who wished to keep their involvement confidential have their pseudonyms enclosed within quotation marks (e.g., "Pseudonym"), with more ambiguous details about their lives provided. One participant requested just before publication to be completely anonymous in the text, and so that biography is not included here.

Mamie Cavell Adderly was born in 1939 in Columbia, South Carolina, and later raised in Philadelphia, Pennsylvania. Mamie attended Earlham College for one semester, spring 1957, before transferring to complete her baccalaureate degree in economics at Swarthmore College. After graduation, Mamie unsuccessfully searched for sales jobs in private

© The Author(s) 2017

D.-L. Stewart, *Black Collegians' Experiences in US Northern Private Colleges*, DOI 10.1057/978-1-137-59077-0

industry before eventually going to Baltimore, Maryland, and working for the Social Security Administration (SSA). Mamie did not marry and does not have any children.

William Allison was born in 1933 in Nashville, Tennessee, where he was also raised. William began attending DePauw University in 1950, majored in speech, and graduated in 1954. After college, William served as a medic in the US Army. After the military, William taught at the American School in the Philippines, serving middle-class Filipino and American families, and later completed a master's degree in public administration at the University of Pittsburgh. William's career spanned both public service and private enterprise, including being the deputy director of the Federal Community Services Administration during President Jimmy Carter's administration. William is the father of one daughter.

Lesley Aranha was born in Washington, DC, in 1938 and would spend her childhood also in DC. Lesley began attending Allegheny College in 1956 and graduated in 1960 with a major in elementary education. While pursuing a career teaching in public schools, Lesley earned her master's degree in special education and developmental education from George Washington University while married with three children. After 35 years, Lesley retired on her 55th birthday.

"Denise Baisden" was born in 1937 in Atlanta, Georgia, where she was also raised. Denise attended Ohio Wesleyan University from 1954 to 1958 and graduated with a double major in sociology and psychology. After graduation, Denise spent time living and working in various locales across the country in public service agencies. Along the way, Denise finished her master's degree in social work from the University of Southern California while married with three children. Denise retired as a psychiatric social worker for a large health care system in southern California. Denise passed away in August 2014.

Dr. Allen B. Ballard was born in 1930 and raised in Philadelphia, Pennsylvania. He attended Kenyon College from 1948 to 1952 and graduated as a political science major. He would spend significant time abroad developing expertise in Russian history, culture, and politics and completed his doctoral degree in government from Harvard University. Al pursued a faculty career and is a professor of history. He has written two novels and three nonfiction books intertwining his life with the history of African Americans in the USA: *The Education of Black Folk: The Afro-American Struggle for Knowledge in White America* (1973), *One More*

Day's Journey: The Story of a Family and a People (1984), and *Breaching Jericho's Walls: A Twentieth-Century African American Life* (2011).

Mary Barksdale was born in Richmond, Indiana, in 1934. Mary began her studies at Earlham College in 1952 before leaving after getting married and was never able to complete her college degree. She would become employed as a human resources manager for a major truck manufacturing company and was involved in significant levels of community leadership, including public elected office and private governing boards.

Rev. Dr. Robert Bennett was born in 1933 in Baltimore, Maryland. Robert attended Kenyon College through a state scholarship program that paid for high-achieving Black students to go out of state for college due to its segregated education system. Robert entered Kenyon in 1950 and graduated Phi Beta Kappa as a philosophy major in 1954. Robert was ordained an Episcopal priest, took classes in Aramaic from Johns Hopkins University, and would earn his doctorate in Near Eastern Studies from Harvard. He later returned to Harvard to teach in the Episcopal Divinity School.

Daniel Boggan was born in 1945 in Albion, Michigan, and spent part of his early childhood in Greenville, Alabama, before returning to Albion during his elementary school years. Daniel would stay local and attend college at Albion College from 1963 to 1967. During his years at Albion, Daniel switched majors from engineering to complete a double major in history and sociology. He completed a graduate degree in social work from the University of Michigan and worked as a city manager in several cities across the country before working for 18 months at Albion as its first advisor for Black students.

Winfred Bowen was born in 1938 in Texas. At age seven, he moved to Gary, Indiana, where he resided until college. Winfred attended Albion College from 1956 to 1960. Winfred would graduate with a major in biology and minor in chemistry. He then went on to Northwestern University and earned a graduate degree in business.

Dr. William E. Bright, II was born in 1938 and raised in Highland Park, Michigan. He attended Albion College from 1956 to 1960. At Albion, William majored in biology and minored in chemistry and would go on to become a professor of education and international development manager.

"Kirston Brick" was born in 1946 in New York City, New York, and moved to a small town in Ohio due to her father's work as a bricklayer.

Kirston entered college at Oberlin College just at the tail end of the study in 1964 and graduated in 1968 with a major in history focused on European intellectual history. Kirston completed a doctoral degree at Harvard in clinical psychology and public practice and would become a faculty member at a southern historically Black institution. Thereafter, she became the first person of color to hold an endowed chair faculty position at a large, public research university in the Midwest.

Dr. Oscar T. Brookins was born in Yazoo County, Mississippi, in 1942 and later moved with his mother and six siblings to Jackson after the death of his father. He entered DePauw University in 1961 to pursue the 3–2 program in engineering and would graduate in 1965, majoring in math. After graduation, he earned his graduate degrees in economics at Northeastern University and the State University of New York at Buffalo and has spent a lifetime in academia.

"Fern Brown" was born in 1938 and raised in Albion, Michigan. Fern chose to stay local to complete her bachelor's degree and entered Albion College in 1956. She graduated from Albion in 1960 double majoring in history and political science. She would earn her master's degree in education at the University of Illinois at Chicago and pursue a career in teaching.

Dr. Larry Browning was born in 1944 and raised in Springfield, Ohio. He entered Earlham College in 1962 and played football for three years until he was advised to withdraw in his junior year because of his low grades. With the assistance of a new faculty advisor, he did graduate in 1966 and went on to earn two doctoral degrees: an EdD from Harvard University and a Doctor of Dental Medicine (DDM) from Tufts University. Larry practiced dentistry in Atlanta, Georgia, where he passed away in June 2014.

Cynthia C. Carpenter was born in 1930 in Cambridge, Massachusetts, and grew up on the campus of the Hampton Institute in Virginia. She graduated from Earlham College in 1951, where she pursued a biology major and psychology minor. After college, she spent some time working with the American Friends Service Committee in Chicago and Ohio and began her career as a primary school teacher in Illinois in 1965. Cynthia earned her master's degree in counseling in 1978 and worked as a school counselor thereafter.

Edward G. Carroll Jr. was born in 1938 in Baltimore, Maryland, and later moved to New York City, where he completed high school. Edward attended Ohio Wesleyan University from 1956 to 1961, during which time he enrolled for one spring semester at Morgan State University, a historically Black college in Maryland. Edward served in the Air Force on active duty from 1961 to 1968 and then transferred to the Air National Guard. He would earn a master's degree in journalism from The Ohio State University and return to Baltimore to teach journalism at the University of Maryland for three years. Edward then went into government work with the US International Trade Commission, and later worked in public relations at the American Petroleum Institute.

Geraldine T. Copeland was born in 1936 in Chicago, Illinois, and later moved to Harvey with her family. Geraldine attended and graduated from the Oberlin College Conservatory of Music as a music education major; she was enrolled from 1953 to 1957. Although she did not receive any offers for teaching positions upon graduation, she married and moved to Texas working temporarily as a domestic. Eventually, Geraldine was able to enter the teaching profession and earned her certification from Sacramento State University. She would later earn a master's degree in counselor education from the University of New Hampshire and ended her career as a guidance counselor.

Patricia Daly was born in 1934 in New York City, New York. The family moved several times before finally settling in Anacostia, Virginia, and Washington, DC. Patricia attended Ohio Wesleyan University from 1953 to 1957, where she initially majored in art before adding a double major in philosophy. After graduating from Ohio Wesleyan, she attended DC Teachers College (now the University of the District of Columbia) and then earned a master's degree from Columbia Teachers College. She would become an art teacher in DC public schools after spending some time working in the South for Dr. Vincent Harding who was heading the Institute of the Black World.

Dr. Russell J. Davis was born in 1935 and raised in the northwest quadrant of Washington, DC. Russell would attend Ohio Wesleyan University from 1952 to 1956, graduating with a major in pre-physical therapy. After graduating from Ohio Wesleyan, Russell earned his certification and master's degree in Physical Therapy from New York University, as well as his doctorate in Public Administration from George Washington University. In his career, he was among the first to spearhead the creation of a comprehensive department of Physical Medicine and Rehabilitation at Howard University, a historically Black institution, where he also orchestrated the creation of the School of Allied Health Professions.

Willis "Bing" Davis was born in Greer, South Carolina, in 1937 and raised from infancy in Dayton, Ohio. Bing attended DePauw University from 1955 to 1959, where he played basketball and competed in the field events on the track team. He graduated as an arts major and then attended Dayton Art Institute and Miami University, where he earned a master's of education degree, as well as pursuing graduate studies in ceramics at Indiana State University. Bing would return to DePauw in the 1970s as a faculty member in the art department and as the Coordinator of Black Studies. In 1976, Bing left DePauw to become an assistant dean of the Graduate School at Miami University and assistant professor of art until 1978. Thereafter, he served as the director of the new Paul Robeson Cultural and Performing Arts Center at Central State University, a historically Black college. Bing remained on the faculty at Central State for 20 years before returning to Dayton in 2004 to establish the Davis Art Studio and EbonNia Gallery.

Richard Dean was born in 1941 and raised in Washington, DC's southeast quadrant. Richard attended DePauw University from 1960 to 1964, where he was an art major with an emphasis in marketing, advertising, and design. He was also active in extracurricular activities: Richard entered the Air Force Reserve Officer Training Corps (ROTC), played intramural basketball and varsity baseball, and was an All-American football player, and as an alumnus he would be an inaugural inductee to DePauw's Hall of Fame. After graduation, he was commissioned as a Second Lieutenant and served briefly on active duty. He would play football professionally for the St. Louis Cardinals and eventually retire from the military as a reservist at the rank of Second Lieutenant. Following other professional success in printing, Richard moved to Connecticut and is currently an independent printing broker.

Henry Deering was born in 1941 in Cincinnati, Ohio, where he was also raised before leaving for DePauw University in 1959, attracted by the 3–2 engineering program with Purdue University. After graduating in 1963 with a degree in chemistry, he completed two years of graduate study in chemistry at Howard University. During his career, Henry worked as a chemist at Hercules Incorporated in Delaware and would later become involved in the War on Poverty government initiative. Henry worked for the Internal Revenue Service for over 20 years and then became licensed as an enrolled agent offering tax preparation services.

"**Rose Jackson Enco**" was born in Cleveland circa 1940, grew up in Atlanta, Georgia, and then the family returned to Cleveland. Rose attended Ohio Wesleyan University, beginning her college career there in 1958. Rose graduated as an education major in 1962 and taught first in Cleveland Public Schools. She earned her master's degree in education from Ohio University and followed her husband to upstate New York, where she was the only Black teacher in a predominantly White school district for the majority of her career.

Dr. Ora Dee Fant was born in 1945 in Dayton, Ohio, where she was also raised. Ora attended Oberlin College; her class entering in 1964 doubled the population of Black students on campus. While at Oberlin, Ora double majored in sociology and psychology and went on study abroad. After Oberlin, Ora completed her doctorate in psychology at Boston College while working at Vassar College assisting in the transition to coeducation and the increase in Black student enrollment. After leaving Vassar, Ora worked as a consultant and then went into private industry. She later retired to "go play" and work with several nonprofit organizations. Ora served on Oberlin's Board of Trustees from 1994 to 2000.

Clyde Francis was born in Monongahela, Pennsylvania, in 1932 and raised in Linesville, Pennsylvania. Clyde attended Allegheny College from 1950 to 1954, where he graduated with a double major in history and political science. After graduation, Clyde applied and was accepted to several graduate programs and desired to work for the State Department. However, the "draft was hanging over [his] head," so he decided to enlist in the US Navy and served for four years. After his discharge, he worked for some time in insurance and then in the banking industry.

Dr. Mildred Denby Green was born in 1938 and raised in the Tidewater area of Virginia. Although Howard University was her first preference, she was first accepted at Oberlin College Conservatory and began studies there in 1955. In 1957, Mildred left Oberlin to transfer to The Ohio State University and graduated from there in 1959. After graduation and a move to Oklahoma, Mildred earned her doctorate in music education with a focus in music history from Oklahoma University. Mildred would spend her career at Owen College as Dean of Women and choir director, and then after the merger she served as a faculty member and choir director at LeMoyne-Owen College, a historically Black college in Memphis, Tennessee.

Richard Hammond was born in 1934 and raised in Chillicothe, Ohio. He was offered a small scholarship to attend Ohio Wesleyan University in 1952, but had to leave in 1954 after only two years due to finances.

After leaving Ohio Wesleyan, Richard worked initially as a Greyhound porter and then passed the postal service exam in Columbus. He would retire from the postal service with 32 years of service. Though he never finished his own undergraduate degree, he was part owner of a bar off campus at Ohio State University through which he was able to help many students earn money to stay in school.

Dr. Sybil Jordan Hampton was born in 1944 in Springfield, Missouri, at Fort Leonard Wood during her father's military service. After the war, the family returned to Little Rock, Arkansas. Among the second cohort of Black students to integrate Central High School in Little Rock, Sybil would choose to attend Earlham College. She was a student from 1962 to 1966 and she majored in English literature. After graduation, she wrote the grant for the first Upward Bound program at Earlham and staffed it that summer. Sybil would earn two master's degrees from the University of Chicago and completed her doctorate in college teaching and academic leadership in higher education from Teachers College. Sybil had several other professional roles in higher education at Iona College, the University of Wisconsin at Madison, and Southwestern University. Sybil retired in 2006 from the Winthrop Rockefeller Foundation, where she had been president. Sybil served on the Board of Trustees at Earlham for six years.

Marylyn Harrison was born in 1941 and raised in New York City, New York. Marylyn matriculated to Oberlin College in 1958 and graduated in 1962 with a major in French. Marylyn took a job as a reservation agent for Eastern Airlines after graduation and then began her teaching career in Fair Lawn, New Jersey. Marylyn continued to teach and earned a master's degree from Fairleigh Dickinson University in human development and group dynamics. She later switched to a career in financial planning.

Chuck Hatcher was born in 1942 in Cincinnati, Ohio, and then raised in Yellow Springs, Ohio. Chuck began college at The Ohio State University but transferred to Earlham College in 1963 and graduated in two and a half years in 1966 with a major in biology. After college, Chuck enlisted in the US Army and completed officer school, serving briefly in Korea. Chuck was a limnologist for the Fish and Wildlife Service, but experienced significant discrimination in graduate school at the University of Michigan. Chuck would marry another Earlham student, Ruth Ann, who completed the interview with him. In 1969, Chuck and Ruth Ann would go back to Earlham to be head residents in the residence halls; Chuck co-directed the Upward Bound program.

Ruth Ann Hatcher was born in 1948 on Chicago's south side to an interracial couple. At 16 years of age, Ruth Ann was admitted to Kalamazoo College, Earlham College, and Oberlin College and would choose to attend Earlham. She entered in 1964 and graduated in 1968 with a major in English. Ruth Ann would go on to earn her master's in English and completed coursework for the Doctor of Arts in Teaching from the University of Michigan. She would marry another Earlham student, Chuck, who completed the interview with her. In 1969, Ruth Ann and Chuck would go back to Earlham to be head residents in the residence hall; Ruth Ann worked in admissions.

Harvey Hawks was born in 1937 in Battle Creek, Michigan, and raised on a farm outside of Marshall. Harvey would attend Albion College, beginning his studies there in 1955. He changed his major in the middle of his senior year from physics and math to chemistry in which he had better grades. However, he decided to leave the college late in the fall of 1958 to work full-time at Kellogg's. After two years and strong encouragement from his father, he took two community college courses in advanced calculus and metallurgy to "get [his] feet wet again." Earning A's in both those courses, Harvey enrolled in Tri-State College in Angola, Indiana, and graduated in the spring of 1963 with a degree in aeronautical engineering. After finishing his degree, Harvey moved to southern California and worked for General Dynamics and retired in 1995 from The Boeing Company in Seattle.

Faye Hines was born in 1945 and raised in Louisville, Kentucky. While still in high school, Faye was very active, protesting segregation in Louisville, and her mother's job and the mortgage on her home were threatened if she was arrested again. Faye attended Hope College from 1963 to 1967, where she double majored in English and Spanish and spent a semester abroad in Bogota, Colombia. As more Black students began attending Hope during her junior year, she helped to start the Black Student Union. After graduation, Faye went to New York City's Lower East Side to work with students in the projects and earned a graduate degree in counseling from New York University. She worked as a counselor at Lehman College and then spent several years in Antigua, owning and operating a tourist bar and cottages. Upon her return to the States, Faye returned to guidance counseling at Boys and Girls High School and retired from there after 20 years.

Stan Jackson was born in 1930 and raised in Steubenville, Ohio. Stan attended Kenyon College from 1948 to 1952 and majored in political science. After graduation, he was conscripted into the US Army. Upon completing his tour of duty, Stan went into civil service, working for the SSA office in Columbus, Ohio, and studying law at Franklin University in the evenings. Stan would later be promoted to the SSA payment center in Chicago and he continued studying law part-time at Chicago-Kent College of Law and earned his bachelor of laws degree (LLB). Thereafter, Stan was promoted to a professional position with the Department of Health, Education, and Welfare in Baltimore, Maryland, from which he would retire in 1983.

Dr. Vivian Hopkins Jackson was born in 1948 in Hampton, Virginia. After a series of moves between Virginia and Maryland for her father's job, the family eventually settled in Norfolk, Virginia. Vivian attended Oberlin College in 1964, entering as a biology major but graduating in 1968 majoring in sociology. After graduation, Vivian would earn her master's in social work at Howard University and later pursue a doctorate in social welfare part-time at Case Western Reserve University. She worked in direct practice in hospital and health centers and later worked for the National Association of Social Workers in their national headquarters, while working part-time in private practice, consulting, and raising her family. Vivian recently retired from Georgetown University, where she had been an assistant professor and senior policy associate in the Center for Child and Human Development.

Betty Johnson was born in 1938 in Baltimore, Maryland, and raised in the northeast quadrant of Washington, DC. Betty would attend Allegheny College from 1955 to 1959, where she majored in sociology. After graduation, Betty worked for two years as a secretary for the Central Intelligence Agency and then completed graduate school at Howard University, a historically Black college, in social work. When not working in the home with her children, Betty had several different jobs, including school social work and hospice care, from which she would retire.

Karl Johnson was born in 1934 and raised in the predominantly Jewish neighborhood of Glenville in Cleveland, Ohio. Karl would attend Wabash College for two years from 1952 to 1954, where he was pursuing a major in political science with a minor in English. Upon leaving Wabash, Karl returned home briefly to study at Case Western Reserve University before leaving college to enlist in the US Air Force, where he served for four years as a Korean-language specialist. After the military, Karl would earn his bachelor's degree from Central State University, a historically Black college in Ohio, where his father served on the Board of Trustees. After unsuccessfully attempting to break into television media, he eventually worked with the Cleveland Board of Education in community relations and then for the district radio station, WBOE. Karl now owns his own business in local tourism.

Ralph W. Jones was born in 1946 and raised in Indianapolis, Indiana. Although he was accepted at Howard University, his mother refused to allow him to attend, and instead he went to DePauw University. He began college in 1964, late in the focus period of this study. Although he was doing well academically at DePauw as a political science major, Ralph left school in 1968 after three and a half years to get married. Despite never finishing his college degree, Ralph had a successful career working in corporate insurance in northeast Indiana.

Elizabeth M. Kitterman was born in 1944 and raised in Charlotte, North Carolina. Elizabeth would attend college at Earlham College from 1962 to 1966, where she graduated as a math major. After marrying her college sweetheart, they stayed in Indiana for several years. Elizabeth was working for Westinghouse until she was laid off, suing unsuccessfully for employment discrimination. Due to her husband's civilian work in the military, Elizabeth lived in Puerto Rico and Panama, and then returned to the continental USA.

Sarah W. Lawrence was born in 1943 and raised in Hempstead, Long Island, New York. Sarah would begin college in 1961 at the Oberlin College Conservatory of Music. Sarah struggled academically as a music education major at Oberlin, but did not want to change her major to performance. In 1963, she decided to transfer back to New York first to Mannes College of Music and then to Hofstra University, where she would earn her bachelor's degree. Thereafter, she pursued a career as a music teacher and received several accolades, including 1989 Teacher of the Year at Monrovia Unified School District, where she taught for 18 years.

Ritten Edward (a.k.a. "Edd") Lee was born in 1925 in Brighton, Alabama, and was raised in Piper and Marion, Alabama. Edd attended Earlham College at the early end of this study's focus, from 1946 to 1950. He graduated with a double major in sociology and psychology and went to graduate school at the University of Connecticut to earn a master's degree in social work. Following graduate school, Edd worked mainly in neighborhood houses focused on mental rehabilitation for youth and the elderly. In 1969, Edd became the first Black trustee of Earlham's Board of Trustees and served for nine years. His memoir, *I Heard the Preaching of the Elders—An Odyssey: From Alabama Coal Fields to Earlham College and Beyond*, will likely appear in October, published by Outskirts Press. He now publishes an annual Black history calendar called *Blacfax*. The second oldest participant, at the time of our interview, Edd was 87 and a half years old.

Dr. Samuel Lewis was born in 1928 in Brewton, Alabama, where he was also raised. Sam began college during the early years of this study's focus at Hope College in 1947. He would graduate pre-med with a double major in chemistry and biology. After graduating from Hope in 1951, Sam earned a master's degree in zoology from Howard University and then entered medical school, thereafter completing two years of military service in the US Army. A heart disease specialist, Sam practiced at DC General Hospital and maintained a private practice with four offices between DC and Baltimore. Sam retired in 1989.

Bill Lowry was born in 1935 and raised on the south side of Chicago, Illinois. Bill attended Kenyon College from 1952 to 1956, where he was a three-sport student-athlete. He would graduate as a history major and earn a master's degree from Loyola University Chicago while working full-time. Bill was engaged in activism in Chicago, including being on the board of the Catholic Interracial Council. He started his own award-winning television show, *The Opportunity Line*, a clearinghouse for employment and training for African Americans. Bill is Trustee Emeritus at Kenyon, having served 25 years on its board. Professionally, Bill worked for 30 years at Inland Steel Company as the Corporate Director of Personnel and Recruitment and then served as Vice President for Human Resources and Administration at the MacArthur Foundation. At the time of our interview, he was Special Assistant to the President of The Chicago Community Trust.

Rev. Dr. Chauncey Mann was born and raised in 1933 on a farm in Elizabeth City County, Virginia. Chauncey left high school to enlist in the US Coast Guard, beginning as a steward's mate and eventually qualifying for aviation electronics. In 1950, he went to the Korean War with the Coast Guard and ended his military service after four years. Returning to complete the 12th grade, Chauncey began his college career at Allegheny College in 1956 as a math major and student-athlete in football and track. After three years, he had used up his GI Bill benefits and could no longer afford tuition. He finished his bachelor's degree in religion by correspondence from the University of the Pacific. Chauncey would work for the postal service, become an adjunct faculty member in math at a community college, and then enter the ministry as a Baptist preacher. He pastored a congregation for 37 years.

Rev. Kyle McGee was born in 1942 in Columbus, Ohio, where he lived through elementary school and then the family moved to Dayton. Kyle would attend DePauw University for college from 1959 to 1963, where he majored in chemistry initially and then graduated as a philosophy and religion major. After graduation, Kyle earned a master's of divinity degree from Yale Divinity School and completed a chaplaincy training program at the Rikers Island correctional facility. Following seminary, he was the first Black priest to serve as rector at a large Episcopal congregation in downtown Dayton. He would later become the first Black and first Protestant chaplain at Georgetown University, where he served for nine years. He then moved to Connecticut to become the head of the diocesan urban ministry program.

Dr. John Herbert Niles was born in 1938 and raised in Washington, DC. Herb attended Allegheny College from 1955 to 1959, graduating with a bachelor of science degree in biology. After Allegheny, Herb graduated in 1963 from Howard University College of Medicine and completed a residency in obstetrics and gynecology. He then enlisted in the US Army serving stateside at several Army hospitals. Herb is a highly regarded surgeon and taught briefly but chose private practice, where he is still active. Herb is actively involved with Allegheny College and has been a member of the Board of Trustees since 1992, receiving an honorary degree, Doctor of Humane Letters, from the college in 2015.

Margaret Ralston Payne was born in 1946 and raised in Louisville, Kentucky. Margaret attended Kalamazoo College at the tail end of the focus period for this study, beginning her studies in 1964. She entered as a math major and switched to psychology, studied abroad in Sierra Leone for her junior year, and graduated in 1968. Margaret completed a master's degree in cognitive psychology at Kent State University and completed all coursework requirements for the doctorate but was unable to finish due to marriage and parenting. She would later become the first Black woman to be Assistant Dean for Developmental Services at Kent State. Margaret was a member of the Ohio Association of Women Deans and the National Association of Women Deans.

Donald Peppers was born in 1935 and raised in Cincinnati, Ohio. Donald attended Kenyon College from 1954 to 1958 and switched majors in his junior year from pre-med to German and Languages and made dean's list from then on. After graduating from Kenyon, Donald would earn his law degree from The Ohio State University in 1962 and pass the Ohio bar exam. He practiced law in Cleveland, Ohio, and was still active at the time of our interview.

James E. Peters was born in 1932 in Baltimore, Maryland. After completing high school, James began college at Morgan State University, a historically Black college, for one year. He then received grant aid from the state and significant financial aid from Kenyon College to transfer there in 1950. In the summer of 1953, James received his draft notice and he had to interrupt his studies to serve for two years, stationed in Arkansas and then Georgia. James returned to Kenyon in 1955 to complete his degree and graduated in 1956 as a political science major. He took some law classes at the University of Maryland and, in 1962, became the first Black person to work in the CIA in the Office of Security.

Jeannette V. Phillips was born in 1940 in Batesburg, South Carolina; later moved to Englewood, New Jersey; and then finally settled with her family in Toledo, Ohio. Jeannette began college in 1958 at Ohio Wesleyan University and majored in sociology. After graduation in 1962, Jeannette was hired by the YWCA as an assistant director of their teenage program. When her husband was moved to St. Louis, Missouri, Jeannette followed and was hired on at the YWCA in St. Louis and then later worked in recreation therapy for the Missouri Institute of Psychiatry. After another move for her husband's job brought them back to Toledo, Jeannette worked as a manager for the Bureau of Vocational Rehabilitation. Another move took them to New Jersey, where she eventually became the Director of Personnel for the Passaic County Board of Vocational Education. While in New Jersey, Jeannette earned her master's degree in public administration. Their last move before retiring to Florida was to Connecticut, where they formed their own company, Phillips Packaging, Inc. and Jeannette's primary job was with the City of Stamford, eventually serving as the executive director of social services.

Ed Rhodes was born in 1933 in Cumberland, Maryland, and was raised there until the tenth grade when he was sent to live with an uncle in Washington, DC, to attend Dunbar High School. Ed attended Kenyon College from 1951 to 1955 and graduated as a political science major. After college, Ed took the federal civil service exam and was offered a government job. Just a year later, he was drafted into the US Army and served for two years. He had a successful career as a member of the Senior Executive Service with the federal government, including with the Health, Education, and Welfare Department; the Environmental Protection Agency; and the Office of Personnel Management. After retiring from government service, Ed served as the Director of the Office of Procurement for the Washington Metropolitan Transportation Authority. Ed was the first president of the National Association of Black Procurement Professionals and would form his own business that grew to 600 employees, earning $40 million in cash flow.

"Dr. Brenda Root" was born in 1938 and raised in Cleveland, Ohio. Brenda transferred from Syracuse University to attend the Oberlin College Conservatory of Music from 1957 until her graduation in 1961. She studied music education at Oberlin and spent her junior year abroad in Salzburg, Austria. After graduation, she taught music in Cleveland Public Schools and earned a master's degree in music education from Case Western Reserve University. Brenda would later earn a doctorate in music from the University of Illinois at Urbana-Champaign and pursue a faculty career teaching at the University of Wisconsin at La Crosse, Wichita State, and the University of Wisconsin at Madison. She moved with her family to Burkina Faso and taught music in Ouagadougu, as well as at Zaria Children's School in Nigeria. Upon their return to the USA, Brenda taught in the Gilford County Schools until she retired.

Dr. Ruth Holland Scott was born in 1934 in Albion, Michigan, where she was also raised. Ruth would stay local and attend Albion College from 1952 to 1956, where she majored in sociology and education. Segregationist hiring policies at school districts between Albion and Chicago prevented her from securing a secondary school teaching position; however, she was able to find placements through the Cleveland Board of Education. Ruth earned her master's degree in education from Kent State University and received a certificate in administration from the State University of New York at Brockport. Ruth taught English in various districts across New York State and then went into public service and later banking. In 1997, she was awarded an honorary doctorate in humane letters from Alfred University and Albion College awarded her an honorary doctorate in sociology in 2000. She is currently the owner of Scott Associates Consulting, Incorporated. In 2014, Ruth published a memoir about her life, *The Circles God Draws.*

Rev. Ronald Spann was born in 1943 and raised in Ann Arbor, Michigan; his mother's family had been in Ann Arbor for five generations. Ronald attended Kalamazoo College from 1961 to 1965, majored in Spanish and linguistics, spent his junior year abroad in Spain, and completed his Senior Individualized Project in Provencal, Mexico. After graduation, Ron received a Woodrow Wilson Fellowship to study linguistics at the University of Rochester and from there went to seminary. Ron took a year off to live in Guatemala, working alongside the significant Afro-Caribbean population there. After seminary, Ron became rector of an Episcopal parish in Michigan.

Dr. Frank D. Starkey was born in 1944 and raised in Indianapolis, Indiana. Frank would attend Wabash College from 1962 to 1966 and major in chemistry. After graduation, he went on to Brown University to earn his doctorate in chemistry. Following graduate school, he accepted a faculty position at Illinois Wesleyan University in Bloomington and then moved with his family to the East Coast. There, he worked as the human resources manager for the premiere research laboratory of General Electric and retired from there in 2010.

Dr. "Tanya Summers" was born in 1947 in Brooklyn, New York, as a second-generation New Yorker. Tanya began her college career at Kalamazoo College in 1963. While at Kalamazoo, Tanya majored in sociology, spent her junior year abroad in Sierra Leone, and completed her Senior Individualized Project in New York City on the unionization of white-collar workers. After graduation in 1967, Tanya worked as a financial aid administrator at three different institutions, including public and private traditionally White colleges and a historically Black institution, where she was director of financial aid. She then earned master's and doctoral degrees in public administration, and then pursued a faculty career at an urban southern traditionally White university.

Jacqueline Huggins Burt Tolliver was born in 1944 and raised in Louisville, Kentucky. Jacqueline would travel north to attend Albion College from 1962 to 1966, where she double majored in English and sociology and minored in French. After graduation, Jacqueline earned a master's degree, studying part-time, in guidance counseling from Wayne State University. Jacqueline began her career as a social worker in Michigan over a period of seven years, serving as a case worker for children receiving Aid to Dependent Children, as well as for foster and adopted youth. After her daughter entered preschool, she began working as a federal probations officer in Michigan and transferred to Louisville in 1983. Jacqueline retired in 2001 after nearly 27 years of service.

Dr. Adine Ray Usher was born in 1939 and raised in Chicago, Illinois. Adine went to Oberlin College in 1957 and graduated in 1961 with a major in elementary education and a minor in German. Immediately following graduation, Adine earned her master's in the education of the physically handicapped from Teachers College and became the first Black teacher in Port Washington, Long Island in their special education classes for first and second graders. She moved into administration and became a school health coordinator in charge of all services related to children with physical disabilities. Adine returned to Teachers College and received her doctorate in special education in 1995. Thereafter, she went into higher education as a faculty member at Bank Street College in their special education division. Adine now works as an independent contractor and specialist in the education of young people with neuromuscular conditions.

Dr. Frances Walker-Slocum, the oldest participant at the time of our interview, was born in 1924 and raised on Sherman Avenue in the northwest quadrant of Washington, DC. Everyone in DC who was in music had been trained at Oberlin and Frances followed suit behind her older brother. She began her studies at the Oberlin College Conservatory of Music in 1941 and graduated with honors in 1945 as a piano and organ major and member of Pi Kappa Lambda, a music honorary society. She went on to graduate studies at the Curtis Institute, Juilliard, and the Manhattan School of Music, and then earned her doctorate from Columbia University. Frances debuted at Carnegie Hall in 1959 and gave a piano recital of Black composers for the US Bicentennial Celebration in 1976. She also taught music on the faculties of Lincoln University (a historically Black college), the University of Delaware, and Rutgers University. Frances then became the first Black tenured faculty at Oberlin, where she continued teaching and performing until her retirement in 1991. She published a memoir of her life in 2006, *A Miraculous Journey*.

Dr. Robert Wedgeworth was born in Ennis, Texas, in 1937 and raised in Kansas City, Missouri. He would attend Wabash College from 1955 to 1959, majoring in English literature with a minor in Spanish. Following Wabash, Robert earned his master's and doctoral degrees in library sciences from the University of Illinois at Urbana-Champaign and Rutgers University, respectively. After an initial stint working in the Kansas City Public Library, Robert held several academic and association executive positions, ultimately attaining emeritus status at the University of Illinois at Urbana-Champaign. In 2010, he was nominated by President Barack Obama to serve as a member of the Museum and Library Services Board of the National Endowment of the Arts and Humanities.

Earl M. White was born in 1937 and raised in Newport News, Virginia. He attended Ohio Wesleyan University from 1955 to 1959, majored in political science, and joined the Air Force ROTC. After college, Earl served the military for 20 years, retiring in 1979. Earl worked in social services, while earning his master's degree by correspondence from Central Michigan University, and then entered the federal government civil service.

Beauford T. Williams was born in 1933 and raised in Fort Wayne, Indiana. He attended Earlham College from 1951 to 1953, where he met and married Janet Mitchell, with whom he did his interview for this study. Beauford was in the college choir that traveled to other cities to perform and had declared a major in secondary education. Beauford was drafted in 1953 and had to leave Earlham. After serving 2 years in the military, he had a successful career in entertainment for 35 years as a hotel lounge singer with the Holiday Inn and Sheraton resorts. After a long battle with cancer, Beauford passed away on April 22, 2016.

Janet Mitchell Williams was born in 1933 in West Bend, Kentucky, and raised between there and Richmond, Indiana. Janet attended college locally at Earlham College beginning in 1951, where she would meet and marry Beauford T. Williams, with whom she did her interview for this study. Janet also sang in the college choir and had declared a major in elementary education before leaving Earlham in 1953 due to Beauford's enlistment and her pregnancy. Upon moving to Fort Wayne after Beauford's military service, Janet worked in the home raising their children and managing the household finances.

Rev. Jeane Bounds Williams was born in 1931 in Philadelphia, Pennsylvania, and raised in southern New Jersey. Jeane would enter Allegheny College in 1951 as its first Black woman student. Although a strong student in high school, academic challenges and marriage precipitated her leaving college in 1952. After Allegheny, Jeane relocated with her daughter to Washington, DC, where she worked for the Department of the Interior and remarried. After moving to Philadelphia, Jeane worked at the University of Pennsylvania as a cataloger at the Perelman School of Medicine, assistant librarian at Annenburg School of Communications, and finally retired as a circulation administrator at the Biddle Law Library. Upon receiving the call to preach, Jeane was first ordained as an elder with the National Association of Community Churches and later completed ministerial studies to be ordained in the African Methodist Episcopal (AME) Church. While pastoring Ben Salem AME Church in Bucks County, Pennsylvania, she successfully applied for the church to be designated as a national historic site. Jeane organized and chaired the first

Conference on African American Women in Ministry for the AME Church and served two terms as the only minority president of the International Association of Women Ministers.

Dr. Laura Simms Wiltz was born in Fort Valley, Georgia, in 1936 and then spent the majority of her childhood in Fairmont Heights, Maryland, and Washington, DC. Laura would attend Oberlin College, her third choice behind Radcliffe and Wellesley. She began in 1953 and changed majors from biochemistry to sociology. After graduating from Oberlin in 1957, Laura pursued her degree in social work at Columbia University on a scholarship from the National Institutes of Health. She eventually would move to California with her husband for his job and earned her doctorate in organizational behavior and management, studying part-time while raising three children at the John Anderson School of Management at the University of California at Los Angeles. She obtained a faculty position in UCLA's School of Social Welfare and then was the head of the Young Women's Christian Association (YWCA) of Greater Los Angeles for a decade.

Mabel "Midge" Winston was born in St. Louis, Missouri, in 1941 and raised in Kansas City. Mabel would attend Oberlin College from 1959 to 1963, majoring in education. After college, Mabel taught in Long Beach, California, and after 17 years left teaching for human resources and earned an MBA in an executive program. She worked for the National Urban League at their headquarters in New York City and would later become the Director of Training for the YWCA in St. Louis in 1997 and retire from that position.

Leonard H. Yorke was born in the Bronx in New York City, New York, in 1935, where he was also raised. After graduating high school at just 16 years old, Leonard started college at DePauw University in 1952 and graduated in 1956. At DePauw, Leonard was a sociology major and student-athlete. Due to his age, he did not take his first job after college until 1958; he worked at a children's home in Yonkers, New York. Shortly thereafter, Leonard followed his brother to Baltimore, where he still resided at the time of our interview.

Appendix 2

Studying Black Collegians, 1945–1965

The aim of this study is threefold: (1) to document the experiences of Black college students in a set of northern, private, liberal arts colleges prior to federally legislated educational desegregation; (2) to illustrate the nature of racial discourse in the Great Lakes region between 1945 and 1965; and (3) to examine the complexities and nuances of institutional responses to racial diversity during a time when public sentiment about racial desegregation in the USA was fraught. I approached this work through a methodological bricolage (Kincheloe, 2001) of historical and traditional qualitative research methods. Informed by Goodchild and Huk (1990), the scope of this historiography is best described as *contextualist*. By definition, a contextualist scope sees education as linked to a holistic process of cultural and societal change and relies on historiographic methods of intellectual, social, and cultural history. Relatedly, the historiographic analytical lens is the *synthetic cultural history approach* described by Goodchild and Huk as showing both how external influences changed institutions of higher learning, as well as how these institutions and their actors changed society. From qualitative methodology, I applied critical theoretical perspectives (Jones, Torres, & Arminio, 2014) to better incorporate my role as the researcher in the construction of this history alongside the primary source data. In this way, the presumed objectivism of historical inquiry (Novick, 1998) is rightfully disrupted and full

© The Author(s) 2017

D.-L. Stewart, *Black Collegians' Experiences in US Northern Private Colleges*, DOI 10.1057/978-1-137-59077-0

engagement of the social and cultural contexts of these colleges and their students is best revealed.

Research Paradigm

As I have stated, objectivist historiographic approaches were deemed insufficient to sufficiently explore these issues. Though hotly debated in the 1990s, objectivity has been the ideal of professional historical scholarship (Novick, 1998) and these historians relied on the idea that the past existed as a discernibly true, fixed, and consistent reality. Further, historians sought detachment from theoretical frameworks and ideologies in order to adhere to the universalism required of historical objectivity (Novick, 1998). Yet, contrary to biasing historical narratives, Novick (1998) also recounted that other historians have pointed to the necessity of locating history within the epistemological and theoretical paradigms of the researcher as recommended by Scott (2008).

CRT as enunciated by Delgado and Stefancic (2012) and Ladson-Billings (1998) informed my theoretical perspective. CRT foregrounds racism and White supremacy as pervasive, inherent characteristics of sociocultural reality deeply intertwined and interconnected with other oppressive systems (Delgado & Stefancic, 2012; Ladson-Billings, 1998). Through the use of strategies that prioritize racially minoritized people's perspectives, experiences, and sense making (Delgado & Stefancic, 2012), I focus this text on the oral histories of the 68 Black participants with whom I collaborated. Moreover, as a post-structuralist, I recognized the role of individuals, particularly as collectives, in co-creating, co-challenging, and co-resisting existing power structures (Jones, Torres, &Arminio, 2014). The resultant polyvocality leads to a more radical democratization of systems and institutions leading to liberatory futures (Barbules & Rice, 1991).

These ontological assumptions inform an approach to knowledge that intentionally centers the voices and experiences of those closest to the phenomenon under study. Through such a subjectivist approach (Ellingson, 2011; Habermas, 1984; Jones et al., 2014), meaning-making is derived from the insights oflived experiences, including the researcher's. Moreover, through a critical post-structural lens, power is understood to shape those narratives (Jones et al., 2014; Lather, 2003). Therefore, the researcher, as witness to the nefarious effects of power and oppression, must bring those analyses to bear on the data (Bowleg, 2008).

Through such an epistemological stance, research is valued and valuable when its effects primarily seek transformation and greater emancipation for individuals and communities (Lather, 1986). For the researcher who is a member of one or more minoritized communities, researching alongside and within the communities of which one is a member is fraught (Collins, 1986, 1999; Lather, 2003), but is also a practice of resilience and resistance (Collins, 1986, 1999; Zurita, 2001).

Methods

The narrative mode used in this project was oral history (Chaddock, 2010; Chaitin, 2008; Perks & Thomson, 1998; Thompson, 1998). Oral history seemed especially appropriate because its "aim…is to gain first-hand knowledge from people who have lived through different social – historical – political periods and events" (Chaitin, 2008, p. 584). Moreover, oral history has been credited with "including the experiences and perspectives of groups of people who might otherwise have been hidden from history" (Perks & Thomson, 1998, p. ix). While sufficient on its own, this firsthand knowledge was also available through textual material directly produced by some of these Black matriculates, as well as that produced by other students, administrators, and even faculty in student newspapers, college yearbooks, reports, and meeting minutes. Including multiple sources of firsthand knowledge and sense making enriched the understanding of the total institutional context in which these Black matriculates lived and studied. Therefore, both archival material and oral history interviews comprised the data for this project.

Documenting Race

Before the passage of the 1964 Civil Rights Act, colleges were not required to keep data on the race or ethnicity of their students as is now customary. Therefore, few of the GLCA colleges had alumni databases sortable by race. Kalamazoo, Oberlin, Ohio Wesleyan, and Earlham Colleges were exceptions to this, while Antioch College had records of its Black alumni from 1943 to 1968 in a file related to integration and student recruitment efforts, likely created by an administrator, J. Treichler (1969). This enabled me to cross-reference my records of Black students at these institutions with those institutional databases. In some cases, particularly at Earlham, this process corrected racial classifications I had made in error and added names to my list whose pictures had not appeared or I had misidentified in the yearbooks. However, for the majority of institutions, I was limited to making racial classifications based on the limited reliability of visual identifications of Black students from pictures. Moreover, only those whose pictures appeared in the yearbook and were identified by name by the yearbook's editorial staffs could be captured.

It is important to note that race is neither scientific nor biological; rather, it is a social construction (Appiah, 1992; Fields, 1982). Any attempt to "scientifically" (as in "objectively" and "accurately") identify someone else's racial identity is inherently prone to error. Such errors cannot be completely avoided in historical research. Nevertheless, I feel confident that I have produced a reasonably reliable record of the matriculation of Black students at the GLCA colleges between 1945 and 1965.

Researching Race in Educational History

Previously, I have interrogated normative, essentialist approaches to the study of race provoked by the historian's quest for authentic and credible (some might say *objective*) experiences of marginalized groups in higher education (Stewart, 2016). Race and racial classifications, therefore, reflect the ideological construction of social groups, albeit with material effects (Appiah, 1992; Campbell & Oakes, 1993; Davis 1997; Fields, 1982; Holt, 1998; Young, 1990). As Fields (1982) argued, the persistence and ubiquity of race makes it tempting to see race as "transhistorical" (p. 144), as inherently existing across time and space. Processes to ensure bureaucratic compliance through counting and documenting individuals by racial (and other demographic) classifications further that temptation. Studying the lived experiences of those who have been classified by such ideological construction as race and blackness in US higher education consequently involves the use of these same constructed categories. However, how researchers document the consequences of these categories and resultant social groupings can either "naturalize those experiences" as though they were unmediated (Scott, 2008, p. 279) or provoke an analysis of that knowledge itself.

To reckon with these issues, I have argued for the adoption of a critical realist approach for the study of race in educational institutions (Stewart, 2016). By using a realist approach to identity categories (Bell, 1992; Sanchez-Casál & McDonald, 2009), I was able to document and interpret the ways in which the social production of racial categories created opportunities for members of those categories to create (or not) communities of meaning (Moya, 2009) within and beyond the primary identity category under study. Acknowledging racial realism (instead of an essentialized idealism; Bell, 1992) challenged me to consider the factors that were producing the experiences that were being shared or documented (Scott, 2008). In addition, this approach invited me to actively present my own identity as having epistemic salience (Moya, 2009), contributing to the construction of meaning with historical actors.

Identity categories are unavoidable in historical inquiry if we are to take Bell's (1992) advice and take a hard look at systems of exclusion in higher education. Black students, faculty, and staff were systemically denied access because blackness had been defined as inferior. Yet, that production of blackness does not wholly explain the social isolation and segregation that has been documented by other scholars over time (Clotfelter, 2004; Evans, 2007; Waite, 2001; Zimbardo, 1966) and which is confirmed in this study. To narrate the experiences of Black collegians historically required an analysis of how Black students understood the role of their racial identity—its epistemic salience—in these predominantly White GLCA colleges, as well as how categories of gender also moderated their experiences and the meaning they made of them (see Chap. 6). An intersectional understanding of the interaction of racism with other systems of oppression (Dill, 2002), such as gender and social class, gave a more nuanced picture of those students' historical experiences. Failing to apply such an approach would have supported a monolithic treatment of these Black collegians, denying the group's heterogeneity.

Further, I needed to attend in my inquiry to the formation of social groups on college campuses based on social identities. Social groups are not preexisting, but are produced by persistent conditions in the campus climate over time. Those conditions, how students became sensitized to them, and how they became sensitized to each other as viable partners in communities of meaning were worthy processes to document in this study. To do so, I had to see the thing as it became, but resist presuming that it had always been, so that I could trace its development as a historical product.

Archival Materials

I conducted research in the institutional archives, both digital and physical, of the member institutions of the GLCA. Each college had primary documents that addressed questions about the presence of Black students, and whether and how issues of race and the events taking place around the country, particularly in the South, were discussed on campus. To collect such data, I contacted the college archivists at each college and arranged to visit the archives for a period of two to three days physically reviewing materials and then spent several hours once home searching online repositories of digitized student newspapers. Consistent with triangulation in qualitative research (Creswell, 2013; Patton, 2015; Shenton, 2004), I collected different types of materials produced by members of the college communities: photographs and text in yearbooks, newspapers, written reports and memos, as well as meeting minutes, where these were available and relevant to the focus of this study. A complete list of all primary sources reviewed for this study is available following the general reference list in this book.

The following keywords guided my search of student newspapers: Negro and colored (consistent with the common parlance of the 1940s and 1950s to reference Black people), desegregation, segregation, racism, civil rights, integration, and race relations. Hundreds of articles were collected, read, and organized according to the following themes: White students' attitudes about race relations; Black students featured as subjects of articles; Black students' attitudes about race relations; editorials about campus policies regarding race relations and integration; campus events featuring topics concerning race; and campus events featuring Black performers. From the yearbooks, I made extensive notes recording the names of Black students, faculty, and staff, as well as any instances of engagement with Black culture (including parody and mimicry) or discussions of racial issues. I recorded photos of organizations with Black students as members, racialized imagery, newspaper articles, editorials, and letters to the editors concerning issues of race, and visiting speakers and performers who were Black, and/or who spoke about racial issues.

Working with Yearbooks and Student Newspapers

I discuss at length elsewhere the ways that the yearbooks and student newspapers from the GLCA institutions reflected the pervasive whiteness of these campuses (Stewart, 2017). As Black students became increasingly segregated on northern campuses during the early half of the twentieth century, it would be difficult for researchers to obtain evidence of this segregation and its effects on Black students' experiences through reliance on student perspectives directly as would be the case in qualitative methodologies. Moreover, institutional chronicles may also fail to tell a complete story of an institution's history with segregation and racial exclusion. Such chronicles are typically positivist in orientation and intended to present a triumphant, victorious narrative (Goodchild & Huk, 1990). Therefore, authors may fail to capture the unsavory reflections of campus life and student experiences resultant from racial segregation on campus. The primary source materials that would reflect student life are also limited to majoritarian perspectives of the dominant student bodies at these institutions, White men and women.

Alternatively, yearbooks and student newspapers present a largely unrealized opportunity (Greene, 1989) to study student campus life and how racial exclusion and segregation may have been manifested. Begun in the late nineteenth century by students (Johnson, 2010), yearbooks "capture an academic year and preserve it for future generations" (para. 13). The benefit of a yearbook as a historical document is that it supposes to portray student life at a campus across the student body. The portrayal (or not) of racial diversity in the college yearbook can yield important insights into an institution's racial climate, the racial attitudes of the majority White student body, as well as the representations of Black and other racially minoritized students.

Three important considerations can be taken away from this study of student publications (Stewart, 2017). I summarize those implications here. First, student publications are reflections of the social and cultural contexts that produce them and must be understood in light of those contexts. In the mid-twentieth century, the GLCA colleges and the entire country were embedded in societal debates about race relations and integration, especially following the 1954 Supreme Court decision in *Brown v. Board of Education*. Segregation was prevalent in the communities surrounding colleges during this era.

Second, whiteness need not be terrorizing to be all-encompassing. As seen in Chap. 8, the yearbooks did not include evidence of hate speech or racist graffiti and the newspapers did not include coverage of racial hostilities between White and Black students. In fact, racial caricatures and blackface were donned in good fun by White students. Nevertheless, the whiteness of these campuses was no less totalizing than that named by the students in Feagin, Vera, and Imani's (1996) study over three decades later. Racism is racism, not because it is emotionally hurtful, but because of the totalizing effect of racial subordination. A researcher looking for open hostility as the only reliable evidence of racism's effects at these colleges would miss the insights gained by considering the benign faces of racism.

Third, those interested in campus traditions and the nature of student cultures must consult multiple sources for insights into students' lives.

As recommended by Kaestle (1992), using multiple sources of data and situating them in appropriate social and cultural contexts produces a more reliable history. Telling a single story based on an objectivist, realist depiction of historical fact does not reveal the ways that race and racism are always already being enforced. These publications are not neutral repositories of information and photographs, but rather reflect the social construction of history and memory.

Oral Histories

Phase two of this project involved locating, contacting, and interviewing these colleges' living Black alumni who attended between 1945 and 1965. Doing so required the cooperation of the GLCA college alumni offices. As explained by these administrators, *alumni* at these colleges often included both graduates and nongraduates, as long as the student had attended the college full-time for at least two semesters. Of the 13 colleges, 11 assisted with contacting their alumni either by releasing addresses to me or by sending letters on my behalf to maintain the alumni's confidentiality until they agreed to participate in the study. Antioch College and The College of Wooster were unable to assist. Of the 913 Black collegians found through the colleges' yearbooks (with Antioch, Earlham, Oberlin, and Ohio Wesleyan accounting for the majority of that total amount), recruitment letters were sent to 290 alumni, due to availability of current contact information, college cooperation in sending letters, and efforts to maintain proportionate representation. Sixty-eight Black alumni from ten GLCA colleges agreed to participate and followed through with an interview. After successive attempts, I was unable to confirm interviews with the three Denison University matriculates who had returned forms indicating an interest in the study. Of these 68 respondents, 12 (17.6%) had not graduated from the GLCA institution at which they enrolled.

Gender

Of the 913 Black collegians attending the GLCA colleges between 1945 and 1965, 65% were Black men (n = 593) and 35% were Black women (n = 320), an imbalance that does not reflect Black women's much greater representation at historically Black colleges during this period (T.J. Edge, personal communication, July 2016). At this time, both Kenyon College and Wabash College were all-male, single-sex institutions. However, each of these colleges only matriculated 21 and 23 Black men, respectively, to their institutions and so do not overly influence the dominant pattern I

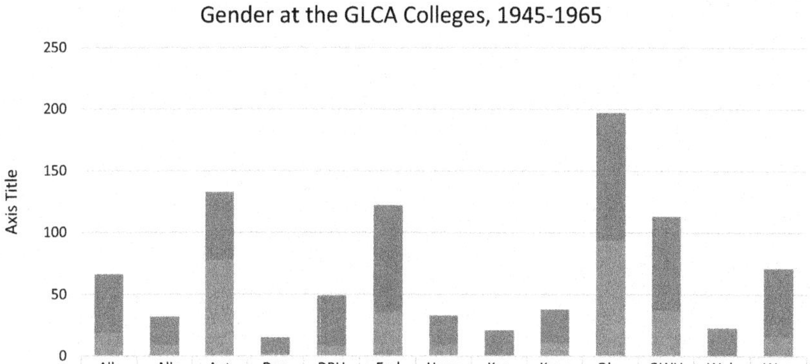

	Alb	All	Ant	Den	DPU	Earl	Hope	Ken	Kzoo	Obe	OWU	Wab	Woo
Men	47	23	55	13	41	86	24	21	27	103	76	23	54
Women	19	9	78	2	8	36	9	0	11	94	37	0	17

Fig. A.1 Gender at the GLCA Colleges. Key: *Alb* Albion, *All* Allegheny, *Ant* Antioch, *Den* Denison, *DPU* DePauw, *Earl* Earlham, *Ken* Kenyon, *Kzoo* Kalamazoo, *Obe* Oberlin, *OWU* Ohio Wesleyan, *Wab* Wabash, *Woo* Wooster

have described. Other colleges had drastic gender imbalances. DePauw matriculated only 8 Black women during these 2 decades, while matriculating 41 Black men. Figure A.1 shows that Albion, Denison, Earlham, and Wooster were similarly lopsided. It is notable that Antioch is the only one of the institutions which matriculated more Black women than Black men. Nevertheless, women were almost on par with men as respondents in this study. Of the participants, 37 (54%) were men and 31 (46%) were women.

Although the focus of this study is explicitly on race and ethnicity, race and racism should not be viewed in isolation but rather in connection with other identities and systems of oppression (Lawrence, Matsuda, Delgado, & Crenshaw, 1993). This study intersects discourses of race and racism and the racialized experiences of Black college students at the GLCA institutions between 1945 and 1965 with the ways in which other systems of inequality also contributed to shaping student experiences and the institutional climate of these colleges during this period. Gender also demarcates these narratives as demonstrated in Chap. 6.

Transcription as Cultural Reflection

Oral history took the form of eliciting stories and interpretations (Chaddock, 2010). As explained by Chaitin (2008), oral history inter-

Table A.1 Numbers of participating black alumni from each GLCA college

Institution	*N*
Albion College	7
Allegheny College	6
DePauw University	8[a]
Earlham College	12
Hope College	2
Kalamazoo College	3
Kenyon College	7
Oberlin College	12[b]
Ohio Wesleyan University	8
Wabash College	3
Total	68

[a]All the participants from DePauw were men
[b]All the participants from Oberlin were women

views are generally guided by open-ended questions that are "person and experience centered" (p. 585). Therefore, my interview questions sought to elicit biographical information, college-choice decision processes, general experiences in college, reflections on the CRM and discourses of race at their institution, and experiences off campus in the local community of their campus. This approach was guided by the belief that "through history ordinary people seek to understand the upheavals and changes which they experience in their own lives" (Thompson, 1998, p. 21). Interviews were all audio-recorded for later transcription by a professional service. Table A.1 shows how many alumni from each institution participated.

The professional service that I used produced verbatim transcripts of each interview. As a result, my and the participants' use of less formal, relaxed speech, and reflecting the incorporation of African American Vernacular English (AAVE; Harris, 2010), was also documented. Thus the transcripts revealed the in-group conversational tone and style sometimes used when Black people speak to each other away from the othering gaze of White people (Harris, 2010). Due to racist stereotypes that depict Black people as inherently less intelligent and which view AAVE and other cultural dialects as reflective of lower intelligence (Harris, 2010), their use is reserved for intra-community conversations. It is not uncommon for Black adults to report being cautioned by their parents to speak "good English" in public and particularly when speaking to White people, and some were required to use only standard English even when at home (Barnes, 2014).

In research, verbatim transcription is common for qualitative research (Creswell, 2013). It is taken to be more authentic and true to what the respondents were expressing (Creswell, 2013). Due to this training, I did not hesitate to allow the professional service I contracted to create verbatim transcripts of the interviews with my participants. However, when participants responded to my transcript verification request, they invariably noted the documentation of their (and my) use of AAVE as "errors" to be corrected in addition to correcting misspellings of names and places they had mentioned. For one participant with whom I conducted their interview over the phone, the appearance of her non-standard English use was cause for great concern. She called me before sending back her transcript to ask me why I had not corrected her non-standard syntax (e.g., usage of the verb *to be*) and clipped endings (e.g., *goin'* for *going*; *cos* or *cuz* for *because*). She explained her concern that by presenting her narrative with her use of "bad English" she would be viewed by the readers of my book as "uneducated" and "unsophisticated." This participant went further to say that she did not want her material to be used at all if I intended to publish it without "correcting" her errors as she questioned my motives for presenting her in that way. She had "worked too hard" to overcome people's racist assumptions to allow all that work to be "undone" by a researcher with suspect motives.

Academic scholars and journalists have argued for ending the practice of requiring students to code-switch between AAVE and Standard English (Harris, 2010; Young, 2009) and correcting quotes in journalistic publications to reflect Standard English (Adande, 2016). In response to Adande's (2016) suggestion that sports journalists stop correcting athlete's grammatical errors in interviews, sociologist Tressie McMillan Cottom wrote the following post on Twitter: "Because we think of discourse as a way that power is structured, syntax matters to sense making. Could be awesome" (Tressie Mc, 2016). Although I agree with Cottom in principle, it is also important to honor how participants want to be reflected in resultant research reports that use what they have shared with us in trust. It would be irresponsible to ignore or deny the racism that may still frame these college-educated and highly accomplished people as "uneducated" or "unsophisticated" for the sake of the supposed authenticity gained by producing a verbatim transcript. Therefore, to maintain the trust of my participants and resist the racist presumptions that may be unconsciously transferred from readers onto these individuals, I have translated all non-standard grammar, syntax, and dialectical pronunciations to Standard

English. There were no instances where doing so would have altered the sense making conveyed by the participant. Although this decision is complicit with racism and internalized oppression regarding AAVE and cultural dialects, I feel this compromise is necessary to prioritize the comfort of my participants with their representations in this text.

Data Analysis

Instead of cutting and slicing the data to perform coding as an analytic strategy (Creswell, 2013; Saldaña, 2013), I adopted Jackson and Mazzei's (2012) approach to "thinking with theory." This approach treats the data in whole chunks making sense of them through the lens of the theoretical frameworks and perspectives that inform the research. For this study, CRT and post-structuralist perspectives provided the lenses through which I understood the archival material and oral histories as data in this research. In this way, the context of the data is retained and is better situated alongside the social and cultural contexts in which they occurred. I believe this approach also complements historiographic recommendations for historians to foreground social and cultural context and reflect multiple perspectives (Kaestle, 1992).

Theoretical Framework

Through slavery and the expulsion of indigenous people from their territory, whiteness came to function as self-identity, as reputation, and as property (Harris, 1993). The legal status afforded to whiteness made it a "vested interest" (Harris, 1993, p. 1725), one that only Whites could possess, "a highly valued and exclusive form of property" (Harris, 1993, p. 1724). In Harris' view, whiteness stands as a form of property that defines social relations and expectations, and has certain functions. Whiteness, explicitly during the Jim Crow segregation era that followed Reconstruction, allowed certain people classified as White to have access to these intangible properties of social mobility (e.g., jobs, education), while denying access to others who were not classified as White. This access, or lack thereof, had material consequences for the ability to gain tangible property as well as for social status and mobility. In a society predicated on racial subordination, as had become the case in the USA by the mid-twentieth century, White privilege became a legally enforceable expectation and "the quintessential property for personhood" (Harris, 1993, p. 1730). Racial classifications were treated as objective fact, instead of as social constructions. Control of whiteness—who could access, use, and benefit from it—was expected to be maintained. Racialized dominant and subordinate statuses came to be reified in the law as claims to whiteness as property were upheld for White people and denied to those deemed to be not White.

Harris (1993) denoted four attributes of whiteness as property: First, although whiteness cannot be transferred between people, it accrues both material and intangible benefits to the owner. Second, whiteness can be experienced and used as a resource through the exercise of White privilege. Third, to be regarded as White conferred reputational property interest. Loss of one's reputation as White, for light-skinned biracial Americans judged to have African ancestry, resulted in a tangible loss of market value in terms of lost wages, access to property, and other monetized legal rights. Fourth, whiteness is defined mainly through the exclusion of others determined not to be White from spaces, participation, and recognition.

As applied to higher education, other scholars have recognized the predominantly White campus as a sanctuary for White students, while being a hostile environment for Black students and other racially minoritized student populations (Chang, Milem, & Antonio, 2011; Feagin, Vera, & Imani, 1996; Harper & Hurtado, 2007; Hurtado, Milem, Clayton-Pedersen, & Allen, 1998). Although not directly applying Harris's (1993) whiteness as property framework, the tenets of her theory are still illustrated through this literature in the multiple ways on traditionally White campuses that whiteness confers material benefits to certain students, is unconsciously enjoyed by those students, is associated with higher status and reputation on campus, and propagates the attitude that those who are not White do not belong and should be excluded from the institution. Elsewhere, I have illustrated how this framework provides a useful lens through which to understand the role of student publications among the GLCA colleges to deploy whiteness to control and limit representations of the campus (Stewart, 2017). In this text, understanding the features and attributes of whiteness as property has shaped my interpretations of the data throughout the text.

Trustworthiness

Beyond asking for participants to verify the accuracy of their transcripts and employing data triangulation, I also employed three other strategies common to qualitative research (Creswell, 2013; Patton, 2015; Shenton, 2004) to buttress the trustworthiness of these data and my interpretations. First, member checking went beyond transcript verification to include checks on my interpretations (Creswell, 2013; Patton, 2015). I did this during interviews by asking clarifying questions that checked my interpretations in the moment. However, as I am applying specific theoretical perspectives and frameworks to these data, I did not elect to invite participants to directly member check the analyses presented in this text. Member checking presumes that participants will make sense of their experiences through the same lenses as the researcher and that if they disagree with the researchers' interpretations then those interpretations are necessarily wrong. Critical theory recognizes that its central tenets are not value-neutral (Delgado &Stefancic, 2012; Jones, Torres, &Arminio, 2014; Ladson-Billings, 1998). Therefore, I employed five peer debriefers (Shenton, 2004) who were versed in critical theoretical perspectives to review the interpretations presented in the text. These scholars pointed out issues where my data did not support my interpretations and recommended places where I could strengthen my assertions based on the data. Finally, I maintained research journals that comprise an audit trail (Shenton, 2004) of my research activities, notes, and a log of the data. In these ways, I have sought to ensure the goodness of my data and instill confidence in my interpretations.

Reporting and Representation

In the summer of 2013, although I am not a fan of zombie fiction, I read a novel by Max Brooks (2006) about the zombie wars. I was intrigued by its subtitle identifying the book as an "oral history." I read it to see an example of how oral history might be approached in literary form. As Richardson and St. Pierre (2005) have written, the process of reporting research is itself a form of inquiry. The structure and organization of the manuscript both imposes constraints and offers possibilities for how the data are presented and therefore understood by the reader. Given the narrative focus of this particular text, Brooks' (2006) choice to foreground stories of the people who directly lived the experiences being reported (albeit fictional) was provocative and exciting. Brooks presented those narratives without further analysis and I was tempted to adopt that approach in its entirety. However, this is still a co-constructed narrative and inclusion of how I made sense of these materials and oral histories is also valid and necessary. I have chosen to foreground the participants' sense making and then comment on the issues and themes raised by their narratives. This is in keeping with the critical paradigm that informs this research.

Summary

This "critical, multi-perspectival, multi-theoretical, and multi-methodological approach" (Rogers, 2012, p. 1)—bricolage research—reflects my perspective that researchers are never free from their subjective standpoints; no one correct telling of an event exists but each retelling reflects a different perspective (Denzin & Lincoln, 2000). As Kincheloe (2001) asserted, bricoleurs do not merely engage in boundary-crossing interdisciplinarity but are deeply aware of the tools available through application of diverse disciplinary approaches and the power inherent in selecting among those tools. This "deep interdisciplinarity" (Kincheloe, 2001, p. 686) allows researchers to transcend formulaic applications of the methodological constraints of one discipline "creating unique possibilities for knowledge construction [and] informed political action" (Rogers, 2012, p. 2).

References

Adande, J. A. (2016, May 18). 'We gonna be championship!': A new approach to 'fixing' quotes. *The Undefeated*. Retrieved from http://theundefeated.com/features/we-gonna-be-championship-a-new-approach-to-fixing-quotes/

Ali-Coleman, K. Z. (2014, March 20). Mom jailed for enrolling kids in school tells her story in new book, film. *Ebony*. Retrieved from http://www.ebony.com/news-views/mom-jailed-for-enrolling-kids-in-school-tells-her-story-in-new-book-film-405#axzz4AMUoTnb7

Alridge, D. P. (2007). Of victorianism, civilizationism, and progressivism: The educational ideals of W. E. B. DuBois and Anna Julia Cooper, 1892–1940. *History of Education Quarterly, 47*(4), 416–446.

American Association of Colleges & Universities. (2007). *College learning for the new global century*. Washington, DC: Author.

American Council on Education. (1949). *The student personnel point of view* (Rev. ed.). Washington, DC: Author.

Anderson, J. D. (1988). *The education of Blacks in the south, 1860–1935*. Raleigh: University of North Carolina Press.

Anderson, J. D. (1993). Race, meritocracy, and the American academy during the immediate post-World War II era. *History of Education Quarterly, 33*, 151–175.

Anderson, T. H. (1995). *The movement and the sixties: Protest in America from Greensboro to Wounded Knee*. New York, NY: Oxford University Press.

Appiah, K. A. (1992). *In my father's house: Africa in the philosophy of culture*. New York, NY: Oxford University Press.

Ballard, A. B. (1973). *The education of Black folk: The Afro-American struggle for knowledge in White America*. New York, NY: Harper & Row.

© The Author(s) 2017

D.-L. Stewart, *Black Collegians' Experiences in US Northern Private Colleges*, DOI 10.1057/978-1-137-59077-0

Ballard, A. B. (2011). *Breaching Jericho's walls: A twentieth-century African American life*. Albany: State University of New York Press.

Barbules, N. C., & Rice, S. (1991). Dialogue across differences: Continuing the conversation. *Harvard Educational Review, 61*, 393–416.

Barnes, H. (2014, April). Talking white and living black: The art of code switching. *For Harriet*. Retrieved from http://www.forharriet.com/2014/04/talking-white-and-living-black-art-of.html#axzz498k5GwLy

Baumann, R. M. (2010). *Constructing Black education at Oberlin College: A documentary history*. Athens: Ohio University Press.

Beals, M. P. (1995). *Warriors don't cry: The searing memoir of the battle to integrate Little Rock's Central High*. New York, NY: Washington Square Press.

Bell, D. (1992). Racial realism. *Connecticut Law Review, 24*, 363–379.

Birnbaum, R. (1988). *How colleges work: The cybernetics of academic organization and leadership*. San Francisco, CA: Jossey-Bass.

Blodgett, G. (2006). *Oberlin history: Essays and impressions*. Oberlin, OH: Oberlin College.

Bowleg, L. (2008). When Black + lesbian + woman ≠ Black lesbian woman: The methodological challenges of qualitative and quantitative intersectionality research. *Sex Roles, 59*(5), 312–325.

Brooks, M. (2006). *World war Z: An oral history of the zombie war*. New York, NY: Crown.

Brown III, M. C., & Davis, J. E. (2001). The historically Black college as social contract, social capital, and social equalizer. *Peabody Journal of Education, 76*, 31–49.

Burton, N. K. (2012, July 9). How did blacks travel during segregation? *The Root*. Retrieved from http://www.theroot.com/print/64178

Cabrera, A., & LaNasa, S. (2000). Understanding the college-choice process. *New Directions for Institutional Research, no., 107*, 5–22.

Callendar, D., & Jackson, J. (2008). Does the fear of debt constrain choice of university or subject of study? *Studies in Higher Education, 33*(4), 405–429.

Campbell, J., & Oakes, J. (1993). The invention of race: Rereading *White Over Black* [Review of the book]. *Reviews in American History, 21*, 172–183.

Carson, C. (1981). *In struggle: SNCC and the Black awakening of the 1960s*. Cambridge, MA: Harvard University Press.

Case Western Reserve University. (2014). *Our history*. Retrieved from http://case.edu/about/history.html

Chaddock, K. (2010). Oral history…as scholarship. In M. Gasman (Ed.), *The history of U.S. higher education: Methods for understanding the past* (pp. 19–29). New York, NY: Routledge.

Chaitin, J. (2008). Oral history. In L. M. Given (Ed.), *The SAGE encyclopedia of qualitative research methods* (pp. 584–586). Thousand Oaks, CA: SAGE.

Chang, M. J., Milem, J. F., & Antonio, A. L. (2011). Campus climate and diversity. In J. H. Schuh, S. R. Jones, & S. R. Harper (Eds.), *Student services: A handbook for the profession* (pp. 43–58). San Francisco, CA: Jossey-Bass.

Chase, S. P. (Ed.). (1833). *The statutes of Ohio and of the Northwestern Territory adopted or enacted from 1788 to 1833 inclusive: Together with the Ordinance of 1787; The constitutions of Ohio and of the United States, and various public instruments and acts of Congress: Illustrated by a preliminary sketch of the history of Ohio; numerous references and notes, and copious indexes* (Vol. 1). Cincinnati, OH: Corey & Fairbank. Center for Archival Collections, Bowling Green State University.

Chickering, A., & Reisser, L. (1993). *Education and identity* (2nd ed.). San Francisco, CA: Jossey-Bass.

Clark, E. C. (1992). *The schoolhouse door: Segregation's last stand at the University of Alabama*. Oxford: Oxford University.

Clotfelter, C. T. (2003). Alumni giving to elite private colleges and universities. *Economics of Education Review, 22*(2), 109–120.

Clotfelter, C. T. (2004). *After Brown: The rise and retreat of school desegregation*. Princeton, NJ: Princeton University Press.

Collins, P. H. (1986). Learning from the outsider within: The sociological significance of Black feminist thought. *Social Problems, 33*(6), S14–S32.

Collins, P. H. (1999). Reflections on the outsider within. *Journal of Career Development, 26*, 85–88.

Creswell, J. W. (2013). *Qualitative inquiry and research design: Choosing among five approaches* (3rd ed.). Thousand Oaks, CA: Sage.

Curators of the University of Missouri. (2016). *History*. University of Missouri-Kansas City. Retrieved from http://www.umkc.edu/history/

Dalfiume, R. M. (1970). Stirrings of revolt. In A. Weinstein & F. O. Gatell (Eds.), *The segregation era, 1863–1954: A modern reader* (pp. 235–247). New York, NY: Oxford University Press.

Davis, D. B. (1997). Constructing race: A reflection. *The William and Mary Quarterly, 54*, 7–18.

Davison, D. M. (1997). Foreword. In P. Murray (Ed.), *States' laws on race and color* (pp. xiii–xxvii). Athens: University of Georgia Press. Retrieved from https://books.google.com/

Day, J. K. (2014). *The Southern Manifesto: Massive resistance and the fight to preserve segregation*. Jackson: University Press of Mississippi.

Delgado, R., & Stefancic, J. (2012). *Critical race theory: An introduction* (2nd ed.). New York: New York University.

Denzin, N., & Lincoln, Y. (2000). *Handbook of qualitative research* (2nd ed.). Thousand Oaks, CA: Sage.

Dill, B. T. (2002). Work at the intersections of race, gender, ethnicity, and other dimensions of difference in higher education. *Connections: Newsletter of the*

Consortium on Race, Gender, and Ethnicity (Fall), 5–7. Retrieved from http://www.crge.umd.edu/publications/news.pdf

Donohue III, J. J., Heckman, J. J., & Todd, P. E. (2002). The schooling of southern Blacks: The roles of legal activism and private philanthropy, 1910–1960. *The Quarterly Journal of Economics, 117*(1), 225–268.

Doyle, W. (2003). *An American insurrection: James Meredith and the battle of Oxford, Mississippi.* New York, NY: Anchor Books.

Eisenmann, L. (1999). Reclaiming religion: New historiographic challenges in the relationship of religion and American higher education. *History of Education Quarterly, 39*, 295–306.

Ellingson, L. L. (2011). Analysis and representation across the continuum. In N. K. Denzin & Y. S. Lincoln (Eds.), *The Sage handbook of qualitative research* (4th ed., pp. 595–610). Los Angeles, CA: Sage.

Evans, S. Y. (2007). *Black women in the ivory tower, 1850–1954.* Gainesville: University of Florida.

Farber, D. (Ed.). (1994). *The sixties: From memory to history.* Raleigh: University of North Carolina.

Farber, D., & Bailey, B. (Eds.). (2001). *The Columbia guide to America in the 1960s.* New York, NY: Columbia University.

Feagin, J., Vera, H., & Imani, N. (1996). *The agony of education: Black students at white colleges and universities.* New York, NY: Routledge.

Federally recognized Indian reservations and tribes. (2010). In A. Truer, K. Wood, W. W. Fitzhugh, G. P. Horse Capture, T. L. Frazier, M. R. Miller, M. Belarde-Lewis, & J. Norwood (Eds.), *Indian nations of North America* (pp. 354–355). Washington, DC: National Geographic Society.

Fields, B. J. (1982). Ideology and race in American history. In J. M. Kousser & J. M. McPherson (Eds.), *Region, race, and reconstruction: Essays in honor of C. Vann Woodward* (pp. 143–177). New York, NY: Oxford University Press.

Finkelman, P. (2006, April 27). *The surprising history of race and law in Michigan.* Michigan Supreme Court Historical Society. Retrieved from http://www.micourthistory.org/historical-vignettes/

Flattau, P. E., Bracken, J., Van Atta, R., Bandeh-Ahmadi, A., de laCruz, R., &Sullivan, K. (2006). *The national defense education act of 1958: Selected outcomes.* IDA Document D-3306. Washington, DC: Institute for Defense Analyses. Science & Technology Policy Institute. Retrieved from https://www.ida.org/idamedia/Corporate/Files/Publications/STPIPubs/ida-d-3306.ashx

Franklin, V. P. (1979). *The education of Black Philadelphia: The social and educational history of a minority community, 1900–1950.* Philadelphia, PA: University of Pennsylvania.

Gasman, M., & Bowman III, N. (2013). *Engaging diverse college alumni: The essential guide to fundraising.* New York, NY: Routledge.

Gates Jr., H. L. (2013). *Life upon these shores: Looking at African American history, 1513–2008.* New York, NY: Alfred A. Knopf.
Goodchild, L. F., & Huk, I. P. (1990). The American college history: A survey of its historiographic schools and analytic approaches from the mid-nineteenth century to the present. In J. C. Smart (Ed.), *Higher education: Handbook of theory and research* (Vol. 6, pp. 201–290). New York, NY: Agathon Press.
Green, V. H. (1947). *The Negro motorist Green book.* The New York Public Library Digital Collections. Retrieved from digitalcollections.nypl.org
Green, V. H. (1949). *The Negro motorist Green book.* The New York Public Library Digital Collections. Retrieved from digitalcollections.nypl.org
Green, V. H. (1956). *The Negro motorist Green book.* The New York Public Library Digital Collections. Retrieved from digitalcollections.nypl.org
Green, V. H. (1963). *The Negro motorist Green book.* The New York Public Library Digital Collections. Retrieved from digitalcollections.nypl.org
Greene, M. A. (1989). Using college and university archives as instructional materials: A case study and an exhortation. *The Midwestern Archivist, 14*(1), 31–38.
Griffin, G., Csete, J., Moerdyk, R. A., & Limer, C. (1983). *Emancipated spirits: Portraits of Kalamazoo College women.* Kalamazoo, MI: Kalamazoo College Press.
Gumport, P. J., Iannozzi, M., Shaman, S., & Zemsky, R. (1997). *Trends in United States higher education from massification to post massification.* National Center for Postsecondary Improvement. Stanford, CA: Stanford University. Retrieved from http://web.stanford.edu/group/ncpi/documents/pdfs/1-04_massification.pdf
Habermas, J. (1984). *The theory of communicative action. Volume 1: Reason and the rationalization of society*(trans: McCarthyT.). Boston, MA: Beacon.
Halberstam, D. (1998). *The children.* New York, NY: Fawcett Books.
Hamm, T. D. (1997). *Earlham college: A history, 1847–1997.* Bloomington: Indiana University Press.
Harding, V. (1981). *There is a river: The Black struggle for freedom in America.* San Diego, CA: Harcourt Brace & Company.
Harper, S. R., & Quaye, S. J. (2009). Beyond sameness, with engagement and outcomes for all: An introduction. In S. R. Harper & S. J. Quaye (Eds.), *Student engagement in higher education* (pp. 1–16). New York, NY: Routledge.
Harris, C. I. (1993). Whiteness as property. *Harvard Law Review, 106,* 1707–1791.
Harris, T. W. (2010, September 17). What's so wrong with 'sounding black?' *Psychology Today.* Retrieved from https://www.psychologytoday.com/blog/colorstruck/201009/whats-so-wrong-sounding-black
Harro, B. (2010). The cycle of socialization. In M. Adams, W. J. Blumenfeld, C. R. Castañeda, H. W. Hackman, M. L. Peters, & X. Zúñiga (Eds.), *Readings for diversity and social justice* (2nd ed., pp. 45–51). New York, NY: Routledge.
Herge, H. C. (1996). *Navy V-12* (Vol. 12). Paducah, KY: Turner Publishing Co..

Hershock, M. J. (2003). *The paradox of progress: Economic change, individual enterprise, and political culture in Michigan, 1837–1878.* Athens: Ohio University Press.

Highlander Center. (2012). *Timeline.* Highlander Research and Education Center. Retrieved from http://highlandercenter.org/media/timeline/

Hirt, J. B. (2006). *Where you work matters: Student affairs administration at different types of institutions.* Washington, DC: University Press of America.

Holt, T. C. (1998). Explaining racism in American history. In A. Molho & G. S. Wood (Eds.), *Imagined histories: American historians interpret the past* (pp. 107–119). Princeton, NJ: Princeton University Press.

Horowitz, H. L. (2005). In the wake of Laurence Vesey: Re-examining the liberal arts college. *History of Education Quarterly, 45*, 420–426.

Horse Capture Sr., G. P. (2010). Chapter four: The plains. In A. Truer, K. Wood, W. W. Fitzhugh, G. P. Horse Capture, T. L. Frazier, M. R. Miller, M. Belarde-Lewis, & J. Norwood (Eds.), *Indian nations of North America* (pp. 142–193). Washington, DC: National Geographic Society.

Hossler, D. (2000). The role of financial aid in enrollment management. *New Directions for Student Services, 89*, 77–90.

Hossler, D., Braxton, J., & Coopersmith, G. (1989). Understanding student college choice. In J. C. Smart (Ed.), *Higher education: Handbook of theory and research* (Vol. 5). New York, NY: Agathon Press.

Hossler, D., & Gallagher, K. S. (1987). Studying student college choice: A three-phase model and the implications for policymakers. *College and University, 62*(3), 207–221.

Hossler, D., & Stage, F. K. (1992). Family and high school experience influences on the postsecondary educational plans of ninth-grade students. *American Educational Research Journal, 29*(2), 425–451.

Hundley, M. G. (1965). *The Dunbar story, 1870–1955.* New York, NY: Vantage Press.

Hunter-Gault, C. (1992). *In my place.* New York, NY: Vintage Books.

Hunter-Gault, C. (2014). *To the mountaintop: My journey through the Civil Rights Movement.* New York, NY: Square Fish.

Hurtado, S., Milem, J. F., Clayton-Pedersen, A. R., & Allen, W. R. (1998). Enhancing campus climates for racial/ethnic diversity: Educational policy and practice. *Review of Higher Education, 21*(3), 279–302.

Hurtado, S., Milem, J. F., Clayton-Pedersen, A. R, &Allen, W. R. (1999). *Enacting diverse learning environments: Improving the climate for racial/ethnic diversity in higher education.* ASHE-ERIC Higher Education Report, *26*(8). Washington, DC: The George Washington University, Graduate School of Education and Human Development.

Hutcheson, P., Gasman, M., & Sanders-McMurtry, K. (2011). Race and equality in the academy: Rethinking higher education actors and the struggle for

equality in the post-World War II period. *Journal of Higher Education, 82*(2), 121–153.
Jackson, A. Y., & Mazzei, L. A. (2012). *Thinking with theory in qualitative research: Viewing data across multiple perspectives.* New York, NY: Routledge.
Johnson, A. G. (2005). *Privilege, power, and difference* (2nd ed.). New York, NY: McGraw Hill.
Johnson, K. A. (2009). "In service for the common good": Anna Julia Cooper and adult education. *African American Review, 43*(1), 45–56.
Johnson, M. (2010, January 27). Yearbooks ending at University of Virginia, other colleges. *Washington Post* [online]. Retrieved from www.washingtonpost.com
Jones, S. R., Torres, V., & Arminio, J. (2014). *Negotiating the complexities of qualitative research in higher education: Fundamental elements and issues* (2nd ed.). New York, NY: Routledge.
Kaestle, C. F. (1992). Standards of evidence in historical research: How do we know when we know? *History of Education Quarterly, 32*(3), 361–366.
Katznelson, I., & Mettler, S. (2008). On race and policy history: A dialogue about the G. I. Bill. *Perspectives on politics, 6*(3), 519–537.
Kincheloe, J. L. (2001). Describing the bricolage: Conceptualizing a new rigor in qualitative research. *Qualitative Inquiry, 7*(6), 679–692.
King, C. S. (1993). *My life with Martin Luther King, Jr* (Rev. ed.). New York, NY: Henry Holt & Co.
Kuh, G. D., Kinzie, J., Schuh, J. H., & Whitt, E. J. (2010). *Student success in college: Creating conditions that matter.* San Francisco, CA: Jossey-Bass.
Ladson-Billings, G. (1998). Just what is critical race theory and what's it doing in a nice field like education? *Qualitative Studies in Education, 11*(1), 7–24.
Lather, P. (1986). Research as praxis. *Harvard Educational Review, 56*, 257–277.
Lather, P. (2003). Issues of validity in openly ideological research: Between a rock and a soft place. In Y. S. Lincoln & N. K. Denzin (Eds.), *Turning points in qualitative research: Tying knots in a handkerchief* (pp. 185–215). Walnut Creek, CA: Alta Mira.
Lawrence III, C. R., Matsuda, M. J., Delgado, R., & Crenshaw, K. W. (1993). Introduction. In M. J. Matsuda, C. R. Lawrence III, R. Delgado, & K. W. Crenshaw (Eds.), *Words that wound: Critical race theory, assaultive speech, and the first amendment* (pp. 1–16). Boulder, CO: Westview Press.
Lester, J. S. (2003). *Fire in my soul: Eleanor Holmes Norton.* New York, NY: Atria Books.
Levine, D. P. (2004). The birth of the Citizenship Schools: Entwining the struggles for literacy and freedom. *History of Education Quarterly, 44*(3), 388–414.
Lewis, J., & D'Orso, M. (1998). *Walking with the wind: A memoir of the movement.* New York, NY: Harcourt Brace & Co..
Lindley, H., Schneider, N. F., &Quaife, M. M. (1937). *History of the ordinance of 1787 and the Old Northwest Territory (A supplemental text for school use).*

Marietta, OH: Northwest Territory Celebration Commission. Folder pOG 1113. Center for Archival Collections, Bowling Green State University.

List of Jim Crow law examples by state. (2016, May 18). *Wikipedia: The free encyclopedia*. Retrieved from https://en.wikipedia.org/wiki/List_of_Jim_Crow_law_examples_by_state

Little, M. H. (2002). The extra-curricular activities of Black college students, 1868–1940. *Journal of African American History, 87*, 43–56.

Long, B. T. (2013). Supporting access to higher education. In M. J. Bailey & S. Danziger (Eds.), *Legacies of the war on poverty, The national poverty center series on poverty and public policy* (pp. 93–120). New York, NY: Russell Sage Foundation.

Lott, E. (2013). *Love and theft: Blackface minstrelsy and the American working class* (20th anniversary ed.). Oxford, England: Oxford University Press. (Original work published in 1993).

McEwen, M. K., Roper, L. D., Bryant, D. R., & Langa, M. J. (1990). Incorporating the development of African-American students into psychosocial theories of student development. *Journal of College Student Development, 31*, 429–436.

McGee, C. (2010, August 22). The open road wasn't quite open to all. *The New York Times* [digital reprint]. Retrieved from http://www.nytimes.com

Meredith, J., & Doyle, W. (2012). *A mission from God: A memoir and challenge for America*. New York, NY: Atria Books.

Michigan, State of. (1885). *Public acts and joint and concurrent resolutions of the legislature of the state of Michigan, passed at the regular session of 1885, with an appendix*. Lansing, MI: W. S. George & Co..

Miller, L. (1970). Very deliberate speed. In A. Weinstein & F. O. Gatell (Eds.), *The segregation era, 1863–1954: A modern reader* (pp. 280–293). New York, NY: Oxford University Press.

Minor, J. T. (2004). Decision making in historically Black colleges and universities: Defining the governance context. *Journal of Negro Education, 73*(1), 40–52.

Moore, N. Y. (2016). *The south side: A portrait of Chicago and American segregation*. New York, NY: St. Martin's Press.

Moya, P. M. L. (2009). What's identity got to do with it? Mobilizing identities in the multicultural classroom. In S. Sanchez-Casál & A. A. Macdonald (Eds.), *Identity in education* (pp. 45–64). New York, NY: Palgrave MacMillan.

Murray, P. (1997). *States' laws on race and color*. Athens: University of Georgia Press. Retrieved from https://books.google.com. (Originally published in 1951).

National Beta Club. (n.d.). *About*. Retrieved June 1, 2016 from https://www.betaclub.org/about

National Park Service. (n.d.a). *List of sites for the underground railroad*. Retrieved October 23, 2012 from http://www.cr.nps.gov/nr/travel/underground/states.htm

National Park Service. (n.d.b). *Underground railroad bing map*. Retrieved October 23, 2012 from http://www.cr.nps.gov/nr/travel/underground/bingmap.htm

New York City Department of City Planning. (2016). *NYC Population: Current and projected populations*. Retrieved May 28, 2016 from http://www1.nyc.gov/site/planning/data-maps/nyc-population/current-future-populations.page

Nidiffer, J. (2010). "Poor" research: The historiographical challenges when socio-economic status is the unit of analysis. In M. Gasman (Ed.), *The history of U.S. higher education: Methods for understanding the past* (pp. 137–149). New York, NY: Routledge.

Novick, P. (1998). *That noble dream: The "objectivity question" and the American historical profession*. New York, NY: Cambridge University Press.

Ogletree, C. (2004). *All deliberate speed: Reflections on the first half century of Brown v. Board of Education*. New York, NY: W. W. Norton & Co..

Ohio Civil Rights Act of 1959. (n.d.). Ohio history central. Ohio History Connection. Retrieved from http://www.ohiohistorycentral.org/w/Ohio_Civil_Rights_Act_of_1959

Onkst, D. H. (1998). "First a Negro…incidentally a veteran": Black World War Two veterans and the G. I. Bill of Rights in the deep south, 1944–1948. *Journal of Social History, 31*(3), 517–543.

Pascarella, E., & Terenzini, P. (2005). *How college affects students: A third decade of research* (Vol. 2). San Francisco, CA: Jossey-Bass.

Patton, L. D., Harper, S. R., & Harris, J. (2015). Using critical race theory to (re) interpret widely studied topics related to students in US higher education. In A. M. Martinez-Aleman, B. Pusser, & E. M. Bensimon (Eds.), *Critical approaches to the study of higher education: A practical introduction* (pp. 193–219). Baltimore, MD: Johns Hopkins University.

Patton, L. D., Ranero, J., & Everett, K. (2011). Engaging race in multicultural student services. In D. L. Stewart (Ed.), *Multicultural student services on campus: Building bridges, re-visioning community, ACPA Books and Media* (pp. 63–80). Sterling, VA: Stylus.

Patton, M. Q. (2015). *Qualitative research and evaluation methods: Integrating theory and practice* (4th ed.). Thousand Oaks, CA: SAGE.

Perkins, L. M. (1993). The role of education in the development of Black feminist thought, 1860–1920. *History of Education, 22*, 265–275.

Perks, R., & Thomson, A. (1998). Introduction. In R. Perks & A. Thomson (Eds.), *The oral history reader* (pp. ix–xiii). New York, NY: Routledge.

Plaut, R. L. (1954). Racial integration in higher education in the North. *The Journal of Negro Education, 23*, 310–316.

Pope, L. (2012). *Colleges that change lives: 40 schools that will change the way you think about colleges* (Rev. ed., H. M.Oswald). New York, NY: Penguin Books.

Report of proceedings in Congress, Wednesday, Feb. 21, 1787. (1787, February 21). *Avalon project.* Yale University College of Law. Retrieved May 20, 2016 from avalon.law.yale.edu/18th_century/const04.asp

Richardson, L., & St. Pierre, E. A. (2005). Writing: A method of inquiry. In N. K. Denzin & Y. S. Lincoln (Eds.), *The SAGE handbook of qualitative research* (3rd ed., pp. 959–978). Thousand Oaks, CA: SAGE.

Rogers, M. (2012). Contextualizing theories and practices of bricolage research. *The Qualitative Report, 17*(7), 1–17.

Rooks, N. M. (2006). *White money/Black power: The surprising history of African American studies and the crisis of race in higher education.* Boston, MA: Beacon Press.

Roosevelt, T. (1957). *The Northwest territory, 1787–1790.* Fort Wayne, IN: Public Library of Fort Wayne and Allen County. (Originally published in 1896). Folder pOG 3088. Center for Archival Collections, Bowling Green State University.

Rudolph, F. (1990). *The American college and university: A history* (2nd ed.). Athens: University of Georgia.

Saldaña, J. (2013). *The coding manual for qualitative researchers* (2nd ed.). Thousand Oaks, CA: Sage.

Sanchez-Casál, S., & Macdonald, A. A. (2009). Identity, realist pedagogy, and racial democracy in higher education. In S. Sanchez-Casál & A. A. Macdonald (Eds.), *Identity in education* (pp. 9–43). New York, NY: Palgrave MacMillan.

Sanders-McMurty, K. (2007). *"Linked together in service": A history of education and philanthropy among the Black elite: The Links, Incorporated, 1946–1996.* Unpublished doctoral dissertation. Atlanta: Georgia State University.

Sayre, N. (1995). *Previous convictions: A journey through the 1950s.* New Brunswick, NJ: Rutgers University.

Schwartz, R., & Stewart, D.-L. (in press). The development of student affairs. In J. Schuh & S. R. Jones (Eds.), *Student services: A handbook of the profession.* San Francisco, CA: Jossey-Bass.

Scott, J. W. (2008). Experience. In A. M. Jaggar (Ed.), *Just methods: An interdisciplinary feminist reader* (pp. 272–282). London, UK: Paradigm Publishers. [Reprinted from *Critical Inquiry, 17*(4), 773–797: 1991].

Serow, R. C. (2004). Policy as symbol: Title II of the 1994 G. I. Bill. *The Review of Higher Education, 27*(4), 481–499.

Shenton, A. K. (2004). Strategies of ensuring trustworthiness in qualitative research projects. *Education for Information, 22*, 63–75.

Sowell, T. (1974). Black excellence: The case of Dunbar High School. *Public Interest, 35*, 3–21.

Statista. (2016). *Percentage of the U.S. population who have completed four years of college or more from 1940 to 2014, by gender* [chart]. Retrieved July 23, 2016 from http://www.statista.com/statistics/184272/educational-attainment-of-college-diploma-or-higher-by-gender/

Stewart, A. (2013). *First class: The legacy of Dunbar, America's first Black public high school.* Chicago, IL: Chicago Review Press.

Stewart, D. L. (2008). Being all of me: Black students negotiating multiple identities. *Journal of Higher Education, 79*(2), 183–207.

Stewart, D.-L. (2015). Know your role: Black college students, racial identity, and performance. *International Journal of Qualitative Studies in Education, 28*(2), 238–258.

Stewart, D.-L. (2016). Race and historiography: Advancing a critical-realist approach. Advance online publication. *Journal of Diversity in Higher Education.* 10.1037/dhe0000017

Stewart, D.-L. (2017). *Whiteness as collective memory: Student publications as historical texts.* Manuscript under review.

Stewart, D.-L. (2017). (In)visibility, involvement, and success: A counter-narrative of Black women in predominantly White liberal arts colleges, 1945–1965. In L. D. Patton & N. N. Croom (Eds.), *Critical perspectives on Black women and college success* (pp. 31–43). New York: Routledge.

Strange, C. C., & Banning, J. H. (2015). *Designing for learning: Creating campus environments for student success* (2nded ed.). San Francisco, CA: Jossey-Bass.

Switala, W. J. (2001/2008). *Underground railroad in Pennsylvania.* Mechanicsburg, PA: Stackpole Books.

Thelin, J. R. (2011). *A history of American higher education* (2nd ed.). Baltimore, MD: Johns Hopkins University Press.

The Wabash [yearbook]. (1962). *Archives and special collections.* Greencastle: Roy O. West Library, DePauw University.

Thompson, P. (1998). The voice of the past: Oral history. In R. Perks & A. Thomson (Eds.), *The oral history reader* (pp. 21–28). New York, NY: Routledge.

Time and Date. (2016). *Indiana's time zones and Daylight Savings Time.* Retrieved from http://www.timeanddate.com/time/us/indiana-time.html

Treichler, J., Hollister, H., & Lemcke. (1947, May 13). *Memorandum from race relations committee. Race relations – Jessie Treichler's File 2/14/1951.* Antiochiana, Olive Kettering Library, Antioch College, Yellow Springs, OH.

TressieMc. (2016, May 18). *Because we think of discourse as a way that power is structured, syntax matters to sense making.* Could be awesome [Twitter post]. Retrieved from https://twitter.com/tressiemcphd/status/733106678053363712

Treuer, A. (2010). Chapter one: The northeast. In A. Truer, K. Wood, W. W. Fitzhugh, G. P. Horse Capture, T. L. Frazier, M. R. Miller, M. Belarde-Lewis, & J. Norwood (Eds.), *Indian nations of North America* (pp. 16–63). Washington, DC: National Geographic Society.

Turner, S., & Bound, J. (2003). Closing the gap or widening the divide: The effects of the G.I. Bill and World War II on the educational outcomes of Black Americans. *Journal of Economic History, 63*(1), 145–177.

United Neighborhood Houses. (n.d.). *About UNH. Settlement house history. What is a settlement house?* Retrieved June 1, 2016, from http://www.unhny.org/about/index.html

Waite, C. L. (2001). The segregation of Black students at Oberlin College after reconstruction. *History of Education Quarterly, 41*, 344–364.

Warren, S. (1990, October). *The Black behind the black and gold.* Retrieved August 27, 2010, from http://www.depauw.edu/library/archives/find/articles/warren.html

Wiley, A. N. (2013). The Dunbar high school dilemma: Architecture, power, and African American cultural heritage. *Buildings & Landscapes, 20*(1), 95–128.

Wilkerson, I. (2010). *The warmth of other suns: The epic story of America's great migration.* New York, NY: Random House.

Williams, J. (2004). *My soul looks back in wonder: Voices of the civil rights experience.* New York, NY: Sterling.

Williams, J. (2013). *Eyes on the prize: America's civil rights years, 1954–1965 (25th anniversary ed.).* New York, NY: Penguin Books.

Woodson, C. G. (2006). *The mis-education of the Negro.* San Diego, CA: The Book Tree. (Originally published in 1933).

Young, I. M. (1990). Five faces of oppression. In I. M. Young (Ed.), *Justice and the politics of difference* (pp. 39–65). Princeton, NJ: Princeton University Press.

Young, V. A. (2009). 'Nah, we straight': An argument against code switching. *JAC, 29*(1/2), 49–76. Retrieved from http://www.jstor.org/stable/20866886

Zimbardo, P. G. (1966). *Physical integration and social segregation of northern Negro college students.* Paper presented at the Eastern Psychological Association conference. ERIC Document Retrieval Service no. ED 025568.

Zipp, Y. (2013, March 10). Kalamazoo College celebrates the 50th anniversary of the K Plan. *MLive.* Retrieved from http://www.mlive.com/news/kalamazoo/index.ssf/2013/03/kalamazoo_college_celebrates_t.html

Zurita, M. (2001). La mojada y el coyote: Experiences of a wetback researcher. In B. M. Merchant & A. I. Willis (Eds.), *Multiple and intersecting identities in qualitative research* (pp. 19–32). Mahwah, NJ: Erlbaum.

List of Primary Sources

Albion College

African American enrollment [First]. (1869). College history files (C.ARC.0061). Albion College Archives, Stockwell-Mudd Library, Albion College, Albion, MI.

Afro-American Union. (1969, undated). College history files (C.ARC.0061). Albion College Archives, Stockwell-Mudd Library, Albion College, Albion, MI.

The Albionian [yearbook]. (1945–1965). Albion College Archives, Stockwell-Mudd Library, Albion College, Albion, MI.

The Pleiad [newspaper]. (1945–1965). Albion College Archives, Stockwell-Mudd Library, Albion College, Albion, MI.

Allegheny College

Allegheny College—Publicity—1960s/1970s/1980s (Folder C1D1F25). Allegheny College Archives, Wayne and Sally Merrick Historic Archival Center, Pelletier Library, Allegheny College, Meadville, PA.

Black Student Statistics (Folder C1D2F26). Allegheny College Archives, Wayne and Sally Merrick Historic Archival Center, Pelletier Library, Allegheny College, Meadville, PA.

History—ABC (Folder RG3 S7 SS2/C5D4). Allegheny College Archives, Wayne and Sally Merrick Historic Archival Center, Pelletier Library, Allegheny College, Meadville, PA.

The Campus [newspaper]. (1945–1965). Allegheny College Archives, Wayne and Sally Merrick Historic Archival Center, Pelletier Library, Allegheny College, Meadville, PA.

The Kaldron [yearbook]. (1945–1965). Allegheny College Archives, Wayne and Sally Merrick Historic Archival Center, Pelletier Library, Allegheny College, Meadville, PA.

Vigrass, J. W. (1949). *The street railway in Meadville 1898–1928.* From the folder labeled "Viagrass, J. William (1952)" in "Course Work 1899–2013" (Record Group 4, Series 2, Box 1), Allegheny College Archives, Wayne and Sally Merrick Historic Archival Center, Pelletier Library, Allegheny College, Meadville, PA.

Antioch College

Anonymous, A. (1946). *Senior paper.* Antiochiana, Olive Kettering Library, Antioch College, Yellow Springs, OH.

Anonymous, B. (1948). *Senior paper.* Antiochiana, Olive Kettering Library, Antioch College, Yellow Springs, OH.

Anonymous, C. (1949). *Senior paper.* Antiochiana, Olive Kettering Library, Antioch College, Yellow Springs, OH.

Anonymous, D. (1950a). *Senior paper.* Antiochiana, Olive Kettering Library, Antioch College, Yellow Springs, OH.

Anonymous, E. (1950b). *Senior paper.* Antiochiana, Olive Kettering Library, Antioch College, Yellow Springs, OH.

Anonymous, F. (1950c). *Senior paper.* Antiochiana, Olive Kettering Library, Antioch College, Yellow Springs, OH.

Anonymous, G. (1950d). *Senior paper.* Antiochiana, Olive Kettering Library, Antioch College, Yellow Springs, OH.

Anonymous, H. (1950e). *Senior paper.* Antiochiana, Olive Kettering Library, Antioch College, Yellow Springs, OH.

Anonymous, I. (1951a). *Senior paper.* Antiochiana, Olive Kettering Library, Antioch College, Yellow Springs, OH.

Anonymous, J. (1951b). *Senior paper.* Antiochiana, Olive Kettering Library, Antioch College, Yellow Springs, OH.

Anonymous, K. (1951c). *Senior paper.* Antiochiana, Olive Kettering Library, Antioch College, Yellow Springs, OH.

Anonymous, L. (1951d). *Senior paper.* Antiochiana, Olive Kettering Library, Antioch College, Yellow Springs, OH.

Anonymous, M. (1952a). *Senior paper.* Antiochiana, Olive Kettering Library, Antioch College, Yellow Springs, OH.

Anonymous, N. (1952b). *Senior paper.* Antiochiana, Olive Kettering Library, Antioch College, Yellow Springs, OH.

Anonymous, O. (1952c). *Senior paper.* Antiochiana, Olive Kettering Library, Antioch College, Yellow Springs, OH.

Anonymous, P. (1953a). *Senior paper.* Antiochiana, Olive Kettering Library, Antioch College, Yellow Springs, OH.

Anonymous, Q. (1953b). *Senior paper.* Antiochiana, Olive Kettering Library, Antioch College, Yellow Springs, OH.

Anonymous, R. (1953c). *Senior paper.* Antiochiana, Olive Kettering Library, Antioch College, Yellow Springs, OH.

Anonymous, S. (1955a). *Senior paper.* Antiochiana, Olive Kettering Library, Antioch College, Yellow Springs, OH.

Anonymous, T. (1955b). *Senior paper.* Antiochiana, Olive Kettering Library, Antioch College, Yellow Springs, OH.

Anonymous, U. (1955c). *Senior paper.* Antiochiana, Olive Kettering Library, Antioch College, Yellow Springs, OH.

Anonymous, V. (1956a). *Senior paper.* Antiochiana, Olive Kettering Library, Antioch College, Yellow Springs, OH.

Anonymous, W. (1956b). *Senior paper.* Antiochiana, Olive Kettering Library, Antioch College, Yellow Springs, OH.

Anonymous, X. (1956c). *Senior paper.* Antiochiana, Olive Kettering Library, Antioch College, Yellow Springs, OH.

Antioch College. (1958–1959). *Syllabus: Senior paper X 389.* Antiochiana, Olive Kettering Library, Antioch College, Yellow Springs, OH.

Race Relations – Jessie Treichler's File 2/14/1951. Antiochiana, Olive Kettering Library, Antioch College, Yellow Springs, OH.

Race Relations (File 3). Antiochiana, Olive Kettering Library, Antioch College, Yellow Springs, OH.

Race Relations-Miscellaneous (File 6). Antiochiana, Olive Kettering Library, Antioch College, Yellow Springs, OH.

Race Relations-Race Relations Committee (File 5). Antiochiana, Olive Kettering Library, Antioch College, Yellow Springs, OH.

Race Relations-Scholarships (File 4). Antiochiana, Olive Kettering Library, Antioch College, Yellow Springs, OH.

Scott, C. (1948, April–June). Why I came to college. Reprinted from *Opportunity: Journal of Negro Life, 26*(2), pp. 1–2. New York, NY: The National Urban League. File 2: Race Relations-General historical info. Antiochiana, Olive Kettering Library, Antioch College, Yellow Springs, OH.

Treichler, J.?. (ca. 1969, June). *Negro or Black graduates and former students of Antioch College – 1943–1968.* Antiochiana, Olive Kettering Library, Antioch College, Yellow Springs, OH.

Denison University

About Shepardson. (1950–1951). Record Group 14 Students. Series SShep. Notebook: Shepardson Club Reports 1946–1953. Denison University Archives & Special Collections, Granville, OH.

Aims and fulfillments of Shepardson Club. (date unknown). Record Group 14 Students. Series SShep. Notebook: Shepardson Club Reports 1946–1953. Denison University Archives & Special Collections, Granville, OH.

At Denison [monthly publication]. (1953–1967). Denison University Archives & Special Collections, Granville, OH.

Borgmann, F. (1951). *Evaluation of the Denison University-Hampton Institute student exchange program, February – June 1950.* Record Group 12 Faculty and Departments. Series DEx. Box: 4, Folder: Hampton Exchange Program 1949–1953. Denison University Archives & Special Collections, Granville, OH.

Borgmann, F. (date unknown). *Survey of Granville businesses.* Record Group 12 Faculty and Departments. Series DEx. Box: 4, Folder: Hampton Exchange Program 1949–1953. Denison University Archives & Special Collections, Granville, OH.

Cephas, S. D. (c. 1951). *My semester at DU in Granville, OH Jan 30-Jun 7, 1951.* Record Group 12 Faculty and Departments. Series DEx. Box: 4, Folder: Hampton Exchange Program 1949–1953. Denison University Archives & Special Collections, Granville, OH.

Constitution of the Denison Cosmopolitan Club. (date unknown). Record Group 14 Students, Series SC. Box: Directory, General A-Da, Folder: Cosmopolitan Club. Denison University Archives & Special Collections, Granville, OH.

Correspondence between Dr. Maylon Hepp and Edward R. Miller. Record Group 12 Faculty and Departments. Series DEx. Box: 4, Folder: Hampton Exchange

Program 1949–1953. Denison University Archives & Special Collections, Granville, OH.
Denison exchange program. (date unknown). Record Group 12 Faculty and Departments. Series DEx. Box: 4, Folder: Exchange Programs. Denison University Archives & Special Collections, Granville, OH.
Hampton exchange program pamphlet. (c. 1951–1952). Record Group 12 Faculty and Departments. Series DEx. Box: 4, Folder: Hampton Exchange Program 1949–1953. Denison University Archives & Special Collections, Granville, OH.
Inter-college community council report. (c. 1955). Record Group 12 Faculty and Departments. Series DEx. Box: 4, Folder: Exchange Programs. Denison University Archives & Special Collections, Granville, OH.
Inter-racial exchange committee report. (1954, April 29). Record Group 12 Faculty and Departments. Series DEx. Box: 4, Folder: Exchange Programs. Denison University Archives & Special Collections, Granville, OH.
Introduction to the American Association of Commons Clubs. (date unknown). Record Group 14 Students, Series SS Social Fraternities/Sororities. Box: 4a, Folder: Denison Commons Club 1917–21, American Commons Club 1921–64 Directories, Brochures, Programs, Etc. N.O.C. Denison University Archives & Special Collections, Granville, OH.
List of Black alumni as of 1973. (1973?). Record Group 10 University Relations and Development. Series LZ, Folder #3: Black Alumni Association. Denison University Archives & Special Collections, Granville, OH.
Program bulletin. (1937–1938). Record Group 14 Students, Series SC. Box: Directory, General A-Da, Folder: Cosmopolitan Club. Denison University Archives & Special Collections, Granville, OH.
Radio script. (1949). Record Group 14 Students. Series SShep. Notebook: Shepardson Club Reports 1946–1953. Denison University Archives & Special Collections, Granville, OH.
Report on the activities of the ICC: Spring Valley pool race. (1958). Record Group 12 Faculty and Departments. Series DEx. Box: 4, Folder: Exchange Programs. Denison University Archives & Special Collections, Granville, OH.
The Adytum [yearbook]. (1945–1965). Denison University Archives & Special Collections, Granville, OH.
The Denisonian [newspaper]. (1945–1965). Denison University Archives & Special Collections, Granville, OH.
Weeks, C. F. (1963, September 20). [Letter]. Record Group 14 Students, Series SC. Box: Directory, General A-Da, Folder: Cosmopolitan Club. Denison University Archives & Special Collections, Granville, OH.
What is Shepardson. (1952). Record Group 14 Students. Series SShep. Notebook: Shepardson Club Reports 1946–1953. Denison University Archives & Special Collections, Granville, OH.

DePauw University

MARK: Religion in Action/Quest [newsletter]. (1946–1950). DePauw Council on Religious Life. Archives and Special Collections, Roy O. West Library, DePauw University, Greencastle, IN.

Philander Smith College (DC225-Folder 1). Archives and Special Collections, Roy O. West Library, DePauw University, Greencastle, IN.

Phillips, C. J., &Baughman, J. J. (1987). *DePauw: A pictorial history, sesquicentennial 1837–1987*. DePauw University: Greencastle, IN (LCC: LD 1618.P55). Archives and Special Collections, Roy O. West Library, DePauw University, Greencastle, IN.

The DePauw [newspaper]. (1945–1965). Archives and Special Collections, Roy O. West Library, DePauw University, Greencastle, IN. Retrieved from http://www.depauw.edu/libraries/about/librarylocations/archives/

The Mirage [yearbook]. (1945–1965). Archives and Special Collections, Roy O. West Library, DePauw University, Greencastle, IN.

Earlham College

Earlham College Faculty Minutes. (1943.September—1958, May & 1958, September—1968, May). Friends Collection and College Archives, Earlham Libraries, Earlham College, Richmond, IN.

The Post [newspaper]. (1945–1965). Digital Collections, Friends Collection and College Archives, Earlham Libraries, Earlham College, Richmond, IN. Retrieved fromhttps://news.arcasearch.com/usinehm/

The Sargasso [yearbook]. (1945–1965). Friends Collection and College Archives, Earlham Libraries, Earlham College, Richmond, IN.

Hope College

The Anchor [newspaper]. (1945–1965). Hope College, Joint Archives of Holland, Theil Research Center, Holland, MI.

The Milestone [yearbook]. (1945–1965). Hope College, Joint Archives of Holland, Theil Research Center, Holland, MI.

Kalamazoo College

The Boiling Pot [yearbook]. (1945–1965). College Academic and Historical Experience (CACHE), Kalamazoo College Archives, Upjohn Library, Kalamazoo College, Kalamazoo, MI. Retrieved from https://cache.kzoo.edu/

The Index [newspaper]. (1945–1965). College Academic and Historical Experience (CACHE), Kalamazoo College Archives, Upjohn Library, Kalamazoo College, Kalamazoo, MI. Retrieved from https://cache.kzoo.edu/

Kenyon College

Freshman Class of 1962. (1958). Greensplade Special Collections and Archives, Kenyon College Library and Information Services, Kenyon College, Gambier, OH.

Freshman Class of 1963. (1959). Greensplade Special Collections and Archives, Kenyon College Library and Information Services, Kenyon College, Gambier, OH.

Freshman Class of 1964. (1960). Greensplade Special Collections and Archives, Kenyon College Library and Information Services, Kenyon College, Gambier, OH.

Freshman Class of 1965. (1961). Greensplade Special Collections and Archives, Kenyon College Library and Information Services, Kenyon College, Gambier, OH.

Freshman Class of 1966. (1962). Greensplade Special Collections and Archives, Kenyon College Library and Information Services, Kenyon College, Gambier, OH.

Freshman Class of 1967. (1963). Greensplade Special Collections and Archives, Kenyon College Library and Information Services, Kenyon College, Gambier, OH.

The Kenyon Collegian [newspaper]. (1945–1965). Greensplade Special Collections and Archives, Kenyon College Library and Information Services, Kenyon College, Gambier, OH.

The Reveille [yearbook]. (1943,1947–1965). Greensplade Special Collections and Archives, Kenyon College Library and Information Services, Kenyon College, Gambier, OH.

Oberlin College

Barbershop segregation controversy (Subjects Folder). Oberlin College Archives, Oberlin, OH.

Black organizations, etc.-clippings (Subjects Folder). Oberlin College Archives, Oberlin, OH.

Hi-O-Hi [Oberlin College yearbook]. (1945–1965). Oberlin College Archives, Oberlin, OH.

The Activist [newspaper]. (1960–1964). Student Publications, Oberlin College Archives, Oberlin, OH.

Ohio Wesleyan College

Le Bijou [yearbook]. (1945–1965). Ohio Wesleyan University Libraries, Archival Collections, Ohio Wesleyan University, Delaware, OH.

The Transcript [newspaper]. (1945–1965). Ohio Wesleyan University Libraries, Archival Collections, Ohio Wesleyan University, Delaware, OH. The Five Colleges of Ohio Digital Collections, http://cdm15963.contentdm.oclc.org/cdm/

Wabash College

The Bachelor [newspaper]. (1945–1965). Archives & Special Collections, Lilly Library, Wabash College, Crawfordsville, IN.

The Wabash [yearbook]. (1946–1965). Archives and Special Collections, Roy O. West Library, DePauw University, Greencastle, IN.

Wabash Oral History Interview Transcripts. Archives and Special Collections, Roy O. West Library, DePauw University, Greencastle, IN.

The College of Wooster

The Index [yearbook]. (1945–1965). Andrews Library, The College of Wooster Archives Collection, The College of Wooster, Wooster, OH.

The Voice [newspaper]. (1945–1965). Andrews Library, The College of Wooster Archives Collection, The College of Wooster, Wooster, OH.

Index

Note: Page numbers followed by 'n' refer to notes.

© The Author(s) 2017

D.-L. Stewart, *Black Collegians' Experiences in US Northern Private Colleges*, DOI 10.1057/978-1-137-59077-0

CPSIA information can be obtained
at www.ICGtesting.com
Printed in the USA
LVOW04*1310290517
536167LV00011B/418/P

9 781137 590763